EDUCATION AND EDUCATIONAL RESEARCH

General Editor: DR. EDMUND KING

THE PSYCHOLOGY OF LEARNING

An Introduction for Students of Education

THE PSYCHOLOGY OF LEARNING

An Introduction for Students of Education

BY

GORDON R. CROSS, M.A., Ph.D. (Cantab.)

PERGAMON PRESS

OXFORD · NEW YORK · TORONTO · SYDNEY

Pergamon Press Ltd., Headington Hill Hall, Oxford

Pergamon Press Inc., Maxwell House, Fairview Park, Elmsford, New York 10523

Pergamon of Canada Ltd., 207 Queen's Quay West, Toronto 1

Pergamon Press (Aust.) Pty. Ltd., 19a Boundary Street, Rushcutters Bay, N.S.W. 2011, Australia

First edition 1974

Library of Congress Cataloging in Publication Data

Cross, Gordon R.
The psychology of learning.

(Education and educational research)
Includes bibliographies.
1. Educational psychology. I. Title.
[DNLM: 1. Learning. 2. Psychology, Educational.
LB1051 C951p]
LB1051.C724   370.15   74–13865
ISBN 0–08–018136–8
ISBN 0–08–018135–X (flexicover)

Printed in Great Britain by A. Wheaton & Co., Exeter

Contents

Chapter 8. Intelligence and Ability 170

Chapter 9. Personality 204

Chapter 10. Educational Technology 222

Introduction

THIS introduction to the psychology of learning outlines and discusses some of the practical implications of the classical and more traditional topics of study as well as recent developments including theoretical models of learning and psycholinguistics for teachers in training. The scope and content of educational psychology has expanded and grown so rapidly that it is hardly possible for experienced tutors to keep pace with the published literature. How much more difficult it is for students to sift out material which is relevant for the work of the teacher in school, especially if they are following integrated or interdisciplinary courses of study.

One of the inevitable and inescapable weaknesses of a textbook of this kind lies in deciding which topics should be developed, mentioned or omitted. It is hoped that the text is no less satisfactory than others in this respect, the choice is subjective and the personal responsibility of the author. Although discussion is focused on how normal children learn, it has not been possible in this book to include styles and techniques of teaching, group methods and the teaching of curriculum subjects including learning to read and write.

In writing this book an assumption is made that educational psychology will maintain its identity and form an integral part of teacher-training programmes, and that insight into human learning and its problems is necessary for a sympathetic and realistic understanding of child behaviour and development. Interdisciplinary studies of general educational theory or courses structured round a curriculum subject are not condemned and ruled out in arguing for the continued existence of psychology as an independent discipline making a special contribution to the training of teachers. Integrated courses have an attractive theoretical rationale; in practice they are exceptionally difficult to organize and implement in a manner which is both easily comprehensible and educationally satisfying for students.

The author is convinced that students should first grasp the essentials of,

1

say, a taxonomy of educational objectives, an hierarchical model of thinking, a cybernetic or feedback principle or a structural theory of language acquisition; then with guidance from subject method tutors, think out for themselves the practical application of principles to specific learning situations. What is envisaged is two stages. In the first, the student acquires (i) technical knowledge and a working vocabulary of terms commonly used in psychology, (ii) skills like test administration, recording observations and the recognition of children with particular difficulties who should be referred, (iii) an ability to critically evaluate an original research paper; and (iv) familiarity with scientific and controlled methods of psychological investigation.

In the second stage, through colloquia, seminars and small group discussion, the contributions of history, philosophy, psychology, sociology, comparative and health education to an educational issue or subject topic are synthesized or interrelated. A student's ability to make a positive and intelligent contribution to discussion and expand his understanding of educational processes is contingent upon prior acquisition of knowledge from the foundation areas. Otherwise discussion will tend to lack meaning for students; it will have no obvious aim or direction and will degenerate into trite comments thrown together in an amorphous collection of snippets and jottings.

The replication of some of the experimental work reported in the text is strongly urged, provided caution is taken in the interpretation of results and not too many assumptions are made on the relevance of limited laboratory investigations for the more complex classroom teaching situation. Practical exercises, tutor demonstration and audience participation, child study and guided observation, visits to special schools and institutions and modern technological aids are all considered essential in helping students gain insight into the learning process and in making personal reading more meaningful.

References and suggestions for additional reading are given in the expectancy that readers will follow up selected topics in greater depth. A great deal of seminar material is nowadays readily available to students in the various collections of readings regularly published in paperback form. Naturally, references to the more recent articles and papers in the leading British journals predominate and this is justified in Britain both on the grounds of wider student access to these publications and an increasing reportage of experimental work in the British educational setting. Cross-cultural studies are important in psychology but again one has to be very careful in weighing up their implications for a national system of education or even a small or specific part of that system.

One of the unsolved mysteries of the classroom is why a suggestion, hint or technique which works on one occasion for a teacher utterly fails on a subsequent yet similar occasion or proves helpful to one teacher but disastrous to another. From experience of observing teachers at work the author is consciously aware of this problem and apologizes for all the subjective comments and interpretations of classroom situations which have no empirical psychological foundation and possibly fail to work out in practice. Having said this it would be stupid to imply that psychology has little of practical value to offer the young teacher. On the contrary, draw from possible alternative suggestions but, above all, learn how to anticipate and know when to take action. A teacher should never assume the role of a distant spectator neither should he be frozen by fear into a state of inactivity. Passive acceptance and feigned unawareness is no solution to a deteriorating classroom atmosphere or incident.

Educational psychologists are often unfairly criticized for adopting an eclectic overview and being inconsistent, one moment taking a cognitive view and the next drawing from behaviourist principles. It is not the aim or function of an introductory text of this kind to defend or take sides with a particular school of thought but to state the case, albeit too briefly and sometimes in an over-simplified and possibly misleading form. In any case, many of the better known contemporary models of learning theory are not only eclectic in the sense of being rooted in two major classical schools but they also borrow heavily from physiological research and advances in the study of communication and information theory.

The danger of writing an over-simplified account of a complex theory is ever-present in an introductory text for student teachers compared with one for specialist psychologists. One attempts to maintain technical accuracy but it is not easy to do so in a subject which is continually developing and is generating far too many personal definitions, notions and concepts for comfortable management by the beginner. Also, there is nowadays so much psychological information available that it is becoming impossible to cope with it all. The day cannot be far off when research will move away from studies of efficient learning techniques to methods of storage and rapid retrieval of information from data banks.

Despite greater understanding of human behaviour and advances in the technology of instruction the old cliché that there is no easy path to learning holds as true today as ever. The teacher has a certain measure of control over the classroom environment and a capacity for making learning a pleasant and worthwhile experience; he points the way and offers guidance, but in the end it is the child's own legs that carry him along the path. It is a tortuous and uneven path with uphill and downhill stretches, plateaus and a surprisingly large amount of back-tracking. In the acquisition of physical skill, language and number many movements and rules have to been unlearned to facilitate subsequent progress and efficiency. Teachers must recognize unevenness as an inevitable characteristic of human development and seek ways of stimulating and motivating children through periods of difficulty.

Finally, learning should never be considered synonomous with rote acquisition of factual knowledge and skills, it encompasses thinking, problem solving and creative production. Foster cognitive development by placing children in decision-making and problem-solving situations whatever their age and however imperfect the initial response. A child progresses towards a full development of his individual potential in thinking only when he is provided with a variety of opportunities in which it may be fostered and practised.

The reading list following this introduction includes the more general textbooks on psychology, teaching and educational research which may prove helpful to student teachers.

Additional Reading

BUTCHER, H. J. (1968) *Educational Research in Britain*. London: Univ. of London Press.
BUTCHER, H. J. and PONT, H. B. (Eds.) (1970) *Educational Research in Britain*, **2**. London: Univ. of London Press.
BUTCHER, H. J. and PONT, H. B. (Eds.) (1974) *Educational Research in Britain*, **3**. London: Univ. of London Press.
CHANAN, G. (Ed.) (1973) *Towards a Science of Teaching*. London: N.F.E.R.
CRAIG, R. C. (1966) *The Psychology of Learning in the Classroom*. London: Collier–Macmillan.
DODWELL, P. C. (Ed.) (1972) *New Horizons in Psychology*, Vol. 2. London: Penguin.
ENTWISTLE, N. J. (1973) *The Nature of Educational Research*. Bletchley: Open University.
ENTWISTLE, N. J. and NISBET, J. D. (1972) *Educational Research in Action*. London: Univ. of London Press.

GAMMAGE, P. (1971) *Teacher and Pupil, Some Socio-Psychological Aspects.* London: Routledge & Kegan Paul.

HILGARD, E. R., ATKINSON, R. C. and ATKINSON, R. L. (1971) *Introduction to Psychology,* 5th edn. New York: Harcourt Brace Jovanovich. Open Univ. Set Book.

KELLMER PRINGLE, M. L. and VARMA, V. P. (Eds.) (1974) *Advances in Educational Psychology,* 2. London: Univ. of London Press.

KRECH D. *et al.* (1969) *Elements of Psychology,* 2nd edn. New York: Knopf.

LOVELL, K. (1973) *Educational Psychology and Children,* 11th edn. London: Univ. of London Press.

McFARLAND H. S. N. (1971) *Psychological Theory and Educational Practice.* London: Routledge & Kegan Paul.

McFARLAND, H. S. N. (1973) *Intelligent Teaching.* London: Routledge & Kegan Paul.

MAXWELL, J. (1969) *Pupil and Teacher: An Introduction to Educational Psychology.* London: Harrap.

MUNRO, M. (1969) *The Psychology and Education of the Young.* London: Heinemann.

OESER, O. A. (Ed.) (1966) *Teacher, Pupil and Task.* London: Social Science Paperbacks, Tavistock.

PEEL, E. A. (1967) *The Psychological Basis of Education,* 2nd edn. Edinburgh: Oliver & Boyd.

STEPHENS, J. M. (1965) *The Psychology of Classroom Learning.* New York: Holt, Rinehart & Winston.

STONES, E. (1966) *An Introduction to Educational Psychology.* London: Methuen.

STONES, E. and MORRIS, S. (1972) *Teaching Practice: Problems and Perspectives.* London: Methuen.

WALL, W. D. and VARMA, V. P. (Eds.) (1972) *Advances in Educational Psychology,* 1. London: Univ. of London Press.

WRIGHT, D. S., TAYLOR, A. *et al.* (1970) *Introducing Psychology: An Experimental Approach.* London: Penguin.

CHAPTER 1

Learning I

Concept of Learning

Students of education are generally surprised when they are first confronted by a technical and seemingly unhelpful definition of learning usually expressed in the following words, "a permanent change in behaviour as a result of experience". This is because young people fresh from school have become accustomed to equate learning with rote memorization as, for example, in revising for an examination. From birth and throughout the life span one learns far more than the recall of facts by heart and the acquisition of competence in skilled activities; to these must be added—attitudes, ideals, mannerisms, prejudices, roles and social skills. What are broadly known as instinctive behaviour patterns are therefore excluded by definition as also are normal growth or maturation processes and temporary states such as those induced by alcohol, drugs and fatigue.

Imprinting

The word "instinct" has tended to become a dated psychological concept and it is nowadays fashionable to talk about innate response tendencies or species—specific behaviour, preferably the latter, because leading ethologists like Tinbergen (1951) have shown that much instinctive behaviour is characteristic of one single species. A behaviour pattern which has been built-in from birth or is innately programmed is said to have been imprinted, and excellent examples of imprinting are to be found in Lorenz's *King Solomon's Ring* (1952) including the classic example of the gosling who follows the professor as he walks about almost immediately from hatching.

In this case the propensity to follow a moving object has been programmed and is innate, whereas the act of attachment has been learned.

This behaviour has been observed in other "precocial species". The term indicates that they can walk immediately after hatching; however, the attachment must occur within a few hours or at the most a day or two from birth. The so-called critical period is of slightly longer duration for a gosling kept in isolation from birth compared with goslings brought up in a group, which consequently have become imprinted to each other.

Fascinating as this behaviour is to general readers it leads to that difficult perennial question raised by student teachers: "why does one have to know so much about the psychological menagerie, surely the child is the proper subject for study?" This is not easily answered because it soon becomes apparent to most students that the relevance of the findings of animal experiments for the work of the teacher in the classroom is often artificial, forced, hypothetical and tenuous. Further discussion of this point inevitably raises another fundamental problem: in the study of behaviour who makes the more worthwhile contribution to knowledge, the ethologist who observes animals in their natural environment or the laboratory psychologist who devises an artificial experiment in an alien environment, and then poses the animal problems which in the context of normal behaviour is unnatural? Also is it valid to compare results of experiments using different species, when it is known that each member of the animal kingdom represents a stage along the evolutionary scale? The results of investigations into phyletic differences in learning by Bitterman (1965) and others suggest that there are marked qualitative differences in performance, and that one should not automatically assume that the processes of learning are the same for all species. Laboratory animals are trained for use in psychological experiments in order to observe and evaluate learning under simple straightforward yet scientifically controlled conditions. One must be fair to experimental workers in the laboratory who often have a different aim compared to the ethologist. Their work is usually more specifically directed towards a single or limited problem and the approach is consequently more rigorous. Unfortunately from the point of view of human learning, animal studies necessarily preclude consideration of language, the varied use of which sets mankind apart from the remainder of the animal kingdom.

The obvious yet elusive aim of every educational psychologist is first to describe and evaluate experimental evidence and then examine its relevance for learning by children and finally to assess its merit in normal educational practice. This approach necessitates a personal selection of material which a more general psychologist will deplore because it has a tendency to produce an unbalanced and somewhat exclusive account of learning. The classroom orientated and highly pragmatic student of education welcomes a reduction in theory and a clarification of concepts even if it incurs a slight loss in scientific detail and accuracy.

Although a broad historical approach to the various learning theories has been adopted, the order has occasionally been modified to show the emergence of two main schools of thought and how they have influenced contemporary research.

Thorndike's Structure of S–R bonds

The earliest theorists, some dating back to Classical times, thought learning and memorizing resulted from the formation of simple associations of words, ideas, objects and concepts "in the mind": the more pleasurable experiences being retained longest; the painful, unpleasant experiences are soon forgotten.

Association by contiguity is a vague theory and expressed in its simplest terms it describes little and explains less; however, from it emerged the implication that rewarded associations have greater permanence, and this proved to be of considerable significance to later investigators. Take an imaginary conversation between a father and his young son as an illustrative example: "What is a ship, Daddy", asks the boy. "Look, here is a picture of a ship in this paper", replies Father and he proceeds to write down the letters "s–h–i–p" in the margin and at the same time talks about the pleasures of seeing ships off the coast at a holiday resort or cruising to exciting places far away in great luxury and so on.

Father next asks his son to spell out the word "ship" and to write it down. He gets it right, and Father praises his correct response, "well done", but becoming bored with the lack of stimulating repartee suggests that the boy draws a picture of a ship, colours it and gives it a name. The boy works at his task with utter devotion until he knocks over and spills his painting jar, is reprimanded, then disappears out of the room and down the garden accompanied by volumes of parental abuse which suggest that he is either a clumsy clot, a moron or worse. This pattern of behaviour illustrates the principle of reward or more technically "reinforcement" of a successful response and its converse.

From a series of experiments in which cats escape from a puzzle box with a release mechanism, Thorndike (1949) developed a narrowly mechanical theory of learning; namely that for each stimulus S there is an associated response R, which become welded together to form a connection or a bond. In the process of learning, "S-R bonds" are constructed, strengthened and organized. He suggested that "laws" or more accurately "statements" could provide a systematic explanation of behaviour, some of these were later reviewed and modified in the light of further experimentation and criticism.

1. The Law of Effect suggests that an S-R connection or bond is strengthened if its consequence proves satisfying or is rewarded, and a bond is weakened if its consequence proves annoying or is punished. This law is an explanation of trial and error learning; for example, a person might make many attempts to solve a problem or perform a skilled action until a correct solution is obtained, subsequent repetition will stamp it in. Conversely unsuccessful solutions or actions are inhibited and extinguished. Thorndike later concluded that the relative effectiveness of reward and punishment are not equal and opposite, reward is far more effective in modifying behaviour than is punishment. Psychologists use the word punishment in a very broad sense, at one extreme to describe the effect of pain obtained from the transmission of electric shocks; at the other, a mild expression of disapproval in a statement such as "wrong", or even an unsuccessful action itself. Similarly, reward does not necessarily imply a material reward such as a prize or food, but includes a sign or comment of approval for a correct and successful action.

Obviously Thorndike's conclusions on the effects of punishment are of considerable significance for parents, teachers and criminologists. Throughout this book under a variety of headings it will be stated or implied time and time again that praise is far more effective than reproof in modifying behaviour. Also, the indirect effects of punishment as, for example, in causing avoidance behaviour should never be overlooked.

2. The Law of Exercise suggests that with practice or repetition a bond or connection is strengthened or conversely a bond is weakened through disuse. Subsidiary to this law is that more frequently and more recently performed actions tend to be repeated and strengthened. In other words, learning is by doing and repetition, or practice makes perfect; as, for example, in memorizing the arithmetical tables by heart. If this kind of learning is without understanding and is solely a result of repetition then it

is called "rote learning", a term which may be applied equally to verbal memory or the acquisition of a physical skill.

Thorndike later became aware of a serious weakness in the law of exercise because it is clear that practice without knowledge of results is quite worthless. Attempt to draw a number of squares with 1-inch sides whilst blindfolded and without feeling the figures by touch or seeing the results; it will soon become apparent that repetition of this kind of activity does not automatically improve personal standards of performance.

3. The Law of Readiness suggests that satisfaction and reward as opposed to frustration and annoyance depend on whether the learner is actively prepared for learning or not. A bond is strengthened or weakened according to the learner's mental adjustment, preparation or readiness. Experienced and sensitive teachers know how easy it is to capitalize on a child's inquisitiveness, interest and genuine enthusiasm for knowledge and how difficult it is to teach the frustrated, unreceptive child. A lost opportunity is not easily regained and the teacher must be quick to spot such critical moments in a child's development. A practical difficulty sometimes arises in making a quick decision as to whether a child sincerely wants a point or question discussed or is simply drawing red herrings and using time consuming diversionary tactics. Readiness in this context must not be confused with the concept of readiness used in the study of growth and maturity; namely the appropriate development time for learning a complex skill such as knitting or riding a bicycle. These activities are not easily learned until a child has reached a certain level of maturation which is determined by a coordination of mental development and physical growth.

Thorndike is generally known by the three major laws of learning. He also proposed five subsidiary or subordinate laws, and these have some educational relevance: (a) The learner must be flexible and vary his approach in attempting to solve a problem until by trial and error he is successful. (b) The attitude or set of the learner is significant in determining his behaviour and success in learning. (c) The learner picks out the fundamental and essential points of an argument or problem and discards irrelevant details. (d) The learner responds to new or novel situations by drawing analogies with past experience or in identifying elements common to both. (e) The learner responds to a given stimulus, then by associative shifting transfers it to a totally different stimulus. This is closely akin to Pavlov's concept of classical conditioning discussed in a later section.

Thorndike's influence on educational thought in the early part of the century was considerable in spite of its rigid and mechanical approach to learning in which trial and error, drill, rote memory and habit formation assume greater significance than understanding, experience, discrimination and motivation. Studying foreign languages by memorizing word lists, history by repeating important dates parrot fashion, geography by cramming facts into rigid regional classifications (the capes and bays approach) and mathematics by tricks and rules of thumb are all illustrative of Thorndike's pedagogy. Human behaviour demands fine discriminations, subtle movements and highly developed thought processes including abstract thinking, yet he never really explained how bonds or connections are chained and organized into complex intricate patterns. However, he later modified his views and it is significant to note that he subsequently referred to trial-and-error learning "as learning by selecting and connecting".

Teachers who constantly enforce mechanical learning to the extreme of overlearning and repetitive perfection in copying are placing serious limitations on a child's intellectual development. They would do well to rethink their basic philosophy in the light of Whitehead's (1950) deprecation of inert knowledge. Also teachers who believe some of the old wives' tales dating back to this period; for example, that children should not be shown marked examination scripts for fear that any errors contained therein, having been seen again, would become stamped in are only deceiving themselves as well as their pupils.

A thorough understanding of a source of error normally proves helpful and this seemingly negative approach often produces positive results and enhances progress. Write out a list of mis-spelt variations of a word frequently spelt incorrectly, underline the correct spelling or write it in block capitals then make comparisons between the spellings. Later when in doubt about the spelling of a troublesome word write out one or two possible versions, look at them carefully and the habit of spotting the correct spelling will quickly develop.

Also, in learning a skilled movement in games such as cricket, golf or tennis, learn how to produce the undesirable stroke automatically and it will reappear less frequently in the normal games situation. The apparent paradox of the competent golfer who knows how to play a sliced or hooked shot to order and yet is normally the straightest of hitters is a constant source of amazement to the beginner who, try as he may, rarely hits the ball along a straight line. The expert recognizes the source of error, understands it and knows what action should be taken to rectify it.

Thorndike failed to reduce human learning to a small number of over-simplified principles, and the dangers of this practice should by now be apparent. Thouless (1958) summed them up succinctly: "The attempts made by some educational psychologists to reduce human learning to the mechanical laws of exercise and effect are strongly to be condemned. They tend to lead to drill rather than to explanation as educational methods, and to treat the purpose of the educational process as remembering where it should be understanding."

Pavlov's Classical Conditioning

Many writers in the past have vividly described the principles of conditioning, but greatest credit for making an experimental and systematized study of the subject is due to the Russian physiologist Pavlov (1941). His classical experiment needs only a brief description; it is the terminology which requires explanation. A hungry dog normally secretes saliva at the sight and taste of food such as meat. In this straightforward situation the food is called an unconditioned stimulus (US) and the salivation is an unconditioned response (UR). Perform some distinctive action such as ringing a bell or switching on a bright light when the dog is next given food and it will again secrete saliva. Repeat this procedure on a number of occasions. Later either ring the bell or switch on the bright light but do not give food to the dog who will continue to respond by secreting saliva. From this experiment one concludes that the bell or the light is now a conditioned stimulus (CS) and the salivation by the dog has become a conditioned response (CR).

As a result of difficulties in translating from Russian to English via German there is still some controversy as to whether conditioned should in fact be "conditional" and response should be termed "reflex". If so, did Pavlov imply that it is only under certain conditions that reflexes are produced? Obviously a whole school of psychology could not have been constructed from the result of one relatively simple experiment with limited implications for human behaviour. By what is known as higher order conditioning the whole process is capable of being extended.

This is best illustrated by returning to the basic experiment in which the dog becomes conditioned to the sound of a bell and taking the procedure a step further. Show some arbitrary stimulus such as a large black square to the dog and it is unlikely to respond to it and it certainly will not produce saliva. Next present the black square without food but ring the bell and the dog will respond by secreting saliva; then finally present the square alone, without either food or ringing the bell, and the dog will continue to secrete saliva. As a result of this process the dog has now become conditioned not only to the sound of the bell but also to the sight of the large black square. If one takes the experiment too far beyond the original stimulus in too many steps conditioning ceases to be effective.

This principle underlies another fascinating phenomena observed not only in animals but in children and adults; namely, that an organism can be conditioned to respond to stimuli which are similar in character, and this is termed "stimulus generalization". A baby severely frightened by a cat suddenly jumping on the pram coverlet, or a young child bowled over by an over-playful dog, could easily develop a fear not only of small animals but also of their inanimate counterparts. The favourite cuddly toy is rejected and the model toy dog begging for charity and sitting peacefully outside the shop is passed with great trepidation. More irrational fears or phobias are thought to be due to the conditioning of involuntary emotional responses. In the case of the white-coat complex, traumatic experience in hospital or a very rough time at the dentist might lead to fear of all white-coated workers including the friendly traffic crossing attendant despite his lollipop image. Possibly fear of lightning or reptiles in children is con-ditioned by observing adults or peers reacting with an unpleasant facial gesture or making a sudden physical movement.

Pavlov was fundamentally a devoted physiologist; therefore, is his con-tribution to educational thought and learning theory too limited to be of value to the practising teacher? Clearly not, if the broad definition of learning given at the beginning of the chapter is recalled. Agreed, verbal memorization of academic material is an obvious and appropriate topic in the field of study called learning, so is emotional growth and personal development. This by no means suggests that they should be studied independently when it is clear from the simplest observation of human behaviour that they are inextricably interlocked.

Many of the great psychologists like Freud, Piaget and Hebb adopted an integrative approach to the study of children, including physical, intellectual and emotional development both in individual cases and in member-ship of a group in a social environment. Pavlov did more than reiterate learning as an association by contiguity; he revealed something of the physiological basis of learning, he explained concepts such as generalization and inhibition and he demonstrated the principles of neuroticism. Reference to a few examples will show the wider significance of conditioning and how it influences learning in the broad definition of the word.

The technique of brainwashing is a form of conditioning to an idea, commonly of a political nature; but only under limited circumstances does it prove effective. For example, with captive groups under severe stress in a prisoner-of-war compound. Lie detectors work on the principle of record-ing on a voltmeter the galvanic skin response; that is, they measure the body's electrical resistance to two types of stimuli which are presented to the suspect. Neutral stimuli are random statements not expected to produce strong reactions, but critical stimuli which are directly associated with the committed crime are likely to produce a positive and very marked response. In countries using lie detectors, recordings alone without corroboratory evidence are not accepted as proof of guilt, but they certainly give interro-gators a firm basis from which further questioning proceeds.

Advertising techniques, particularly those appealing to the emotions or an individual's status, are examples of conditioning by repetition and suggestion, in this case direct suggestion. It is also possible to use subliminal techniques. In a warm cinema flash or project images of cool refreshing drinks on the screen at a level just beyond perception at the conscious stage and wait for the sales to rise. Naturally it has been banned for it is open to abuse by unscrupulous operators, and it is basically abhorrent because individuals are not adequately equipped mentally to resist its force and could be very easily exploited.

Pavlov's demonstration of inducing abnormal or neurotic behaviour in a dog is taken by some psychologists to show how breakdowns in human behaviour might possibly occur. A dog is shown a lighted circle and given food, later it is shown a lighted ellipse but no food is given. Gradually the ellipse is widened until it is nearly the size of a circle, at this stage the dog is unable to discriminate between the figures and its behaviour becomes markedly disturbed. This abnormal behaviour is called experimental neurosis; it can also be observed in cats. A cat will normally not take alcohol but may be induced to do so if given alternate food rewards and electric shocks on the successful completion of a problem. Failure to discriminate, together with experimental neurosis, will cause him to consume increasing quantities of alcohol in his milk until a good-looking, healthy cat becomes what can only be described as an unkempt back-alley moggy. Fortunately the cat can be conditioned by successive rewards back to normal behaviour and its alcoholic penchant will disappear.

Whether it is valid or not to draw direct comparisons between human neurotic behaviour and experimental neurosis in animals is debatable, but evidence accumulating from the practice of behaviour therapy in clinical psychiatry should not be ignored or overlooked. A very readable account of this subject and covering such topics as aversion therapy in the treatment of alcoholics and drug addicts is to be found in Meyer and Chesser (1970).

Pavlov's direct contribution to educational practice appears limited, probably because he is best known in the West for his basic study of animal conditioning. To the elements of this process shared with man he gave the name, "first signal system". Speech in man is the "second signal system"; it is being investigated by his followers and from it is emerging important contributions to the study of language development in children.

Skinner's Operant Conditioning

In classical conditioning the response or reflex which is elicited by a known stimulus such as salivation at the sight of food, the contraction of the eye pupil in very bright light or a jerk of the knee when sharply tapped is commonly called "respondent behaviour". This is easily differentiated from operant behaviour in which the response is emitted by an unknown or unrecognizable stimulus. Nearly all human behaviour is emitted whether it is reading a book, typing a letter or riding a bicycle and is therefore operant. Skinner (1953) recognized the significance of operant behaviour and investigated it first in rats and pigeons and later in children to demonstrate principles of programmed learning. Instrumental conditioning has been likened to a practice known to animal trainers in circuses for centuries; namely, follow a successful performance with an immediate reward.

In his experiment with pigeons Skinner's apparatus typically consists of a puzzle box with a disc at which a bird pecks and is rewarded with grain. The lever mechanism which releases the grain can be linked to record the number of pecks made and also regulated to give complex variations in the time intervals between rewards. Clearly, in an operant behaviour experiment the strength of the stimulus is not measured directly and is irrelevant, therefore it is the rate of response which is significant. The strength of the operant is determined by the total number of responses over a specified period.

In Pavlovian conditioning the organism responds passively to the stimulus but in operant conditioning the animal actively brings about his own reward, it reacts positively and exerts some measure of control over its environment. The technical term used by Skinner to describe a reward is "reinforcement"; positive reinforcement includes rewards such as food, a prize, praise and success; negative reinforcement includes punishment, rebuke and dissatisfaction caused by an unsuccessful performance. In Skinner's language, reinforcement is *contingent upon* response and reinforcement always strengthens the probability of a response. After making an adjustment to the mechanism in the Skinner puzzle box each peck at the disc is not automatically rewarded, therefore reinforcement becomes partial or intermittent.

Throughout life human behaviour is not constantly and immediately rewarded, it is frequently delayed in voluntary pursuits such as fishing and collecting. The child investing pocket money in a savings scheme is learning the principle of delayed reward; but thank heaven he does not really understand what he is doing because in an inflationary world he is more than likely to lose part of his investment in the long run. The gambler operating a one-armed bandit or fruit machine is working to a schedule of intermittent reinforcement.

Skinner made the interesting observation that if a pigeon happens to be behaving in a certain way or adopts a specific posture, such as standing on one leg when he makes a successful action and is rewarded, he will continue to behave in that manner on subsequent occasions when seeking a reward. This is known as "superstitious" behaviour, it is common in adults and children alike, as for example in wishing for a lucky number before throwing a dice, putting on a favourite piece of clothing before attending an important function, or walking slowly to the batting crease in cricket in possible anticipation of a quick exit.

By changing the schedule of intermittent reinforcement it is possible to study the effect of a variety of rewards on a bird's behaviour from fixed intervals, say every minute, to fixed ratios, say every fifth peck. If pecking is considered to be analogous to work then variations in work habits can be planned, observed and recorded. In fact so many patterns of work output have been recorded in response to different schedules that no firm conclusions have been made; only broad generalizations emerge from the experiments, such as fixed ratios tend to give higher outputs than fixed intervals and that variable intervals give higher outputs than fixed intervals.

Obviously if no further rewards are forthcoming the pigeon will discontinue his pecking activity and the response gradually disappears by a process known as "extinction". Whereas reinforced activity leads to learning and non-reinforcement results in extinction; the two are not equal and opposite because in spontaneous recovery the original activity is rapidly relearned and total decay is rare. This is of comfort to the struggling student looking ahead to an examination and saying, "I will never remember all this material even if I do manage to understand it now". Look upon a final written examination as delayed reinforcement and continuous coursework assessment as a form of partial reinforcement.

Teachers must constantly seek to praise children's work or behaviour in a variety of ways and as expeditiously as is possible. Praise for a good answer, credit for an original suggestion, points in a competition, marks for a slip test, grades for a commendable essay, acknowledgement of an act of kindness are of personal significance to each and every child in the class. The good teacher encourages and praises the child frequently and is effective; the dull teacher monotonously burbles little more than "yes" and only occasionally nods assent or ticks a piece of written work, good or bad without comment.

An outstandingly successful teacher of difficult children claimed that the whole of her approach was based on the philosophy of praise and reward, constantly informing children of the good in their work and behaviour whereas before they only ever heard how bad they were. In praising the minimum contribution no matter how slight and in encouraging the smallest step forward she achieved remarkable results both in the improvement of social conduct and in the acquisition of elementary academic learning skills. To an independent observer it was the variety of ways in which she managed to encourage, praise and reward deprived children which was so impressive, it represented patient and positive reinforcement at its best.

From the outline of Skinner's contribution to learning theory it is clear that in many ways his views are nearer to Thorndike's laws, particularly the "law of effect", than to Pavlov's concept of classical conditioning. However, Skinner recognizes the significance of classical conditioning in his acknowledgement of secondary reinforcement. A neutral stimulus such as a bright light or a clicking sound, which in itself is not a reinforcing stimulus, can acquire the power to reinforce or condition. It achieves this by repeated association with a reinforcing stimulus such as food. The light or click become secondary reinforcers; the original stimulus, food, remaining a primary reinforcer. Visualize an extension of this process until a generalized system of reinforcement is built up.

This model of the basic principle of secondary reinforcement in learning complex behaviour patterns becomes clearer if a gradual step by step progress towards an ultimate goal is imagined. One step reinforces the next until success is achieved. This process of reinforcement, "shaping", is sometimes described as reinforcement by successive approximations. The technique is used by the experienced classroom teacher who is skilled at framing a series of questions which lead in consecutive and logical stages to the solution of a problem. This is partly the reason why it is considered bad practice, except in speedy revision, to dart round a class questioning child after child or to ask generalized questions which evoke a choral response. What is normally required is the analytical questioning of one or two children. This proves a far more profitable experience all round, not only for the two children directly questioned or to the class as a whole, but also for the teacher as an exercise in self-evaluation.

Shaping is as important in the acquisition of skill as it is in learning complex academic material and together with the principles of feedback or knowledge of results it plays a fundamental role in the construction of programs for programmed learning techniques. These technical terms are specifically discussed later in this book in the chapter on educational technology.

Skinner is undoubtedly a strict behaviourist in his approach to learning, yet his theories tend not to produce a causal explanation of learning but descriptions of stages in the acquisition of knowledge or skill. His contribution to education has been of significance and the implications of his shaping techniques are profound in practice, but he is frequently criticized for his minimum recognition of the role of attitudes, emotion, insight and motivation in human learning.

Hull's Need Reduction

An appraisal of the direct contribution of Hull's (1952) theories to educational thought and practice inescapably leads one to the conclusion that it has been minimal. However, his influence on the broader experimental and purely theoretical study of learning has been of some importance even though his basic theories are nowadays considered limited and dated. His research methods and techniques, particularly in the construction of mathematical models, lead to significant advances in the study of behaviour.

Hull was a more systematic behaviourist than Thorndike and like him placed great emphasis on the law of effect and reinforcement. He interpreted reinforcement in terms of "need reduction". An animal has basic needs such as food, shelter and warmth; for example, if it is hungry it needs food and consequently develops a drive, in this case a hunger drive. As a result of successfully searching for food it eats, feels satisfied and the hunger drive is reduced. The expression need or drive reduction describes this process. The basic model once established is developed by introducing principles of secondary reinforcement to build up a comprehensive theory of learning.

The immediate question which arises from this brief and simplified introduction is whether human behaviour can be fully explained by the reduction and ultimate removal of a need and how does the theory apply to less obvious needs including affection and social status? Only by enlarging the concept of human drives well beyond the narrow confines of biological necessities is sense made of the basic model; therefore one must include motives such as curiosity and competition in the category of a need. Even so it is difficult to see how learning takes place when there is no obvious need to be reduced and the intrinsic reward is negligible.

According to Hull, learning is maximized when need reduction is great and when there is only a short interval between response and reinforcement. Parents and teachers of young children know only too well the perils of ignoring immediate need reduction. It sometimes proves beyond the realms of human patience to instantly satisfy the demands and cravings of children gluttonous for attention, praise and recognition. Older children are fortunately less demanding regarding immediacy, their needs may be delayed. Marked homework returned after a month has passed, school cricket victories announced in the winter term and examination results published so late that the occasion as well as the facts have been committed to oblivion are as exciting and stimulating to a child as baked beans to a gourmet.

Hull's experiments with rats in mazes brought about the observation that they run faster as they approach their goal; human behaviour is exactly the same, whether under competitive conditions or performing a skilled operation or solving a difficult problem—output rapidly increases as soon as the final stretch is in sight. The educational implications of this are quite clear; set a series of attainable objectives rather than one long-term objective and make progress towards it in progressive steps. A further observation of significance is that each reinforcement in learning represents a fraction of the total amount remaining to be learned. In the early stages of learning a great deal remains to be learned, in the later stages only a little remains, therefore a curve on a graph plotting learning against time generally shows decreasing gains.

All the theorists discussed to date take a rather mechanical view of learning, considered to be more appropriate to animal behaviour and to the earliest stages of human learning than to normal adult human behaviour which is actively organized and purposeful. In many practical situations and in problem solving which demands abstract thought, trial and error is uneconomic, conditioning is at a minimum and reward is but a minor source of motivation.

CHAPTER 2

Learning II

Tolman's Sign Learning

Theories of learning in which insight, goal-directed behaviour and expectancy are considered more significant than S–R bonds and conditioning are generally known as cognitive theories. For Tolman (1959) random trial-and-error behaviour is much less important than the comprehension of a problem and the active organization of thought processes to facilitate its solution. Consequently he has been described as a purposive behaviourist. Probably the clearest description of Tolman's viewpoint is drawn from an analogy with map reading. Conventional signs on a map show the reader possible paths and give some indication of the easiest route to be taken. This route is consciously chosen by the map reader after he has weighed up alternatives in the light of past experience and in the expectancy of straightforward progress to the destination or goal based on skill in map interpretation.

Similarly the learner follows a cognitive map "in the mind". He follows environmental signs and pointers towards a goal: the signs are means to an end, rewards and the like indicate possible directions of behaviour. Place learning experiments were devised to demonstrate purposeful behaviour in which rats learned to run through blocked mazes and were forced to choose alternative routes.

It was from studies of latent learning that Tolman and Honzik (1930) developed a theory of sign learning. Three groups of rats are required for a typical latent-learning experiment in a maze.

Group A receives no food reward over the whole of the experimental period of 15 days.
Group B is given food each day.
Group C is given food on the eleventh day of the experiment.

The errors in running the maze remain quite high for the Group A rats who received no food reward. Group B rats who were regularly rewarded reduced the number of errors from day to day as might be expected from normal learning procedures. However, Group C rats showed a pattern of learning equivalent to the Group A rats over the first 10 days: but on the eleventh day, the day on which they were first rewarded, they suddenly began to make as few errors as Group B rats (see Fig. 1).

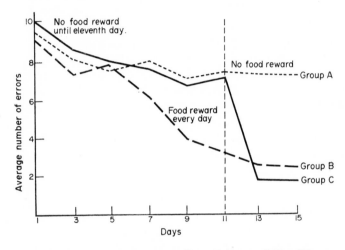

FIG. 1. Latent learning in rats (from Tolman and Honzik).

From this kind of experiment it is presumed that Group C rats were learning their way about the maze in the first 10 days in spite of not being rewarded. In experiments in which the later-rewarded rats perform better at maze running than the regularly rewarded rats it is suggested that the later-rewarded rats thoroughly explored every aspect of the maze in the early trials and were therefore better equipped for running the maze in the final stages of the experiment. There are many teachers who believe that the child who wrestles with a novel problem or difficult technique and masters it is in many ways at a greater educational advantage in the long term than the child who picks it up quickly, possibly with limited under-standing, then lets it fade fairly rapidly out of memory.

Hull did not accept Tolman's explanation of latent learning, arguing that some kind of reinforcement was taking place before the later-rewarded rats were given food. He has shown experimentally that habit strength is not necessarily dependent on a large amount of reinforcement and that in Tolman's experiment the principles of need reduction were operating in the exploratory activity of the rats. Such need reduction or reinforcement was in itself latent and was therefore only revealed on the eleventh day when food was introduced. The food only further reduced the need of the rats.

In purposeful or goal-directed behaviour there is expectation that behaviour will bring about a result and expectation is acquired by weighing probabilities before taking a course of action. Learning is facilitated when the expectation is fulfilled. Finding a route across a fairly strange town when only a few prominent landmarks are known illustrates the principle. The traveller expects to arrive at his destination and although he does not necessarily know the most direct route he weighs the probability of making a successful turn at each junction. It is only when he arrives at his final destination that he has learned the route. This not only illustrates the significance of expectancy in learning, but clearly indicates that learning is not necessarily the same as performance. Tolman maintains that learning is the result of repeated confirmation: that is, if an expectation is confirmed then the probability of learning is increased, if it is not confirmed it is decreased. Unlike the behaviourists who argue that rewards and punishments reinforce and extinguish responses, Tolman maintains that they are simply informational signs which open up possible lines of behaviour.

Purposeful and exploratory behaviour is of the utmost value in the education of the child whether at home or in school. On no account take the jaundiced view that learning by discovery is simply another excuse for play and that time devoted to it could be better spent in direct and formal teaching. This attitude shows a complete misunderstanding of the role of play in physical and mental development and reveals ignorance of the variety of processes by which children learn. Conclusions from experiments show that material learned by children using discovery methods is more readily understood and retained for a longer period than material learned parrot-fashion from prepared sets of notes and rules.

Children should be encouraged to discover knowledge and learn how to utilize it under guidance. The art of discovery is in itself an example of habit formation which a child has to learn. A pupil's first attempt to use this technique might produce some utterly appalling results but improvement soon comes with practice and standards rise quickly. Too many teachers are concerned about the perfect copy; the meticulous notebook, the flawless project and the impeccable exercise, all worthy ideals ultimately, but not at the expense of limiting a child's normal educational development. Imperfect and original contributions are of greater personal significance for the individual child than the outpourings of the teacher's mind commonly communicated in the form of dictated notes. There are a few occasions when dictation is valid but in normal classroom work it is an educational practice which must be strongly deplored. The artificial conditions imposed during teaching practice, especially if a tutor is present, understandably make a student teacher think and act as if he were the sole source of purposeful activity. He soon realizes this is a delusion when the tutor begins to show greater interest in the contribution and work of the children than in his pedagogic rituals.

Another common fallacy is that exploratory techniques are more appropriate in Nursery and Primary rather than Secondary School education. Yet this misconception is certainly not self-evident to teachers with experience of activity methods, field studies, museum projects, games and simulation techniques in higher education. The value of learning by activity and discovery holds true whatever the age or ability of the learner. If in the act of self-evaluation it is felt that these techniques are too time consuming then the planning and organization is probably at fault, not the activity.

The "Gestalt" School

One of the great paradoxes in education is that a theorist like Hull who devoted most of his life to a direct study of learning made little impact on current educational thought; whereas Gestalt psychologists like Köhler (1929), Koffka (1935) and Wertheimer (1945) who were more fundamentally interested in the study of perception and thinking, exerted tremendous influence on contemporary educational practice. Progressive educators like Dewey (1910) (who belonged to an eclectic group called functionalists) were concurrently extolling the virtues of learning by understanding, analytical thinking, creativity and self-motivation, consequently their sympathies lay more with the cognitive gestaltists and added impetus to a movement running counter to mechanical learning and conditioning.

The conclusions drawn by Köhler (1925) from his observation of learning in apes were geometrically opposed to those of Thorndike. One marked point of divergence between them stemmed from attempts to explain insightful behaviour. Insight is often described as the sudden solution of a problem, it demands a valid intellectual assessment of the problem's total structure. Emphasis is placed on the word "sudden" as opposed to the laborious processes associated with trial-and-error learning. A person who has solved crossword puzzles has often experienced the feeling of finding in his thoughts the correct solution to a question he has for long been attempting. The answer suddenly comes to mind and it even occurs when the solver is currently thinking about different clues to another problem.

Köhler observed insightful behaviour in chimpanzees who reached bananas suspended from the roof of their cage by piling one box on top of another; they also drew bananas into the cage by joining two sticks together thereby putting them within easy reach. This intelligent behaviour seemed to display little in common with the actions of Thorndike's cats in puzzle boxes. Köhler's interpretation of these experiments was that the chimpanzee reorganized the perceptual field of his immediate environment consisting of objects like the cage, food, sticks and boxes. The animal's facility for mental reorganization enabled it to "see" the solution to the problem. Insight is the reorganization of a perceptual pattern and it cannot occur without past experience. Köhler criticized Thorndike's experimental method because the cat inside the puzzle box could not see the release mechanism and would therefore gain no insight into the problem, only by making trial-and-error movements could it possibly succeed.

The role of insight in learning is not easily assessed because it is a rather diffuse concept not strictly defined and difficult to explain. Whether the concept itself is basically inadequate or not, teachers should provide situations and frameworks in which the insightful solution of problems is likely to occur. Clear and logical perceptual organization of material to be taught is prerequisite to efficient learning.

Imagine a classroom teaching situation in which a lesson is divided into parts; one of which is the teacher's exposition, the other is individual work by the children on exercises, free composition or problem solving. How frequently is a teacher disappointed by the attempts of individual children to comprehend the exercise or to solve the problem? In spite of a seemingly lucid introduction the teacher's personal expectation remains unfulfilled.

Before rushing off muttering about the quality of the intake think back to the instructions given to the class and go over them step by step, then note the exact points in the exercise where the children made errors in their thinking. Mistakes may possibly have resulted from the following sources:

1. *Giving poor, incomplete and misleading directions.* This is practically demonstrated in a psychological experiment in which Fig. 2 is shown to a group of students who are asked to memorize it. Later they are requested to recall the names of the two towns on the chart. Generally they have difficulty in doing so. Shown the chart again they will not only see the names

β			π		
	E			I	
U	R	H			
	Σ	L	O		
	E	I			
	D	A	N		

FIG. 2.

quite clearly because they have consciously looked for them, but they will also realize how easy it was to be deceived by a simple verbal instruction such as "memorize" when it should have been "look over this diagram carefully". Writers of thrillers often use this device; namely, by a process of suggestion the actual culprit is made to appear less likely to have committed the crime than a number of innocent suspects. The thriller writer intends to mislead, the teacher does not and should not unless he is purposely using it as a specific teaching technique to demonstrate a principle. A skilled teacher with able children can carry a class along a path offering "evidence" at each and every step to support a "hypothesis" then finally blow it up in one devastating argument, an effective technique if used sparingly.

2. *Assuming children understand a point or principle,* which is self-evident to the teacher, but is completely novel to the class or has been previously used

colloquially in a different context. It is not surprising that a student fresh from the field of battle with difficult classes and "lively" children takes less kindly to a psychological definition of "behaviour" because his thoughts have become narrowly orientated as a result of self-involvement. Howlers commonly result from poor insight, the child tries to make common sense out of the limited material and ideas he has at hand.

3. *Teaching by analogy rather than giving genuine explanations.* All teachers are occasionally guilty of this kind of false reasoning, particularly when they are not sure of their ground; but not, one hopes, so blatantly as in this instance: "Sir, why does compression produce heat?" Reply, "Have you ever blown up a tyre with a bicycle pump?" "Yes, sir", "Now you know". Know, yes, an example; but he still does not know how or understand why heat is produced. Quite a lot of the so-called explanations of psychological processes are merely analogies or descriptive illustrations. Similarly incomplete explanations lead to poor insight; for example, it is common to read that language is learned by a child imitating sounds, but how does the child first learn to imitate?

It was previously stated that the Gestalt psychologists were basically theorizing about perception; for instance, Köhler described insight as the reorganization of perceptual patterns. The implications of results of experimental investigations into the nature of perception is of significance for educationalists and merits further consideration. "Gestalt" is the German word for pattern or configuration. To the Gestalt psychologists it is the *whole* pattern which is important rather than the sum of its parts or the total number of individual perceptual elements it contains. Look at a reversible figure and according to the organization of the observer's perceptual field either two faces or a vase may be seen (Fig. 3).

Perception actively alternates between figure and background. Study a set of illusions (Fig. 4) or an "impossible" figure (Fig. 5) and notice how perception of the individual parts or components is determined by the wholes containing them. Designers put this to good effect when they recommend that rooms with low ceilings should be papered with vertically striped wallpaper and that striped dresses should be worn to give an illusion of height.

The concept of a learner actively organizing his perceptual experiences makes a strong argument against trial-and-error methods, S–R bond building and habit stamping by mechanical processes. Concentrate on the group of circles in Fig. 6 and mentally organize them into different patterns.

Fig. 3.

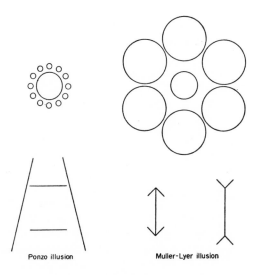

Ponzo illusion   Muller-Lyer illusion

Fig. 4.

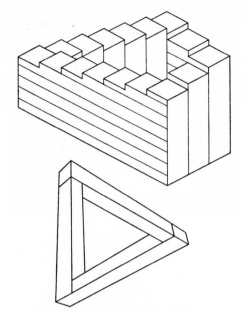

FIG. 5. From Gregory, R. L. (1967).

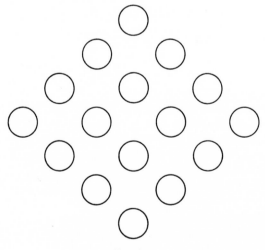

FIG. 6.

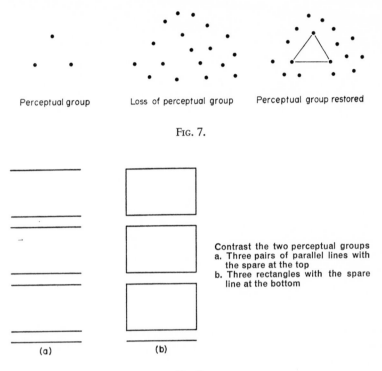

Perceptual group   Loss of perceptual group   Perceptual group restored

FIG. 7.

Contrast the two perceptual groups
a. Three pairs of parallel lines with
the spare at the top
b. Three rectangles with the spare
line at the bottom

(a)   (b)

FIG. 8.

What makes a good pattern or Gestalt and has it special properties? The properties enunciated by Kaffka in the so-called "laws of prägnanz" were assumed to be equally applicable to both learning and perception.

1. *Law of similarity.* Dots, shapes, colours and sounds which are basically similar but differ only in detail constitute a whole or a perceptual group. Köhler demonstrated that similar pairs of nonsense syllables are more easily memorized than heterogeneous pairs (Fig. 7).

2. *Law of proximity.* Parts, lines and shades which are close together in space form a good perceptual group (Fig. 8).

3. *Law of closure.* Closed figures are more readily perceived and recalled than open figures (Fig. 9).

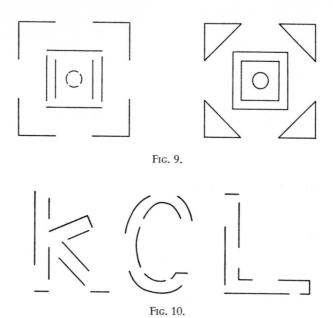

FIG. 9.

FIG. 10.

4. *Law of good continuation.* Objects lying along a straight line appear to continue as a straight line, and broken or open figures tend to be completed or closed (Fig. 10).

The attractiveness of learning by insight was immediately apparent to progressive teachers; so too were the implications of the Gestalt concepts of perceptual organization. A seemingly impossible and haphazard mass of detail in an apparent jungle of facts has to be broken down and reorganized into relatively simple patterns or wholes to bring knowledge within the grasp of children's learning capacities. The patterns should be easily recognizable, meaningful and, if possible, related to past experience. To ask a very young child or a dull person of any age to solve mentally the problem: if all "A"s are F, and all "B"s are F, therefore all "A"s are "B"s— true or false?, is merely making an invitation to guesswork. However, substitute A for apple, B for banana and F for fruit and the answer is only too obvious.

Provide an easily recognizable framework within which children are required to make personal contributions; for example, blanks in incomplete sentences or sums, tabulated note headings for guidance and completion, boxes for the insertion of detail on maps and so on. Make use of mnemonic devices to aid the recall facts: for many SOH CAH TOA is the basis of elementary trigonometry. Use key letters: in stalactite, C is for ceiling therefore hanging down; and in stalagmite, G is for ground therefore growing up from the floor. Point out perceptual groups in spelling; baker, butcher, draper and stationer are all service occupations, stationery is sold by the stationer, therefore by elimination stationary means standing still.

Occasionally ask a child to complete a partially worked problem, having provided enough information for him to work towards a solution. Stimulate further interest in a topic by not ending on a note of finality, suggest there is more information to be explored and indicate how it can be found or followed up.

Many of the aphorisms of the "master of method" have roots in Gestalt theory; "hang new knowledge on old pegs", "work from the known to the unknown" and teach "whole–part–whole" methods. In other words organize teaching material into a recognizable pattern, make effective use of past experience and constantly show how parts fit into the pattern as a whole. In teaching a physical skill such as a golf swing if too much emphasis is placed on one isolated movement, say the rotation of the hips, the path and rhythm of the complete swing frequently breaks down and causes disastrous results. In the teaching of mathematics a lengthy step-by-step solution of a problem does not always prove helpful until certain key steps are identified and shown in their relationship to the problem as a whole.

Adults and children alike learn when they understand meaningful patterns: for older and more able children the patterns may be larger and more complex, but for younger and less able children they should be smaller and more simple in structure. It is probably true to say that the larger the pattern that is grasped and comprehended, material is more effectively learned and a skill more fluently performed.

Obviously two opposing schools of thought, divided fundamentally on the interpretation of experiments in learning could not coexist for ever, no matter how deeply they were entrenched. Advances in the physiological study of the nervous system, the use of more sophisticated laboratory equipment than simple mazes, the development of computer programs and progress in information theory and communication studies have all brought fresh approaches to the study and practice of learning. Armies are no longer marshalled under two main banners, the quest for knowledge of human behaviour is conducted by small groups of investigators across many frontiers; research is now highly specific and resources from many inter-related disciplines are being tapped and incorporated.

Servo-mechanisms and Theoretical Models

A thermostat to control temperature, a governor to control the speed of rotation of a motor and a valve to control the pressure of steam are all relatively simple mechanisms whereby output is modified or controlled by a regulator. A servo-mechanism is a refinement of this basic principle in which discrepancies between the required output and variations in the input load are reduced to a minimum and are virtually eliminated (Fig. 11).

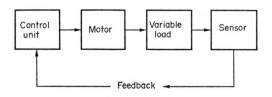

FIG. 11.

In domestic gas or oil-fired central heating systems the advertising agents have laid great stress on automatic, self-regulating performance demanding the minimum of human attention. An efficient system quickly corrects and stabilizes a discrepancy such as a drop in temperature—in an inefficient sys-tem there is too much fluctuation in the output between hot and cold.

In a good-quality sound amplifier, negative feedback consisting of most of the undesirable elements of the output signal is literally fed back to an earlier part of the circuit where distortion is low. This return signal is inverted and therefore cancels out practically all the distortion in the final output where the feedback and input are balanced. Many sophisticated servo-mechanisms are used in complex automated industrial operations and in analogue computers or simulators and they all work on the same basic principle of series of negative "feedback" loops. The adjective "negative" is used because the correction process is always opposite to the discrepancy.

Has the above mechanism any physiological counterpart in human behaviour and could it be developed into an explanation of learning in the higher organisms? A change in the size of eye pupils to adapt to variations in the intensity of illumination is an example of a self-regulating system, in bright light the pupils remain tiny but in dullish conditions they become dilated to admit more light. Many other physiological examples are found in the sensory processes and they function to maintain stability or "homeostasis".

Human behaviour tends to be homeostatic; man adapts to infinite changes in the environment and leads a relatively stable life, but he also engages in much purposive, goal-seeking behaviour. Is it possible to construct a machine which displays this kind of behaviour? A fascinating and ingenious machine is Grey Walter's (1961) *machina speculatrix* which not only performs complex movements and operations but plugs itself into a recharging circuit when its power falls below a critical level. Computer design has reached a very advanced stage in a relatively short period of time and sophisticated programs have been written for them. Programs exist which enable a machine to play draughts like a champion, to solve difficult theorems like a wrangler and to translate foreign languages directly. Compelling as these performances by a machine appear at first sight they are as nought compared with the intricate workings of the human brain save in speed and perseverance. A machine that genuinely innovates or creates beyond the planning of the human programmer has yet to be invented.

In the present state of the art of computer design attempts to make direct comparisons between the human brain and machines tend to be of limited value; however, this need not invalidate the findings of contemporary research workers who examine principles such as feedback in the context of human behaviour. It is also significant to note that some of the basic principles utilized by the technologist in industry have been discovered and demonstrated independently by the neuro-physiologist in the laboratory. If a servo-mechanism loses stability through feedback distortion there is a consequent drop in the efficiency of the machine, similarly if the normal feedback loop in a higher organism is disrupted simple muscular performances become impaired. A speaker listening to his own voice on a recorded tape played back with a delay of, say, one second can be reduced to a gibbering idiot. Observing your own handwriting movements through a television device with delayed visual feedback produces similar consequences. Clearly, skilled performance deteriorates if the servo-mechanisms of the nervous system are in any way impaired.

Feedback principles have been observed and recorded in human behaviour long before the advent of machines and computers under the more generalized term, "knowledge of results". In a target activity like archery, shooting or throwing for treble twenty in a game of darts knowledge of the results of previous aims or throws directly affects subsequent performance; if the first throw is on target then an attempt is made to repeat precisely the same action, if it is too low an adjustment is made to throw the dart higher. Knowledge of results has a significant functional role at all levels of intellectual behaviour, including abstract thought processes and in modern practical technology by a process which is colloquially described as "trouble-shooting". Skinner effectively exploited the principle in designing programs for teaching machines, but more of this later.

Psychologists tend to differ as to the exact function of knowledge of results in learning and thinking; is it a secondary reinforcer in the Hullian sense, is it an incentive and motivator of behaviour or is it simply a means of providing information which is utilized in planning successive stages in the solution of a problem? These points are discussed by Annett (1969) in his excellent and readable *Feedback and Human Behaviour*, some of them will be referred to under the heading of motivation.

Of the many series of experiments which have led to the construction of feedback or cybernetic models those by Deutsch and Clarkson (1959) are of particular interest because they confirm predictions made about insightful behaviour. It will be recalled that Tolman also researched in this area, but Deutsch and Clarkson came to different conclusions after they had found evidence for failure of insight in rats in the experiment shown in Fig. 12.

The rats were familiar with the geography of the alley maze, having found food in both boxes on previous runs.

First problem. No food has been placed in box 1 which is near the rat's starting point. The rat runs to box 1 along a short alley, does not explore the second short alley to the same box but goes straight to box 2 taking the long alley. There is no food reward in either box on this occasion.

Second problem. Both short paths are blocked near the first box. The rat runs towards box 1 along one of the short alleys, finds it blocked then

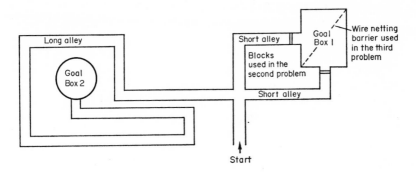

FIG. 12. From Deutsch and Clarkson (1959).

runs along the other short alley towards the same box rather than take the long alley to box 2. Again no food reward is found in the box.

Third problem. Construct a wire mesh barrier in box 1, watch the alley taken by the rat then place food on the side of the barrier opposite to this short alley chosen by the rat. Next time the rat enters the maze, according to Tolman's theory of latent learning it should choose the other short alley to box 1 as it "knows" the plan of the maze and the location of the reward. In fact, it does not—the rat takes the long alley to box 2.

Deutsch predicted that in the third problem the rat would take the long alley rather than the other short alley because the goal directed behaviour in search of food via one short alley has become "linked" to the other alley. As food-seeking via the two short alleys is linked, the longer alley is chosen as the alternative. Before food was introduced into the experiment, namely, in the first and second problems, no such associations or linkages could have been formed. The key word in the explanation of the predicted maze-running of the rat is "linkage". The model of behaviour Deutsch proposes from the experiment is a closed circuit of behaviour chains in which analysers and links receive, process and transmit impulses. Whereas in a typical S–R chain the circuit is open; in this model, the chain is closed by the introduction of feedback loops between successive links and the control unit in the organism.

There is apparently nothing difficult about the model so far, it is merely an intricate set of feedback loops until the function of the analyser is examined. The analyser is a program in the computer sense of the word which responds to all kinds of stimuli; according to Deutsch, it is determined by heredity. In the above experiment the animal is motivated by hunger, it moves from the analysis of one environmental clue to the next and from a weaker to a stronger stimulus.

As stated this is an over-simplification of the model but it serves to illustrate integrated contemporary thought on the nervous system, behaviourism, feedback loops and computer techniques. Deutsch's model is basically too simple to explain complex human behaviour; for example, concept formation and generalization which demand analysis of many competing clues or stimuli (Fig. 13).

Drawing a direct analogy between the human brain and computing machines often proves misleading to students, particularly if simple compu-

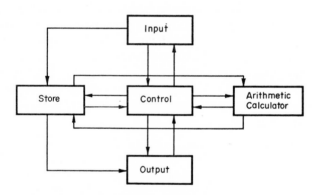

Control: Console with human operator (teleprinter)
             Commencement and sequence of operations
             Clear the store for new data
Input: Program—precise instructions about method of computation
             Data—figures to be processed, normally in binary code
Store: Storage of data and of data generated in the calculation
Arithmetic
 calculator: The mechanical process of computation
Output: Display on panel
             Print out on punched cards or paper tape

FIG. 13.

tational techniques on electrical or hand calculators are confused with digital computer operation. Before commencing to calculate or process data which has been recorded on a punched card or tape in binary code, the digital computer must first read its instructions from a prepared program. It only reads when it is commanded to do so by the control unit under human supervision. The control unit is the master mind of the computer because it initiates the input flow of data, reads the program, transfers and retrieves data to and from the memory store and it gives instructions to print-out the completed calculation. In spite of limitations in the physical storage capacity of its memory and in the number and complexity of mechanical operations which can be performed within the calculation unit itself, the computer is nevertheless tremendously flexible because of the infinite number of programs it reads. As yet, the "ability" or as some have called it the "artificial intelligence" of the computer is a direct function of the skill of the designer and the intelligence of the human programmer.

A different and more cognitive concept of feedback loops is the Test–Operate–Test–Exit or TOTE unit devised by Miller, Galanter and Pribram (1960). Each unit is called a "Plan" and sequences of plans are built up to form a complex hierarchical structure. As an illustration, part of the series of plans, used by a golfer in setting up his stance for a shot, is given in Fig. 14. Obviously from each stage in the sequence or plan there is feedback, behaviour is modified or adapted by knowledge of results. This is the basis of the practical art of "trouble-shooting" in industry, step-by-step diagnostic testing in a logically planned sequence until the error is discovered. For a complicated cycle of operations such as in a branch of the electronics industry diagnostic plans need to be published in advance as they enable a relatively inexperienced operator to locate trouble quickly and efficiently, otherwise lack of experience would have compelled him to make little better than random trial-and-error movements.

In teaching difficult skills and problem solving or the comprehension of obscure literary passages a sequence of well-thought-out plans leads to more efficient learning and it helps students to diagnose mistakes more readily. Complex plans of this kind are sometimes programmed in the Socratic question and answer style; for example, medical students can be taught something of the principles of diagnosis fairly effectively in a minimum period of time.

That the general standard of lesson preparation by student teachers is

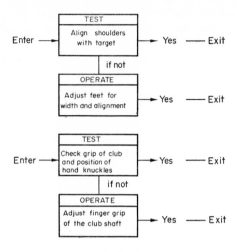

FIG. 14.

gradually declining is sometimes voiced by experienced tutors, particularly if a lesson is observed without prior access to the student's lesson plan. Is it a dying art in which logic and order are sacrificed to amorphism and flexibility? A well-prepared lesson need not and should not be inflexible, an alert teacher has access to alternative plans should the original not prove appropriate or workable in practice. Pupils from the fifth form upwards are conditioned to the idea that knowledge constantly overflows subject barriers and that frontiers slowly expand. No wonder many student teachers find difficulty in adjusting to the narrower confines of the discipline of formal learning with younger children. Unless they are prepared to plan their teaching with care and an awareness of the stage of mental development of the class a satisfactory adjustment will not be achieved.

The student requested to teach a principle or topic about which he has certain misgivings, possibly because he does not thoroughly understand the problem or has imperfect and limited knowledge of the subject, tends to adopt a defensive role and sometimes suggests alternatives with which he is more familiar. Eventually persuaded to explore the unknown he is surprised by the good response of the class to the lesson and feels the sense of achievement and self-satisfaction which comes with mastery of the unfamiliar. The student's success can only in part be attributed to reading, comprehending and memorizing in preparation for the lesson, but also to the logical organization of material in his mind in response to the oft repeated question, "how do I explain this material and in what order?" Conversely, an unprepared lesson on a subject well known and over familiar to the teacher is too frequently badly planned, poorly organized and consequently ill-received by the class.

The model proposed by Deutsch has been criticized for its limitations, Lunzer (1968) has hypothetically constructed a different feedback model of an eclectic kind which represents an attempt to bring together under one system many of the heterogeneous fragments of learning theory. Students might question whether or not this is a valid technique; yes it is, provided it is understood that a model is temporary and it will become obsolete and ultimately it will be discarded when it is shown to be impractical or too limited. The technique of matching experiment and practice against theoretical concepts in structural models is acceptable to all scientists, whether pure, applied, social or however described. In the advanced study of Geography it has proved invaluable; it has added precision and direction to the subject. The construction of theoretical models in psychology also marks an advance in methodology. Contemporary research workers tend not to become so deeply entrenched in personal beliefs and theories. Rather than uneconomically spending time and energy in attacking, defending and counter-attacking opponents they prefer to adopt a more open and flexible approach; namely, the objective examination of possibilities in a drive towards a common goal, the extension of the frontiers of knowledge.

Basically the Lunzer model consists of three units: a comparator, a selector link and an effector system. The latter corresponds to reflex, muscular and perceptual-motor movements in the organism and needs no further explanation. A comparator system has a program similar to the I.R.M. in imprinting but is capable of modification through a process akin to conditioning. It is also a detector system in which environmental cues are filtered and matched against the built-in program. If the match is perfect then there is no learning, but this a very rare occurrence. The selector link is very similar to the main control unit in a digital computer; it is a switching mechanism which governs both the comparator and effector systems. The basic links or triangular units composed of link–comparator–effector are built into complex patterns or structures termed "strategies" and these in turn are organized into a network or hierarchy of strategies called "schemata".

The concepts of strategy and schema are probably new to readers and as these terms frequently occur in the study of thinking and memory they merit attention. A strategy is a planned sequence of events commonly associated with decision making; it takes many forms from say a carefully planned move in a game like chess to intelligent guessing in an elimination game like "animal, vegetable or mineral". Schema sounds a more difficult concept but in fact is quite simple if one pictures a filing system in the mind in which the whole of a person's past experience is stored. By assimilation, sensory data and information is incorporated into the schema. Bartlett (1932) used the term in his studies of memory and described the schema as a frame of reference into which all manner of sensory inputs from the external environment or from within the organism itself are assimilated. The framework is by no means fixed, it constantly changes shape and capacity to accommodate new data.

Lunzer's model additionally stresses the total relationship between strategy and schema. For example, a child wanting to move from one room to another room in his home is aware of the spatial layout of the house: this is the schema; the route he actually takes is the strategy. Schematic concepts are nowadays considered absolutely essential in the study of behaviour. Lunzer looks upon his triangle link–comparator–effector as a cybernetic representation of Piaget's dictum that the modification of behaviour patterns necessarily involves an assimilation of environmental cues into a schema.

One of the signs of an inexperienced teacher is that he relates little new factual data, fresh ideas, novel concepts and untried movements to the past experience of children; yet later in that same lesson by some magical or divine technique he expects children to build up an insightful and logical solution to a problem about which they have no real foundation or background knowledge whatsoever. In defence he will no doubt refer to the validity and merit of the question and answer technique; so show him a file cover containing a blank piece of paper and suggest that you would like to question him on its contents. By then he should realize the significance of the schema. How many discussion periods in college fall flat because the participants have insufficient knowledge to make worthwhile points, observations and suggestions?

Reverting to Lunzer's model; the complex hierarchies of strategies and schemata and the connections between links are not considered to be innate, they are the result of learning. The model, as one must come to expect, by no means adequately and fully explains or describes all human behaviour; the nature of the basic regulating structure inherited at birth remains hypothetical; to date no one has established a firm neuro-physiological equivalent to the links, strategies and schemata in the brain.

Earlier it was suggested that current research in behaviour takes the form of highly specialized investigations into precisely defined and apparently isolated topics. Practical research into an enormously complex subject has necessarily lead to fragmentation but this must not be taken to imply that human behaviour, *per se*, is disjunctive. The fact that topics like concept development, memory, motivation and skill are given separate consideration in this or any other text in no way suggests that they are only loosely related. Fragmentation in the study of educational psychology is a real danger and one suspects that many student teachers only gain an imperfect insight into the unity of the discipline. With due warning, the topic approach need not prove too unrewarding for the reader. There is no real justification for this approach other than that it makes it easier for the student teacher, who is not a trained psychologist, to pick out parts which are directly relevant to his work with children.

Chapters 1 and 2
Additional Reading

BLIGH, D. A. (1972) *What's the Use of Lectures?* London: Penguin.

BLODGETT, H. C. (1929) The effect of the introduction of reward upon the maze performance of rats. *Univ. of California Publications in Psychology*, **4**, 113–34.

BORGER, R. and SEABORNE, A. E. M. (1966) *The Psychology of Learning.* London: Penguin.

BROADBENT, D. E. (1964) *Behaviour.* London: Methuen Univ. Paperback.

BROADBENT, D. (1970) "Review lecture". *Proclamations of the Royal Society*, Vol. 1, pp. 333–50.

BUGELSKI, B. R. (1956) *The Psychology of Learning.* London: Methuen.

DEUTSCH, J. A. (1960) *The Structural Basis of Behaviour.* London: Cambridge Univ. Press.

ESTES, W. K. (1972) *Learning.* In Dodwell, P. C.

HILGARD, E. R. and BOWER, G. H. (1966) *Theories of Learning*, 3rd edn. New York: Appleton–Century–Crofts.

KATZ, D. (1951) *Gestalt Psychology.* London: Methuen.

MACE, C. A. (1968) *The Psychology of Study*. London: Penguin.

McGEOCH, J. A. and IRION, A. L. (1952) *The Psychology of Human Learning*. New York: Longmans.

MELTON, A. W. (Ed.) (1964) *Categories of Human Learning*. New York: Academic Press.

MILLAR, S. (1968) *The Psychology of Play*. London: Penguin.

OSGOOD, C. E. (1953) *Method and Theory in Experimental Psychology*. London: Oxford Univ. Press.

PAVLOV, I. P. (1927) *Conditioned Reflexes*. London: Oxford Univ. Press.

SKINNER, B. F. (1954) *The Science of Learning and the Art of Teaching*. In Lumsdaine, A. A. and Glaser, R. (Eds.).

SKINNER, B. F. (1959) *Cumulative Record*. London: Methuen.

SLUCKIN, W. (1954) *Minds and Machines*. London: Penguin.

SLUCKIN, W. (1965) *Imprinting and Early Learning*. London: Methuen.

SLUCKIN, W. (Ed.) (1971) *Early Learning and Early Experience*. London: Penguin.

STONES, E. (1968) *Learning and Teaching: A Programmed Introduction*. London: Wiley.

THYNE, J. M. (1966) *The Psychology of Learning and Techniques of Teaching*, 2nd edn. London: Univ. of London Press.

TINBERGEN, N. (1953) *Social Behaviour in Animals with Special Reference to Vertebrates*. London: Methuen.

WATSON, J. B. (1957) *Behaviourism* (revised edition). Chicago: Phoenix Books.

CHAPTER 3

Memory

Perception

The Classical controversy as to whether learning and memory should be considered as one process or two separate and continuous processes need not worry education students unduly. Current psychological experiments and investigations into the physiology of memory have tended to prove inconclusive on this point.

Apart from physiological conditions like colour-blindness, sensory deprivation, slow adaptation and brain damage, the normal sensory processes are frequently imperfect and sometimes grossly distorted. Everyday examples of this are referred to as illusions and include those of the Gestalt figure and ground kind previously noted (p. 29) or POLITE NOTICE . Apparent movement observed in a spiral design constantly moving upwards or felt when sitting in a stationary train and the adjacent train moves out slowly also fall into this category. An illusion is normally due to incomplete or ambiguous information reaching the sense organs and to an unfulfilled or modified anticipation of sensory input based on past experience.

The learner in the active organization of his perceptions sometimes makes errors in a search for symmetry, rhythm and meaning. If he is not certain what he is looking for, say specific characteristics of an object under a microscope or listening to musical reproduction from various loudspeakers he will almost inevitably be easily deceived by what he sees or hears. The seemingly impressive loudspeakers with startling impact in the showroom often become a source of irritation and fatigue when heard at home due to their insistent coloration when fed a variety of program material. Affective states including attitudes, beliefs, boredom, inhibition, level of anxiety, motivation and preservation of self-image all influence perceptual reception in various ways at different stages in the cognitive development of the child and the adolescent. For a detailed and very readable account of the psychology of perception readers are recommended to Vernon's (1962) fascinating work.

Broadbent's Model of Selective Attention

Attention or the registration of perception is a highly selective process, an organism makes no attempt to assimilate the total number and variety of percepts that make up the environment at any given moment. Other than in the case of intense and unusual percepts like a bright flash and a loud bang people tend to perceive only what they want to perceive and this often imperfectly.

Consider the student who keeps looking at his watch during a boring lecture. Each separate occasion he does so is probably not specifically remembered, if neither the occasion nor the precise time has been registered then nothing has entered the memory store. However, assume that he registers one of the occasions when he looks at his watch, say, 10 minutes to one because he is restless, hungry and observant of the lecturer looking up at the clock at the back of the room before hurrying on. At one o'clock he might recall the incident, then promptly forget it for good. Similarly, having scanned for an unfamiliar telephone number in a directory the caller has probably forgotten it by the time he has completed his conversation. In both these cases information is said to have been registered in the primary or short-term memory store and has not passed into the secondary or long-term memory store.

The concept of a two-stage or dual storage memory system although not new in psychology has only recently been scientifically investigated by research workers such as Hebb (1949) in neurophysiology and Broadbent (1958) in the study of communication. Students familiar with contemporary popular music know what is meant by the term reverberation when it is used to describe the re-echoing of sound. Hebb's dual trace mechanism is a theory based on reverberatory activity in the neural system. He says that the input of a stimulus produces a neuronal discharge and sets up reverberatory activity in the brain and this may be equated with short-term memory. If the period of reverberation is short in duration, the "activity trace" which it makes soon dies out or decays. On the other hand, if the period is more prolonged and there is repetitive reverberatory activity, then structural changes occur in neuronal connections. This results in the formation of "structural traces" and these may be equated with long-term memory.

Broadbent postulates a double-storage system with a filter and channel between the two memory stores. Information first reaches the short-term memory store, which has a very limited capacity, and only a fraction of it is passed selectively by a filter to the larger long-term memory store (Fig. 15).

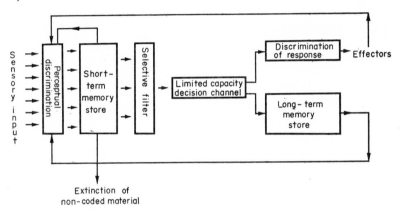

FIG. 15. Hypothetical model of attention and memory (after Broadbent, 1958).

1. Attention to competing sensory stimuli is highly selective and it depends both on the intensity and uniqueness of the sensory input and on the vigilance and state of arousal of the individual.

2. The short-term memory store is of limited capacity and only holds information for a very short period of time, possibly about 5 seconds, unless material is rehearsed and recirculated. Memory traces tend to decay rapidly and unwanted or non-coded material is extinguished or forgotten.

3. A selective filter picks out information an individual wants to pay attention to and, in Broadbent's words, "it has a permanent bias towards passing novel stimuli". In conversation, many of a speaker's words in a sentence are predictable and in terms of information they are therefore redundant.

4. The limited capacity channel is quickly overloaded if too much novel

or "real" information is to be handled in a short space of time. If the information demands are small an individual can attend to more than one set of data at a time and respond to a greater number of stimuli, and vice versa when the information demands are heavy. Information or skill which has been over-learned makes little demand on decision-making processes and is channelled automatically. The first stage of a complex process, once recognized, is handled in the same way because the later stages of the sequence are redundant and require no decision making.

5. The long-term memory store of past events may be likened to a filing system with a complex system of cross-references. Material is forgotten due to interference from competing information rather than spontaneous decay. Retention of material is affected by rehearsal, going over it in the mind of the learner, and it is important that if possible it should occur within half an hour.

6. An effector is a body organ like a muscle which moves in response to a signal transmitted along the nervous system.

7. Note recirculation via feedback loops.

What are the implications of the two-stage theory of memory, Broadbent's model in particular, for current educational practice in the classroom? If little of the total information imparted or discussed in a lesson is channelled through to the long-term memory store, how does the teacher increase the probability that significant and valuable material is selectively passed through the filter to be retained by the child? As Broadbent has suggested, this depends both on the nature and organization of the information and on the personal characteristics of the individual child including degree of attention and drive.

In psychological terms the teacher has first to gain the attention of a class, implying focusing or channelling the children's sensory perception to the task in hand, and then to maintain their vigilance or concentration at an optimum level between under-arousal and over-stimulation. Children at a low level of arousal pay little attention to what the teacher is saying; they are easily distracted by other equally bored peers or by environmental factors external to the classroom such as noise from a game of football on a nearby pitch or a class singing in the hall. A high level of arousal suggests over-excitement with a consequent impairment of performance or a lowering in standard of attainment due to anxiety. Motivation or drive is the subject of a separate chapter.

Visiting tutors commonly observe an otherwise creditable lesson virtually disintegrate in the transition period between the teacher's exposition and the commencement of individual work by children. More often than not, it is because children fail to register all the instructions given by the teacher. Either too much information is given in a very short period of time and this overloads the memory store, or it is unstructured and lacks a clear logical sequence. Worse still is the constant interruption of individual work in the form of a running commentary by the teacher on how he would like the exercise to proceed. This leads to frustration in children, simply because they mentally rebel against paying attention both to their own thoughts in working through the exercise and to the teacher's voice in the background. In modern parlance he is nothing but audible wallpaper. A defence mechanism is likely to be adopted by the child, particularly if he cannot discern which of the teacher's remarks are significant or relevant: he enters a state of habituation, remaining only partly tuned in to the teacher yet sufficiently alert or vigilant should something occur to arouse him like a bang on the blackboard. Ultimately he either switches off altogether and risks getting on with his work or else joins his colleagues in asking endless trivial questions.

The almost certain way of ensuring a smooth transition to individual work is to obtain 100 per cent attention from the class, give out instructions slowly, clearly and logically, afford an opportunity for the children to ask questions about difficulties and then let them get on quietly with the minimum of interruption. Children need to use their short-term memory in solving problems, planning approaches and organizing material and must not have their perceptual mechanism overloaded by the sound of the teacher's voice, however well intentioned and helpful he wants to be.

Short-term Memory

Recent research into the nature and characteristics of short-term memory have been summarized most excellently by Welford (1968) in *Fundamentals of Skill*; in making many references to this source the author is deeply indebted and also takes full responsibility for adapting his material for use in an educational context. That many of the research techniques in the investigation of short-term memory involve the repetition of nonsense syllables and other material which seems to have little in common with normal memorizing activity in the classroom is no excuse for dismissing it either as irrelevant or of little consequence compared with long-term retention. Readers are warned that not all psychologists agree on the existence of a separate short-term memory store; those who do support the dual theory say little about its location in the central nervous system, its capacity and how it actually codes and retrieves data.

What is the function of the short-term memory store and has it any relevance for the educational development of children? Obviously it holds information until it is of no further significance and therefore decays, or it rehearses and passes on material to long-term storage. As a temporary hold it also allows time for decision-making until further data is received. In dictation there is usually a slight delay between the spoken word and the shorthand written in a notebook because the secretary waits for additional information to make literary sense out of what is heard. In attending to a long sentence, the earlier parts are probably stored if there is too much information to grasp in a single span. Similarly in problem solving, data and strategies are temporarily held in store whilst material is reorganized, coded and calculated. The economy of this lies in the number of solutions which can be mentally worked without recourse to physical activity. As a mental jotter it is indispensable.

Most of the characteristics of immediate memory are not unique, they are shared in common with long-term retention and include improvement with rehearsal, familiarity and meaning; or conversely, decay with interference and lack of coding. The limited memory span or store capacity raises several important questions such as, why are the beginnings and ends of a passage or sequence more easily remembered than the middle? Obviously information is not stored in strict rotation otherwise final items would certainly be more readily recalled than earlier items. The brain probably recodes incoming data in a different pattern or sequence.

Teachers need to be constantly aware of the danger of overloading the immediate memory store and should time the presentation of material at a rate appropriate to the handling capacity of the class. Novel and unstructured information with little obvious meaning should be communicated slowly and deliberately so that children have working space to recode and assimilate it to past experience.

The importance of short-term retention may be judged from its role in a variety of thought processes and skills. In problem-solving in the formation of concepts, in reading patterns, in the interpretation of topographical maps, in tracking data and attending to multiple display panels information must be temporarily stored.

Long-term Memory

The teacher who organizes information in the best possible sequence also provides a model which serves as a frame of reference for the child working alone under similar circumstances at some future date. When a person claims that his memory has improved he probably means that he is better able to organize data into meaningful patterns and therefore assimilates it more economically. Treisman (1966) and other researchers would argue that it is the number of cross-connections between items in a cerebral dictionary which is important and that they probably assume greater significance than meaningfulness itself. The greater and richer the variety of cross-connections the more likely it is that data will be accurately recalled.

Whereas the capacity of the primary or immediate recall store is relatively small; that is, in the region of seven digits for most adults, the long-term memory store has an almost infinite capacity and has far greater stability in the retention of data. Information is more permanently filed in it and it is fairly easily retrieved provided there are sufficient cues or cross-references available. Given the necessary cues it is surprising how much of the past can be remembered. With relearning a lot of factual material can be relocated in a relatively short period of time, for instance in revising for an examination.

Analogies between the secondary memory store and filing techniques are currently fashionable, but how this efficient system exactly works in practice is an unsolved mystery. In particular, the method of coding information presents many difficulties because the input is so diverse that it must be transformed prior to permanent storage. Furthermore, it is suggested that at the same time as information is filed, anticipation or expectancy of possible use in the future is also taken into account.

The factors affecting efficiency in remembering are traditionally classified under three main headings:

(i) nature of the material to be retained,
(ii) conditions of practice or rehearsal and

(iii) characteristics and differences of individual learners.

Inability to remember or "forgetting" is discussed later as a separate topic purely for convenience and for no other reason; in life the processes of learning, remembering, forgetting, recalling and recognizing are practically inseparable.

(i) *Nature of the material*

Familiar, meaningful and structured material is more easily retained than unrecognizable, nonsensical and haphazard data. It is easier for readers of the English tongue to remember short pieces of connected prose or verse than lists of isolated words or strings of nonsense syllables. Translate such material into a foreign language, preferably with a non-roman script, say Arabic, Hindi or Chinese characters, and the difficulties are magnified out of proportion. Katona's (1940) experiments suggest that material which is organized and meaningful is not only in itself more easily retained but more readily permits and facilitates the learning of new material. In Great Britain many people regret the adoption of all figure numbers in the public telephone system. How much easier it was to remember associated place names like WIMbledon than 946, or romantic names like ELGar, HOGarth and WORdsworth!

Material which evokes pleasant emotional associations is more easily retained and lasts throughout the whole span of life. For young children an attractive colourful and rhythmical presentation is known to be an asset; but why restrict it to the junior age group? Drabness has no specific virtue in education. The notion that austerity and obscurity are commendable because they make the child adopt the "right" attitude to learning, exercise the thought processes and demand time for absorption and therefore en- hance memory, is as nonsensical as it is uneconomical, yet it is slow to die.

Children sometimes hear adults recount that in certain schools in the past it was considered deplorable to obtain information from an easy as opposed to a difficult textbook and that memory aids for revision were but one step from copying and cheating. Before the current flood of paperback publica- tions, in many college circles it was deemed moronic to read and quote from paperbacks particularly if the tutor thought they had been written for the so-called layman.

A good story-teller with a sense of humour not only stimulates and holds the attention of a class, but also provides a climate in which self-discipline and genuine learning flourish. The colourful, rich and varied experiences narrated by the skilled raconteur, possibly trivial and of little consequence in themselves, often prove to have associations of lasting significance for an audience. No teacher should consider himself competent in his craft until he has learned the art of telling a good story. Obviously a sense of balance is desirable; otherwise, if overdone, only Mr. X's best jokes, or Mr. Y's wartime experiences or Miss Z's travelogue will be recalled by the class and the worth-while content will not register and be retained.

(ii) *Conditions of practice*

In discussing the various approaches to effective methods of memorizing, students most commonly disagree about the distribution of practice time and the organization of material into manageable loads. Unfortunately it is difficult to make generalizations and comparisons between techniques because so much depends on the individual learner and his confidence in a method which personally works for him. Given enough time for revision or study, as opposed to intensive cramming, it is probably better to break down practice into shorter sessions with intervals to recover from fatigue. With over-long sessions the law of diminishing returns operates; a point is reached when it is no longer economical to go on memorizing and it is more beneficial to turn to a completely different type of activity.

It is similarly difficult to reach firm conclusions about the relative efficiency of whole compared with part learning; for example, whether to learn the whole poem in a single unit, stage by stage or in successive coup-lets. If the whole method is adopted certain advantages accrue from over-sight of the work, but it needs a lot of confidence because the initial returns seem to be so disproportionately small. The part method offers the advan-tage of greater motivation which comes with the attainment of successive sub-goals and more immediate feedback. In practice it is generally found that few people adopt a rigid approach to memorizing, most alternate between methods according to the length of material to be learned and its criterion of difficulty.

The superiority of active rehearsal over passive repetition is indisputable whether it takes the form of reciting lines and lists prior to an examination, or in mentally rehearsing the teaching of selected material in preparation for a subsequent lesson. Students often find that as a result of projecting themselves into the learning role of a child they achieve positive success, probably because they have organized their teaching material more effectively in the process of rehearsal. On no account should a tutor accept an argument from a student to the effect that he is unwilling to teach something because he knows relatively little about the subject and that he is afraid of forgetting too much in front of a class. Some of the best lessons come from students who have mastered novel material and techniques in lesson preparation and in doing so have gained insight into difficulties likely to be encountered by children in their learning. Far from meeting difficulty in remembering the content of the lesson, students in their self-evaluation often comment on their over-ambition and inability to get through all the material they had prepared. In revising for examinations it is valuable to mentally rehearse possible solutions to anticipated questions; this not only aids subsequent recall but also the logical organization of answers.

(iii) *Individual differences*

Some intelligence tests incorporate a standardized memory scale and an analysis of these scores suggest that the average memory span varies from two digits at the age of $2\frac{1}{2}$ years, to six digits at the age of 10 years and to about seven digits (plus or minus two) throughout the teen-age years followed by a slow regression to six digits in middle age. Variations in scores between the sexes reflect personal interests, attitudes and experiences, on neutral material there is no significant difference between boys and girls.

There is a positive correlation between memory span and intelligence test scores and this is anything but surprising if the role of short-term memory in problem solving and thinking is recalled. Of more general interest is the argument as to whether speed of learning is correlated with short-term immediate memory or delayed recall or both. Underwood's (1966) experiments suggest that fast learners are superior in both kinds of memory test provided practice time is held constant. A slow learner might be prepared to spend more time in practice and rehearsal but ultimately the advantage will always lie with the fast learner.

The role of motivation in learning and memorizing is too large a topic for discussion under this heading; suffice to say at present that rewards, goals, ego-involvement, intrinsic curiosity and desire to please all affect retention. Similarly aspects of personality, including anxiety states, should not be overlooked.

Individual differences in memory show themselves under a variety of different circumstances. Abernethy (1940) has shown that environmental conditions influence memory; generally more is recalled if a person is tested in the room where the original learning took place. It is possible to form a greater number of associations in a familiar environment therefore there are more cues available to aid recall. Finally, is it reasonable to draw distinctions between different kinds of memory in individuals as one does with personality types, for example, between introverts and extroverts? Gardner *et al.* (1959) used the expressions "sharpeners" and "levellers" to describe the assimilation of perceptual impressions to memory schemata. Sharpeners have a well-differentiated memory compared with the more blurred memory schemata of levellers, therefore recall of past experience is more freely available to them.

Forgetting

In psychological studies of recall and forgetting it is necessary to assume that information has been registered and stored. Quite commonly when a child fails to answer a question and states that he has "forgotten" he means that he never knew the information in the first place. To add further to the child's confusion teachers normally respond with a supplementary question, "why have you forgotten it?" He should really be inquiring as to why the child did not understand or was not paying attention and learning.

The concept of the decay of a neural trace was introduced in connection with short-term memory and Hebb's theory of reverberation, although it is a seemingly commendable model further physiological evidence is needed to establish it as a firm explanation of the process of forgetting. Possibly it represents only one way in which human beings forget. Some students are confused and misinformed about the role of time in forgetting because decay implies fading with time and there is a correlation between the passage of time and failure of memory. Time itself is not a cause of forgetting, it is simply a dimension in which factors such as interference and repression operate (see Fig. 16).

Ebbinghaus (1885) learned lists of nonsense syllables. The retention curve

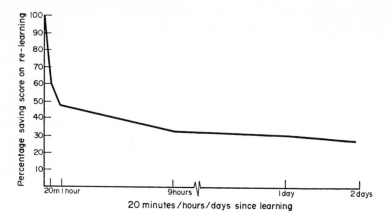

FIG. 16. Retention curve (after Ebbinghaus, 1885).

indicates how much learning has been retained over a given period of time, and the saving score the per cent reduction in time needed for relearning. Subsequent learning demands fewer attempts or shorter time than initial learning, hence "saving score".

The normal method of measuring relearning is to express time saved in the second learning as a percentage of the first learning:

$$\text{Saving} = \frac{\text{First learning trials} - \text{Relearning trials} \times 100}{\text{First learning trials}}$$

For example, if it takes a language student fifteen trials to learn a list of words by heart and a fortnight later he takes only three trials to relearn the same list, then his saving score is:

$$\frac{15 - 3 \times 100}{15} = 80 \text{ per cent}$$

Interference is classified as either "retroactive", in which material learned first is impaired by the learning of later material; or "proactive", in which the learning of the second material is impaired as a result of having learned the first material. The terms become clearer when two simple experimental designs are diagrammatically illustrated. Either nonsense syllables or words from different languages with common roots are selected as material to be learned. First, retroactive interference:

Experimental Group	Learn A	Learn B	Recall A
Control Group	Learn A	Rest	Recall A

Two matched groups of subjects take part in the experiment; an experimental group and a control group. Each individual in the experimental group learns, say, a list of French words (A), then immediately learns a list of Spanish words (B) and is afterwards required to recall the French words (A). Each member of the control group learns the list of French words (A), then engages in some totally different activity or else rests. They are also required to recall the French words (A) after a period of time. If the average scores for recall are significantly greater for the control than the experimental group then it is assumed that the learning of the Spanish words (B) has interfered with the learning of the French words (A). The impairment or interference of the first learning by the second is attributed to retroactive inhibition.

Clearly the extent of the interference is a function of the similarity or difference in the material or data used in the experiment. If the material is so alike that the learner does not easily discriminate between the two sets of data then the probability of retroactive interference occurring is greater. The implications of this in the construction of a school time-table are fairly obvious, one does not learn Latin, Spanish and Italian in successive lessons even if economic use of the language laboratory favours such blocking of periods. Also it is not only between periods that interference occurs, but within periods; therefore plan lessons with changes in the variety of activity in order to keep interference to a minimum.

There is an old Spanish proverb, "lección dormida, lección sabida", which says a lesson slept on is a lesson learned. Could this literally be taken as a statement of fact that relatively little of what one has learned in the previous evening is forgotten during the night. Jenkins and Dallenbach (1924) have shown experimentally that retention is greater after a period of sleep, in the first 2 hours of sleep there is some forgetting but in successive

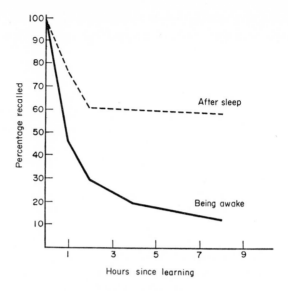

FIG. 17. Retention after sleep compared with being awake
(after Jenkins and Dallenbach, 1924).

hours the amount forgotten represents only a small decremental loss (see
Fig. 17).

Proactive interference:

Experimental Group	Learn A	Learn B	Recall B
Control Group	Rest	Learn B	Recall B

Again, two matched groups of subjects are required to take part as
individuals in the experiment. The experimental group learns a straightforward algebraic solution to a problem in physics (B) having previously
learned in mathematics the principles of say Boolean algebra (A). Each
member of the group is later required to recall the algebraic techniques
learned in physics (B). The control group which has not studied Boolean
algebra (A) in mathematics, but has learned physics, is also required to
recall the algebraic techniques learned in physics (B). If the average scores

for the control group are significantly higher than those of the experimental group then it is assumed that the prior learning of Boolean algebra (A) has interfered with the recall of the algebraic methods learned in physics (B). The interference of the previously learned material by material which has been subsequently learned is called proactive inhibition.

Most of the experimenters in proactive interference, for example Underwood and Postman (1960), have asked for nonsense syllables to be learned and recalled; with more meaningful material, the results are generally much less spectacular and differences are barely significant. Similarly, material which has been over-learned is much less susceptible to interference, proving the necessity for an initial thorough learning of essential basic data and its constant revision.

Interference theory has been put forward as another possible explanation of the phenomena which is characteristic of recalling items in serial order; namely, that the first and last items are more easily recalled than the middle items. As the greatest amount of retroactive and proactive interference is likely to occur in the centre of a poem or a list of items this will prove the most difficult part to learn and recall. It also accounts for the Welsh preacher's concept of a good sermon: "First I tell them what I am going to tell them, then I tell them, and finally I tell them what I have just told them." For a review summary of interference in memory the paper by Slamecka and Ceraso (1960) is recommended.

Of lesser practical significance for students of education are explanations of memory failure under the heading of "motivated forgetting", including Freud's theory of repression. Associations, actions and experiences which, if recalled, would cause displeasure or arouse anxiety tend to be blocked from consciousness. The evidence for this hypothesis is largely clinical and is not easily verified under controlled laboratory experimental conditions.

In the light of current knowledge the only conclusion one draws from a survey of possible explanations of forgetting is that no single hypothesis is adequate; it is a matter of multiple causation. Readers who find this the most inconclusive of conclusions may take comfort in the fact that very little of what is said to have been forgotten is irretrievably lost, given sufficient clues the amount of material an individual is capable of recalling is enormous.

So far the term recall has been used in a generalized manner and no reference has been made to imperfect recall or to the process of recognition. It is usually agreed that people find it easier to recognize a person's face than to recall his name or other personal characteristics, or that it is easier to identify a photograph of a person rather than to describe him in detail. Similarly it is more likely that students will correctly answer the question, "What work of Shakespeare is common to Berlioz, Prokofiev and Tschaikovsky?", than, "What composition is common to the following composers, Berlioz, Prokofiev and Tschaikovsky?", than, "Name one composer other than Berlioz, Prokofiev and Tschaikovsky who used the phrase 'Romeo and Juliet' in the title of a composition". From a study of objective tests of the "true–false" or "cross-out the oddity" type it is clear that recognition is not as difficult as recall; it is much less demanding because of the greater availability of cues and prompts. The confines of recognition are limited, in comparison recall is boundless. Generally it would be wrong to equate scores on a test mainly involving recall with one largely demanding recognition, but there are some marginal examples in which the opposite might occur as a result of misinterpreting cues. If a geography group is asked to name the three main salt-producing towns of Cheshire they generally give the correct answer: namely, Middlewich, Northwich and Sandbach. However, if asked to cross out the odd town in the sequence: Middlewich, Northwich, Nantwich and Sandbach they more frequently delete Sandbach instead of the non-salt producing town, Nantwich.

Teachers realize too well that recognition and recall are not always 100 per cent perfect and magistrates know that even with the best of intentions and highest of motives how difficult it is for a witness to give wholly accurate testimony in evidence. Bartlett (1932) wrote a fascinating account of memory distortion in his comprehensive and now classical publication, *Remembering*. His methods are quite simple to reproduce with small groups of students and they form the basic framework for a worthwhile discussion period. The techniques have been very well summarized by Hunter (1957) who discusses their implications both generally and with specific reference to the spread of rumour and folklore.

In the method of repeated reproduction a subject is required to recall the contents of a picture or to recount a story at intervals. If the period between the intervals is relatively short, the information remembered tends to stabilize at a fixed brevity and subsequent repetition neither adds nor detracts data. Lengthen the period between intervals and the narrative or the description of the picture becomes so distorted compared with the original that it is almost unrecognizable. The transformation tends to be gradual and the inaccuracies incremental. For demonstration purposes this is too prolonged a method, therefore in practice serial production is more widely adopted; that is, the repetition of a story by one person to another as in the spread of scandal, gossip and rumour. Obviously the two methods are not identical yet the conclusions drawn from them appear to have much in common. Serial reproduction is rarely encountered in school and in other learning situations but it is nevertheless a useful simulation technique.

Rumours spread from group to group, person to person at an alarming rate; stories are elaborated, exaggerated and reconstructed as they are passed on. As soon as firm and reliable information is obtained they quickly die. During the war false stories deliberately circulated in neutral countries like Spain soon spread through occupied Europe and were subsequently picked up in one of the sounding boards like Sweden or the Lebanon. It sometimes had quite amusing consequences if, say, the security branch of intelligence, not having been previously warned of the rumour-mongering activities of another branch, reported the original but now grossly distorted rumour back to the country of origin as "reliable information". Rumour was particularly rife prior to "D"-day and the landings in Normandy; as soon as an official announcement of the date and location of invasion was made, it fell to proportions normally associated with war.

Bartlett's method of serial reproduction brilliantly illustrates the spread of rumour and how the process of reconstruction of a story operates in recall, particularly if the narrative is somewhat obscure as it is in "The War of the Ghosts". Read the story (Hunter, page 88) to a volunteer student who is asked to memorize it and repeat it to a second student who has not heard the original reading, then to a third and so on until about seven students are involved. If possible make a tape recording of the narrators for subsequent discussion and analysis; it usually reveals the following points:

(i) An incoherent folk-tale emerges as a firmly structured story with a large injection of personal interpretation to make it rational and meaningful.

(ii) In making it a coherent story there is omission of detail, emphasis of salient features and general over-simplification.

(iii) Shades of meaning, subtleties of argument and nuances are traded for direct expression and lack of ambiguity.

(iv) Personal experience and peer group culture is unconsciously revealed in a conventional literary style characteristic of the narrator and acceptable to the group.

(v) The beginning and the end of the story is more easily remembered but proper names and numbers are not.

(vi) Recounted stories become progressively shorter until a fairly constant brevity is reached; only occasionally is it expanded in search of meaning and in the elaboration of minor points of detail.

Hunter sums up the process of recall in the formulae:

Recall = literal reproduction + imaginative reconstruction.

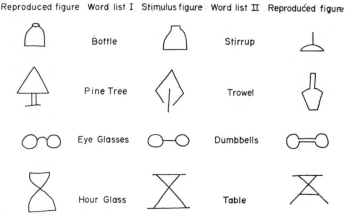

FIG. 18. Stimulus and reproduced figures (after Carmichael, 1932).

Similarly Talland (1968) uses the phrase: "remembering is a constructive process, not mere duplication". Another experiment which illustrates the effect of personal interpretation and suggestion on recall was made by Carmichael *et al.* (1932) on the relationship between stimulus figures and figures reproduced after hearing two different word lists (Fig. 18).

Subjects were shown a set of ambiguous stimulus figures and were told that they would be asked to draw them from memory. Before doing so, the experimenter suggested to one group that a certain figure looked like, say, an hour glass, but to the other group, a table. The word which had been suggested clearly distorted and biased the nature of a subject's recall of the original ambiguous drawing.

It is often necessary for children to learn by heart or commit to rote memory fundamental and basic data for the furtherance of study in a subject; for example, the multiplication tables in arithmetic, verb endings in a foreign language or a skill like riding a bicycle. This is known as "overlearning" and it represents one stage beyond mastery of a subject.

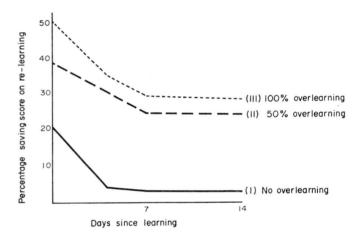

FIG. 19. Overlearning and retention (after Krueger, 1929).

Krueger (1929) showed the effects of overlearning on retention with three groups of subjects: (i) who stopped learning at the point of the first perfect recall, (ii) who carried on learning for half as many trials again as the first perfect recall, that is 50 per cent overlearning, and (iii) who carried on learning for twice as many trials as required for perfect recall, that is 100 per cent overlearning. Figure 19 shows the significant improvement in retention as a result of overlearning not only over the whole session but at given intervals.

As a precautionary note, overlearning can prove uneconomic as many students know to their cost. In revising for examinations students tend to spend too much time going laboriously over material they recognize, understand and already know instead of concentrating on imperfectly known and novel data. This is quite natural because in a typical exercise demanding learning by heart, say, seven possible causes of an event; if in mental rehearsal only six are correctly recalled, it is customary to go over the list of causes time and time again until all seven are perfectly remembered. The trouble with this is that it is not always the same item which is forgotten at each attempt and this leads to anxiety, frustration, fatigue and loss of confidence. There is no need for such pessimism. If it subsequently becomes necessary to reproduce the list of causes under examination conditions it is more than likely that enough clues will be evoked in the time taken to write out the answer to facilitate perfect recall. In over-learning the law of diminishing returns operates and this varies with the nature of the material to be learned.

The ability to relearn quickly is an important mental defence mechanism, it is also time-saving because the learner need not go back to the beginning and spend exactly the same number of hours in learning material on a second occasion. Previously learned information rarely disappears without trace. The extent to which children of different abilities forget basic data in specific school subjects over varying periods of time including vacations needs to be investigated by empirical research. Very little is known about short- and long-term rates of forgetting in different subjects of the curriculum.

RNA and Memory

Traditional psychological laboratory experiments represent but one approach to the study of human memory; on the clinical side there are many investigations into physical and brain disorders, including amnesia in its various forms. In biochemistry fascinating inquiries are made into the role of ribonucleic acid RNA in learning and retention. Hydén (1965) put forward the hypothesis that if deoxyribonucleic acid DNA is directly responsible for the coding or blueprint of genetic inheritance, then RNA may be responsible for the storage of memory in individuals. It is known that electrical impulses, such as those generated or heightened when learning takes place, change the structure of protein molecules. The molecular structures are reproduced over and over again by means of RNA and in so doing reproduce the original pattern of electrical impulses. Learning is therefore a function of RNA and its associated proteins and memory is the storage of protein molecules.

The storage capacity of an RNA molecule is enormous; but what other evidence is there to support Hydén's hypothesis? It has been reported by McConnell (1962) that the amount of RNA in neural cells is increased when an organism is activated as in the learning situation. Furthermore, RNA obtained from conditioned planaria and injected into a second group of planaria will facilitate more rapid conditioning. Similarly there is some evidence that if RNA from trained rats is injected into untrained rats it enhances transfer of specifically learned tasks, see Bahrick and Bahrick (1964) and Fjerdingstad et al. (1965).

There are also suggestions that as a result of inhibiting RNA synthesis in animals it is possible to impair conditioning, learning and memory. Human patients with memory disorders have shown some improvement after the injection RNA or allied drugs. Unfortunately replicas of the reported experiments have not always proved confirmatory and a number are distinctly negative, therefore it is not yet valid to make firm conclusions about the role of RNA in memory. Certainly there has been no breakthrough in research into methods of coding, possibly RNA's role lies more in the transmission rather than storage of information.

Additional Reading

BADDELEY, A. D. (1972) Human Memory. In Dodwell, P. C.

BARLOW, F. (1951) Mental Prodigies. London: Hutchinson.

GREGORY, R. (1967) Eye and Brain. London: World University Library, Weidenfeld and Nicolson.

HERRIOT, P. et al. (1973) Organization and Memory. London: Methuen.

MELTON, A. W. and MARTIN, E. (Eds.) (1972) Coding Processes in Human Memory. Washington D.C.: Winston.

ROBINSON, J. O. (1972) The Psychology of Visual Illusion. London: Hutchinson Univ. Library.

POSTMAN, L. and KEPPEL, G. (Eds.) (1969) Verbal Learning and Memory: Selected Readings. London: Penguin.

CHAPTER 4

Motivation

Concept of Motivation

Some aspects of motivation have already been discussed directly or by implication in the study of learning theories; this was inevitable as learning and motivation are inextricably linked, indeed many claim that motivation is the "heart of the learning process". If learning is defined as a permanent change in behaviour as a result of experience, then motivation is the study of the activation or arousal of behaviour, its strength and direction. The vocabulary of the subject is expansive and continues to grow at a pace faster than an acceptable understanding of its complex nature; it is a splendid example of a polymorphous concept with a diversity of interpretation and classification. Adjectives like *drive, need, goal, urge, impulse, set* and *incentive* commonly occur in the language of psychology to describe basic motives. In the classroom the more readily observed surface motives are generally referred to as *attitudes, interests, rewards, reproof, curiosity, status, anxiety to please* and so forth. This immediately raises the problem as to whether it is necessary or worth while to attempt a classification of human motives; for example, to differentiate between general and specific motives.

Many behaviourists would argue that basic biological needs such as food for the survival of the organism or sex for the survival of the species are the mainsprings of activity. Need results from deprivation; whether it is a natural need as in the case of food by a hungry person, or an acquired need—for example, alcohol or drugs by an addict. The search for food or activity as a consequence of need is called drive.

For the practical teacher the concept of need reduction and drive is too primitive and too distant from the everyday behaviour of children in the classroom where individual needs are subtle, complex and quite often completely hidden and disguised. An hierarchical structure of needs says

66

little about human behaviour, it is simply a convenient method of classification. It is possible to think of an arrangement analogous to a gearing system
in which a large cog drives several smaller and decreasing cogs until the
required ratio is obtained. However, this is not a very satisfactory model
because it would have to be exceedingly complex to account for all the
possible combinations and permutations of human motives. Also, motive
and behaviour are not always predictable. Much social behaviour is of this
kind; for example, the person who remains silent rather than upset a host
and friend, or finds it hard to come to a decision about someone who
continually gives offence, whether he should be ignored or confronted.

Other classifications of motives prove equally unsatisfactory in the quest
for causal explanations of man's propensity for action. The well-known
dichotomy, intrinsic and extrinsic motivation, is useful to the teacher as a
general description, yet much that is intrinsic to a person, like reading a book
for enjoyment, was once extrinsically motivated in the home and in the
early years of school. Probably it is wiser for students to forget academic
classifications of motives and first look at the relationship between an
organism and its environment in a broad general sense, then talk about
specific motives for particular aspects of human behaviour like learning
poetry, skills in athletics, aesthetic appreciation and manners in public.

Clearly if learning and motivation are very closely related then it is
necessary to make reference back to learning theory for possible explanations and suggestions. Readers should be familiar with two of them: the
need reduction hypothesis supported by the behaviourists and man's
purposeful behaviour advocated by the cognitive theorists. To these may
be added the role of the unconscious in motivation as proposed by Freud.
There is no need to restate these theories because the implications are fairly
self-evident.

What is the function of motivation in a cybernetic or feedback theory of
learning? The elements of a servo-mechanism including a closed circuit, a
regulator and stability of output have been discussed but where does
motivation fit into the analogy with human learning? Annett (1969) would
argue that the whole idea of fitting motivation into a feedback circuit is
superfluous because motivation, *per se*, is feedback in action. Knowledge of
results or feedback signals error information which in turn releases corrective action. He arrives at this conclusion from an examination of the incentive and reinforcement effects of motivation. Incentives make for greater

and more sustained effort, for speed and accuracy; in short, they increase drive. On the other hand, reinforcement is said to reduce drive.

Teachers tend to capitalize on the incentive function of reward, particularly when they set standards of performance and provide information about the learner's position relative to that standard. Annett rightly points out the almost insignificant value of knowledge of results without reference to a standard or level of performance, a target or a goal. With an incentive it is the promise of reward which is effective because the actual reward is made *after* the required behaviour change. Also the reward should be given in small increments rather than in a single unit, otherwise it will no longer function as an incentive. Skinner's pigeons kept on working because a few pellets of food were insufficient to satisfy the needs of hungry birds.

Knowledge of results not only provides information of the kind normally associated with the word "result", that is, a score, mark or percentage, but it also determines a plan or strategy for the next performance. This assumes, of course, that a person has reached a level of maturity in thought development which enables him to look back and overview his past performances. Certainly young children are not capable of this kind of thinking, neither are some intellectually retarded adults.

An efficiently functioning servo system maintains stability and in the living organism it is also functionally desirable to maintain a homeostatic state. Contemporary psychologists recognize the significance of the regulation of human behaviour and the necessity for a state of balance between a high and low state of arousal. Normally when a child is bored he is underaroused and the monotony sends him in search of stimulation, but when he has become over-active or over-aroused he might seek peace and quiet. The tendency towards balanced activity is a classical example of a regulatory system. A well-planned school time-table should cater for this essential need. Many experienced teachers will strongly deny the concept of balance, too often they see and hear too much over-aroused activity and precious little of the under-aroused state. A suggestion that less able children tend to be over-active because they more frequently express themselves in overt behaviour rather than engage in thinking deserves investigation, but it would have to take into consideration many variables including desire to please and peer group conformity. Possibly differences in personality should also be considered; it is well known that some individuals take more kindly to the routine monotony associated with dull repetitive tasks than others who are driven to desperation by sensory deprivation and lack of stimuli. A homeostatic theory of motivation is postulated not only on evidence derived from observed behaviour but also from the study of neuro-physiological processes in the brain.

It is known that the hypothalamus controls important body functions such as the regulation of temperature and the organization of metabolism, functions typically compared with a thermostatic control in a domestic central heating system. Recent physiological research into reward and punishment by electrical stimulation of the hypothalamus suggests that this is the centre of motivation in the brain. Furthermore, the reticular formation which controls the state of arousal in an organism is located immediately below the hypothalamus and also appears to function like a servomechanism. The significance of the adjacency of these centres and their regulatory function is not yet fully understood but it is noteworthy that they are located in the deeper or basal centre of the brain.

To the young student teacher motivation is of double significance in that he has to constantly motivate himself in the preparation of lessons, essays and coursework; also he has to learn how to motivate children in the actual practice of teaching. Unfortunately there is no simple straightforward and logical method of classifying either motives or the factors which are said to affect motivation. Purely for the convenience of readers an arbitrary division is made into the following categories: objectives and goals, self-concepts and ego-involvement and social group influences.

Objectives and Goals

It is said that a learner must feel an urge, desire or need to learn; few will dispute this. Also there are times when the learner wants to know how he is progressing and where it is leading. With young children motivation is almost by necessity extrinsic, for they have insufficient intellectual maturity to comprehend long-term objectives; however, they quickly respond to other forms of motivation in which objectives are more immediate, clear and generally attainable. Older children want to know the specific end-product, goal or target of learning quite implicitly and as they become more sophisticated and mature in outlook they like to feel that the ultimate aims are worth achieving and desirable. Too often in education in the past the content of the school curriculum and methods of teaching have been dictated by what a particular teacher decides is a need, rather than what individual children feel is needed.

The fact that pupils' needs are rarely expressed in the classroom, especially in large and formal classes, should not be taken as an indication that they do not exist. It is a courageous child who publicly admits to limitations in his attention, comprehension or skill at computation. This aspect of motivation looms large in arguments between teacher-dominated versus child-centred education, yet if one looks at the controversy objectively the inescapable conclusion is that under both régimes the teacher ultimately determines what has to be learned and attained. In the formal and traditional case it is obvious to an outside observer who is determining needs; in child-centred education it is less obvious, but it is still the teacher who is setting the goals at the planning stage.

Responsibility for the determination of objectives lies with the teacher whose duty it is to present them to children in logical and meaningful statements. All too frequently one comes across examination syllabuses written in the broadest and most generalized terms and one suspects that they are deliberately presented as vaguely as possible in order to maintain maximum flexibility in covering a compass of topics. They serve little useful function other than to frustrate uncertain candidates and to shield unimaginative examiners. On the other hand, how stimulating it is to read a well-thought-out syllabus with clear objectives stated in unambiguous terminology. It is the right of every fee-paying candidate in any subject to demand from a public examination body a statement of its objectives, if it cannot provide one then it has no business to attempt to evaluate a candidate's performance in that subject.

It is strongly recommended that as a practical exercise each student teacher should examine part of a syllabus and attempt a classification of objectives using either the well-publicized model of Bloom (1956) or one of the composites which can be found in Beard (1970) or Stones (1970). In a subject like English it is a more difficult exercise to complete than in mathematics or the physical sciences, but it will prove worth while especially if followed up in group discussion. The statement of aims must be realistic and attainable by the majority. If it contains long-term objectives it should also specify sub-objectives in an hierarchical structure or chain of intermediate goals. Hierarchical is used in the sense that before a learner progresses from one stage to another it is assumed that he has assimilated and thoroughly understands all that has gone before.

Bloom (1956) and his co-workers began their specific investigation into curricula development and evaluation by collecting information on teaching objectives from a wide cross-section of educational authorities and sources. From an analysis of the data they constructed a classification of educational objectives in the cognitive domain. It is called a taxonomy because the classification is hierarchical in the sense that each level makes successively greater demands on intellectual skill and incorporates all that has gone before. A classification based on specific relationships of this kind is valuable in subsequent evaluation and provides a more than useful guideline in test design and content analysis. The second part of the group's work, a taxonomy for the affective domain, was published by Krathwohl *et al.* in 1964, but, of course, attitudes and the like are far more difficult to classify objectively. Attempts have also been made to classify objectives in the psychomotor domain, notably by Guilford (1958) and Simpson (1966).

TAXONOMY OF EDUCATIONAL OBJECTIVES
Cognitive domain
Bloom's classification of educational goals

1. KNOWLEDGE
   (*a*) Knowledge of specifics   (i) terminology
                                    (ii) specific facts
   (*b*) Knowledge of ways and means of dealing with specifics
                                    (i)   conventions
                                    (ii) trends and sequences
                                    (iii) classifications and categories
                                    (iv) criteria
                                    (v)   methodology
   (*c*) Knowledge of universals and abstractions
                                    (i) principles and generalizations
                                    (ii) theories and structures

2. COMPREHENSION
   (*a*) Translation
   (*b*) Interpretation
   (*c*) Extrapolation

3. APPLICATION

4. ANALYSIS
   (*a*) Elements

(b) Relationships
(c) Organizational principles
5. SYNTHESIS
    (a) Production of a unique communication
    (b) Production of a plan
    (c) Derivation of a set of abstract relations
6. EVALUATION
    (a) Judgement in terms of internal criteria or evidence
    (b) Judgement in terms of external criteria or evidence

Knowledge is equated with the normal psychological process of recalling data, categories and principles from the memory store. Comprehension implies understanding the consequences of events, a reorganization of material and translation to alternative verbal statements and to symbols at an elementary and somewhat restricted level. Application suggests the use of abstractions such as notions and general ideas in particular and concrete situations. Analysis is the reduction of a communication to its constituent parts to demonstrate its hierarchical structure of ideas, the nature of the relations between ideas and the identification of patterns of ideas which assist understanding. Synthesis is the rearrangement of elements to form a unique communication; namely, a new whole or pattern which was not previously identifiable. Evaluation takes two forms: making judgements about internal consistency including the recognition of fallacious arguments, and making comparisons with other works of excellent quality and standard.

Objections to a specific statement of objectives prior to teaching are often based on their limited use by practising teachers and examining authorities and are couched in such terms as: "if objectives are so fundamentally important why is it that very few teachers are prepared to state them, and even if requested to do so, find difficulty in classifying them clearly?" Setting aside teachers who never consciously think directly about objectives but acquire them incidently by tradition or from textbooks and syllabuses, what are the arguments of those who believe that formally stated objectives are not necessarily helpful and desirable in the education of children?

Many of the objections are centred round the need for flexibility in lesson planning, particularly in a subject like criticism in English literature, where it is exceedingly difficult to predict the course and outcome of a particular lesson. Also, if evaluation is an important by-product of a taxonomy of objectives how does a teacher evaluate a pupil's critical faculty objectively or assess his creativity and originality? Good teachers are adaptable and flexible in their approach; they know how to exploit a good point as it arises in a lesson and how to vary their technique in the light of the previous average level of knowledge of the class. Too close an adherence to stated objectives might possibly make a teacher dogmatic in his approach and overemphasize certain objectives at the expense of those which are less easily stated but are nevertheless equally as important. Finally there is the very real problem of teaching classes of children of mixed ability; in a number of subjects of the curriculum there would be too many objectives for a teacher to handle with confidence and an acceptable degree of competence.

On the credit side, surely it is far more desirable that a teacher should have a clear and attainable goal in sight rather than meander aimlessly along ill-defined paths? A prior statement of what a teacher intends to accomplish should not be so rigid as to prove a real hindrance to learning. Nobody expects to accomplish all his objectives at the first attempt, initial objectives are capable of modification in the light of practical experience. Material which has been classified in a taxonomy is more easily evaluated; of course, there are difficulties in attempting an objective assessment of activities like criticism and creativity, but they do not have to be strictly quantitative in nature.

Everybody in the practice of education is aware of a recent proliferation in printed and technological aids for the teacher including new syllabuses, courses of study and changes in curricula. Many of the innovations are accompanied by extravagant claims to the effect that they promote and facilitate thinking and problem-solving and represent a break away from traditional rote learning. A taxonomy of objectives is a useful yardstick in the evaluation of novel ideas and often shows that the modern technique is nothing but a rearrangement of older material at the level of Bloom's lowest category, knowledge. Some examination authorities would find it helpful to look at Bloom's hierarchy and scrutinize their marking schemes to see what proportion of marks is awarded purely for memory work. It would certainly prove mandatory should the trend towards objective test-ing gain momentum.

Not all psychologists accept Bloom's taxonomy as being definitive, there are valid reasons for the adoption of Gagné's (1965) model as an alternative.

Many find it is more logically structured and more firmly based on psychological principles. Modified and hybrid systems of classification are to be found in Beard (1970) and Ausubel and Robinson (1969), or applied to specific subjects like mathematics in Avital and Shettleworth (1968), and geography in Lessinger (1963).

In a later publication, Bloom (1971) examines mastery learning in children and estimates that possibly 90 per cent are capable of attaining stated educational objectives. He bases his argument on the factor of time available for learning concepts in school. Too many children are expected to work at approximately the same rate of progress in many subjects of the curriculum, and a large proportion of those who fail, do so because they have not been given sufficient time in which to master concepts.

Skinner, of course, also recognized the factor of time in his study of programmed learning. In working through a linear program children follow the same path towards a common ultimate objective, it is the pace or rate of progress which differs for individual children. A well-designed program facilitates progress and maintains pupil interest in the subject.

The concept of mastery learning raises two important problems. How does the teacher motivate and sustain ego-involvement in the slow-learning child, who could easily become bored to death with a narrowly repetitive and small incremental step by step approach to learning? The educational fare would have to be carefully planned, rich and varied. Secondly, what exactly is meant by mastery and how is the concept evaluated in a subject like human geography compared with the acquisition of physical skill? What proportion of knowledge of a given subject or how many principles have to be grasped before making a confident assertion that mastery has been attained?

A poor performance of a physical skill in public is immediately revealed, limitations are fairly obvious; likewise, errors in grammatical usage or in arithmetical calculation. For many subjects of the school curriculum it would be difficult to say whether knowledge, concepts and principles have been mastered perfectly or not. Through suggestion, generalization and spurious argument it is easy to conceal what in fact is a fairly low level of achievement or a deficiency in comprehension.

Self-concepts and Ego-involvement

A simple exercise which often stimulates lively discussion is to ask student

teachers at the beginning of their course in education to list under two headings aspects of teaching practice which they find pleasurable and satisfying
and those which are not. Without informing them in advance and towards
the end of the course they are again asked to list their views under the same
headings and these are compared with the original list. Without going into
the psychological background of many prevalent statements to the effect
that absence from children certainly makes the heart grow fonder of them,
there will also be many positive references to the pleasure teachers obtain
from teaching a class in which intrinsic motivation is evident, ego-involvement is maximized and realistic levels of aspirations are a prelude to worth-
while achievement.

Intrinsic motivation implies drive from within, and this is possibly
derived from genuine personal interest in a subject and the deep pleasure it
gives. In the process of stimulating and sustaining interest two broad inter-
actions may be identified; one in which the child is expected to catch some
of the infectious enthusiasm a teacher has for his subject, in the other, the
teacher is expected to channel the broader interests of a child's everyday life
into a specific learning situation or focus them on a particular topic. Secondary school children engage in a tremendous range of cultural activities and
have a wealth of unexposed interests besides the more general and superficial liking for games, popular music, films and television. Valid contributions in chemistry from a keen photographer, in physics from a "high-
fidelity" enthusiast with a knowledge of radio circuits, in botany by the
young gardener, in history by a frequent visitor to museums, and in
geography by the overseas traveller, not only add to the practical aspects
of a period and give a genuine sense of realism but they also have an indirect
impact on the subsequent self-motivation and interest of the contributor.
Beware, children are quick to detect the bogus teacher who attempts to
cash in on something popular and precious to the children's peer group
culture.

In the same way recognize the natural curiosity of children and the
satisfaction they gain from manipulating and tinkering. Many of them
seem to learn very efficiently by exploration and physically handling
equipment. Harlow (1953) demonstrated quite forcibly that the term
"*monkeying about*" is more than a colloquial expression! Moreover, it is not
restricted to young children either: go into a large departmental store before
Christmas, visit the toy department and observe the parents enthusiastically

playing with the latest development in mechanical gadgetry. Curiosity is a natural and powerful motivator. Adults who enjoy solving puzzles published in newspapers and magazines love the mental exercise it affords, puzzles on an advertisement panel in a train or billboard evoke enormous curiosity, particularly if they challenge a person's so-called intelligence.

The total absorption of a person in a hobby where the visible rewards seem small or the total participation of a learner in recreational problem-solving has been described as "ego-involvement"; it is at its maximum when mental capacities are challenged. Self-judgements of success and failure in a given task may be interpreted as a function of "level of aspiration". The level is a standard or goal a person sets himself; if performance exceeds the expected level then the learner feels successful, if it falls below the level, he not only feels unsuccessful but possibly a deep sense of failure. A pupil who expects a Grade One in C.S.E. and obtains a Grade Two might feel he has failed because a Grade One pass is said to be equivalent to an "Ordinary Level" pass in the lowest grade of G.C.E. Similarly, an Upper Second Class Honours degree graduate will interpret his degree class in terms of failure if it debars him from going on to research and a higher degree.

The standard a person sets himself is not only a reflection of confidence in performance, but of his total personality including temperament, adjustment and attitude. A permanent feeling of failure, of under-achievement and of imperfection is a serious symptom of instability and the causes are not easily investigated. Possibly such a person has too deep a concern with standards which are externally imposed in a highly competitive situation, rather than with a realistic level of aspiration which he knows he can attain by regular application to study and practice with normal effort. A skilled teacher knows by experience of a child's past performance where to pitch the standard and this is generally only a little way past the previous level. Occasionally the incremental steps are varied according to the rate of progress in achieving or failing to maintain preceding standards. Skinner made the maximum use of incremental learning in developing his theory of reinforcement and in its application to programmed teaching.

In some academic subjects it is not always easy to detect whether a child is setting himself a realistic standard or not; a marked drop in attainment could reflect boredom which comes with too easily achieving a low level of performance, or withdrawal because it is felt that the work is too difficult and demanding. Teachers of skills, say in physical education and handicraft, have better opportunities to adjust the personal performance of children to individual aspirations. For example, in circuit training in the gymnasium pupils compete against their own targets as well as against group norms. One of the arguments in favour of broad ability banding in large comprehensive schools as opposed to rigid streaming is that children are less likely to have constant feelings of failure if taught in fairly homogeneous groups or sets. The onset of frustration when the slow and dull child grows tired of comparing himself with those who take everything easily in their stride also marks the beginning of maladjustment to the learning situation. Sooner or later this manifests itself in idleness, aggression and truancy. Not every Sunday morning hacker on the local course aspires to be a Jack Nicklaus in the world of professional golf; the average club golfer is satisfied to know he is improving his standard by a periodic reduction in his handicap.

Festinger (1942) investigated changes in levels of aspiration of college students: they were given achievement scores which were said to be above or below those of (i) high school students representing a lower prestige group, (ii) other college students and (iii) graduate students representing a higher prestige group. A college student told that his performance was lower than that of high school pupils generally raised his subsequent level of aspiration, but if told it was higher than that of graduates he lowered his level. This study and other similar investigations by Sears (1940) and on achievement motivation by McClelland (1953) warn of the inherent danger in allowing unrealistic levels of aspiration to lead to successive feelings of failure and of too much ego-involvement leading to a rise in anxiety. Teachers should take note of this and also of an even more critical stage in distress which often arises when a child is so externally motivated to achieve a high level of performance that he feels totally pressurized. Parental dominance of this kind is probably even more dangerous because it evokes a deep conflict in the child between personal distaste for a subject and anxiety to please a respected and loved figure.

An athlete striving to attain higher standards of performance, a craftsman dedicated to improving and extending the skills at his disposal, a designer searching for novel methods of expression and creativity in his art and the scholar aspiring to standards of excellence in his thinking and writing are all showing evidence of achievement motivation. McClelland *et al.* (1953) assessed the achievement motive of individual subjects from the stories they related about pictures which had been presented to them or projected. The technique known as the "Thematic Apperception Test" is described as a projective method because the subject unconsciously discloses aspects of his personal motivation in telling a story.

Several attempts have been made to design questionnaires which would be easier and quicker to administer to large groups than a projective test, but on the whole they have failed to correlate highly with results obtained from the Thematic Apperception Test. What is required is a reliable method of discriminating between general achievement motivation and the more specific, academic motivation; and between children who are motivated because they are afraid of failing and those motivated because they obtain pleasure from being successful.

The natural tendency of children to identify with admired and revered adults, especially at the age of adolescence, often acts as a desirable motivational force. Provided, of course, it is at a level of maturity where identification is with general qualities and characteristics, say a congenial teacher's mastery of his subject, as opposed to seeing him purely as a sex-symbol. Critical and autobiographical accounts of student's patterns of education, including reasons for selecting certain subjects for Advanced level study, commonly disclose the extent to which the personality of teachers affected their choice. This holds true both on entry to the sixth form and in choosing specialized subjects for study in particular colleges and universities. The teacher who infects children with genuine enthusiasm and love for a subject, whatever his scholastic imperfections, is a tremendous asset to a school and he is not always the dominant character in an extraverted sense of the word. His main armament seems to be in the use of suggestion; in discussion he proposes rather than presses alternative points of view and hypotheses and he takes an idea from a pupil, reformulates it and consciously makes that person feel that it was his original contribution. In other words, by guidance and suggestion he provides a situation or climate in which initiative and ideas come from the pupils themselves and he uses their contribution to stimulate further critical and creative thinking. At all levels, worth-while contributions from pupils must be encouraged, they work far harder at a task if they believe it has risen directly from one of their proposals and therefore accept responsibility for it. Also positive suggestion that mastery of a difficult skill or performance is attainable is far better than the pessimistic prediction "You will never get it right, Jones, as long as you live". If he will never get it right why waste time in harassment?

On taking over a class which has become accustomed to a monotonous routine of passive participation a teacher attempts to stimulate activity by extrinsic motivational methods. There are other times when a class is over-active and needs a reduction in tension, a calmer ethos and a more equable climate for productive work. Similarly with individual children, a balance between states of over- and under-anxiety is highly desirable and some-times essential. In the chapter on personality development (Chap. 9) reference is made to a number of investigations into the relationship be-tween learning efficiency and level of anxiety. They tend to arrive at con-clusions which are seemingly in conflict with each other. This is not surprising considering how much depends on personality traits like intro-version and extraversion and on factors like the degree of complexity of material to be learned and the intellectual ability of the learner. The more complex the task the more likely it is that a highly anxious and introverted student will be adversely affected, yet there is convincing evidence available to suggest that the most able students with high-anxiety ratings tend to produce better performances or scores under pressure.

One possible explanation of the general hypothesis that extraverted children tend to be more successful than introverted children is that the latter spend too much time worrying about what they have to learn and the rate of progress they set themselves. High-anxiety pupils probably learn more unnecessary and irrelevant material than the low-anxiety pupil who makes a more direct and economic approach to the heart of the required learning. Such pupils could very well overload their mental capacities for processing data and become hopelessly confused, their perceptual system might function with poorer discrimination under stress and the finer points of a problem are neither appreciated nor recognized. A number of researches report that it is only in the case of high-ability pupils that high anxiety enhances performance. With average and less able groups of students high anxiety generally produces the opposite effect. Studies of secondary school children by Hallworth (1961) and of primary school children by Rushton (1966) tend to point in the same direction; therefore it is safe to say that deliberate action to charge the emotion of a class up to a pitch of frenzy in the expectancy of improved performance is wholly misguided; it might possibly motivate a few but will certainly impair the majority.

Social-group Influences

The desirability of intrinsic motivation and its greater effectiveness is not disputed, but shortcomings in the strength, constancy and direction of human drive necessitate external motivation. Children at work in a formal class or in small groups, competing individually or co-operating jointly are subject to influences and pressures both from the teacher and the peer group. Young children generally show an anxiety to please their teachers, they love to be recognized and they want to make a good impression on those in authority. As they grow older and reach adolescent development, status and acceptance by the peer group assumes greater significance and motives become more complex, conflicting and concealed.

From the study of behaviourism and operant conditioning it soon became evident that praise and reward were far more effective in motivating learning than punishment and reproof. Whereas the results of reward are usually predictable the effects of punishment are not; it tends to produce undesirable consequences including suspicion, dislike and ultimate rejection of authority and hatred of the culture and learning it upholds. Unfortunately this is the probability which must be weighed in making a decision as to the type of punishment which should be imposed. Neither can it be made without taking into account the personality of the individual involved. Estes (1944) investigated the effects of punishment on rats under experimental conditions associated with operant behaviour and concluded that it temporarily suppresses a response rather than extinguishes it and that intermittent punishment is more effective than frequent punishment. With human beings it is not easy to investigate the psychological consequences of punishment. Although it apparently acts as an immediate motivator, excessive punishment is apt to prove highly dangerous, particularly if it causes a child to develop an aversion to school and learning from a young age.

This is not the same as saying that fear of punishment for a stupid act, like attempting to lift a red hot metal bar with bare hands, or darting across a main road without first seeing if the way is clear, has no part to play in controlling behaviour. Children have got to be protected and for personal survival they need to learn how to sense danger, but again it is far more effective to achieve this by positive preparation before the event than by punitive action after it. Hence the necessity to learn habits like kerb drill, safety precautions in handling laboratory materials, the inspection of gymnastic equipment and to walk not run near the edge of a swimming pool.

If praise is far more effective as a motivator than reproof, should teachers necessarily accept a low standard of performance or a poor answer without some form of correction? False praise under such circumstances would prove meaningless and is quickly detected as being hypocritical by the class. Undoubtedly part of the art of teaching lies in knowing how to set tasks and pose questions at a level which a child may reasonably be expected to answer either immediately or with the aid of a cue or prompt. This demands from the teacher both a capacity to judge the attainment and intellectual development of individual children and an ability to frame appropriate questions.

A fundamental dictum of Skinner's theory of programmed learning is that children are expected to make progress in small incremental steps and that reward comes with feedback or knowledge of results of a successful response. A teacher must never adopt a superior attitude towards a class by intentionally showing them how little they know or proving how incompetent they are in skilled activities. Neither does it serve any useful purpose to attempt to catch children out with obscure questions which they will almost certainly get wrong. There is nothing clever about this mode of conduct, it reflects an immature approach to teaching and leads to face-saving behaviour in children. Instead of admitting genuine difficulties which normally lead to diagnostic and corrective work, children will cover up personal deficiencies and conceal their true feelings. One of the aims of teaching is to eliminate incorrect and undesirable responses, not to eliminate the interest of a class in a subject.

Knowledge of results has been known to educators in various forms from the earliest recorded times. Tests and measurements of progress whether for personal information or competitive purposes have been so universally employed as motivators that they have acquired the tendency to determine educational needs rather than serve them. In primary schools attractive colourful star-studded charts, merit tables, performance leagues and ladders of progress are often conspicuous. Whereas one teacher might find that they create an atmosphere of competitive and purposeful activity, another would dismiss it all as so much wall decoration or an advertisement hoarding to promote the virtues and achievements of the gifted. The truth lies somewhere between the two points of view. Competitive leagues certainly motivate some children, of this there is no doubt, but what effect have they on the less fortunate whose burden in life seems to be to support the rest of the league on their shoulders? In order to minimize personal sense of failure a workable compromise is to inform children of their attainment and progress in the normal routine of classroom work, to announce test and examination results in a straightforward order of merit without ostentatious display and to foster competition by the publication of credits awarded to house groups rather than to individuals.

In some secondary schools it is painful to observe a deadly dull cycle: set homework, test homework, record marks, further question and answer, with a minimum of discussion a maximum of note making and dictation, set homework and test. The schedule of testing is so frequent that pupils become conditioned to the routine and the incentive effect is lowered to negligible proportions except on the occasions when the teacher takes positive measures to counteract poor and dropping performances. Judged solely by grades in formal examinations such a system obtains results, but at what cost in terms of long-term educational objectives? Testing to fill up a few empty columns in a teacher's mark book or purely to check on the satisfactory completion of homework is largely a waste of time, the main function of a test should be to provide diagnostic information.

It has been found difficult to generalize on the effect of competition on attainment; it is even more difficult to comment on the effect of motivation on public compared with private performance. So much seems to depend upon the temperament and personality of the individual that it would be folly to draw conclusions until more research evidence is gathered. Some children excel themselves if called to the front of a class to solve a problem on a blackboard, others suffer a partial mental black-out and agonies of frustration. Students at university also respond in different ways to public and private environments: for some the crowded library and lecture hall is an anathema and for others the solitude of a quiet room is a living hell. Reaction to an appearance before an audience is not easily predicted either, fortunate are those who thrive on it and are not overwhelmed. In the group situation the teacher should generally aim at reducing the anxiety and worry of over-tense individuals and at raising the vigilance of the lethargic. O'Connor (1968) makes some sensible and very practical suggestions on the reduction of anxiety in the classroom and her methods of praising an individual's contribution are well worth reading.

Arousal and Vigilance

The desirability of reducing anxiety in children should not be assumed to be synonymous with low levels of arousal, attention and vigilance. A class in a state of habituation needs new stimuli to make it alert and ready for renewed learning and performance. Unusual stimuli of an intense kind are most effective in gaining attention or for initial motivation. This was clearly shown in Berlyne's (1966) study of children's reactions to complex and colourful designs. Many students are aware of the impact of a good "opening gimmick" to a lesson because it quickly focuses attention on a topic, but be cautious and moderate in its use for vigilance needs to be maintained once aroused. Occasionally in practice what should have proved a good opening is wasted because it has led to over-excitement and subsequent control problems or to the formation of a "wrong set" or attitude to learning. Children probably expect a "gimmick" to be followed by something less challenging than usual and certainly more fun, when in actual fact the teacher's aim might have been exactly the opposite: a dramatic opening to something difficult or complex.

Another potential danger lies in the presentation of too much intensive and competing stimuli at one time like displaying all the goods in a shop window. It causes a form of mental indigestion and ultimately a sensory knock-out. The inexperienced student teacher, over-anxious to impress his prowess in the use of teaching aids, sometimes falls into this trap as he darts from wall chart to overhead projector, from film strip to tape recorder without pause. Sustain motivation by a normal presentation of material at a steady and unhurried pace. Some of the more desirable aspects of presentation would include:

(i) Making material meaningful by the use of straightforward unambiguous language and clear demonstrations.
(ii) Relating new material to previous knowledge and in the initial stages of learning pruning all unnecessary detail.
(iii) Breaking down complex material into parts within the grasp of the learner, the parts should be directly related to the whole and they should be presented in a logical sequence.
(iv) Choosing appropriate colours and rhythmical patterns to make attractive designs.

(v) Demonstrating in a realistic manner to show how something may be used in actual practice, followed by immediate practice and an opportunity for pupils to gain insight into uneconomical and wrong methods and their possible consequences.

(vi) Suggesting that mastery is possible and there is room for improvement, that further learning is rewarding and opens up new and exciting fields for exploration.

(vii) Planning changes of activity well before the onset of boredom and fatigue or the kind of frustration which leads to withdrawal.

It has been found difficult to generalize on the circumstances and methods of motivating children in the classroom beyond emphasizing the desirability of moving from extrinsic to intrinsic motivation. It is also difficult to judge the true level of motivation of individual children in a large class. Beware the artful cunning of those who are apparently motivated and achieve little. Recognize and accept the genuine motivation of the quiet, unobtrusive and self-effacing pupil, for his qualities are not always immediately evident.

Students are likely to find specialist books and papers on motivation rather difficult to read and narrowly technical. It is therefore advisable to consult a general textbook on learning like Hilgard, E. R., and Bower, G. H. before turning to, say, Peters, R. S. and Vernon, M. D. Further references to achievement motivation will be found in Chapter 9, "Personality".

Additional Reading

ATKINSON, J. W. (1964) *An Introduction to Motivation.* New York: Van Nostrand.

ATKINSON, J. W. and FEATHER, N. T. (Eds.) (1966) *A Theory of Achievement Motivation.* New York: Wiley.

BERLYNE, D. E. (1960) *Conflict, Arousal and Curiosity.* New York: McGraw-Hill.

BINDRA, D. and STEWART, J. (Eds.) (1966) *Motivation: Selected Readings.* London: Penguin.

BIRNEY, R. C. *et al.* (1969) *Fear of Failure.* New York: Van Nostrand.

COFER, C. N. and APPLEY, M. H. (1964) *Motivation: Theory and Research.* New York: Wiley.

FESTINGER, L. (1957) *A Theory of Cognitive Dissonance.* Stanford: Stanford Univ. Press.

GAGNÉ, R. M. and BOLLES, R. C. (1959) A review of factors in learning efficiency. In Gallanter, E. H. (Ed.).

HECKHAUSEN, H. (1967) *The Anatomy of Achievement Motivation*. New York: Academic Press.

JONES, M. R. (Ed.) (1958) *Nebraska Symposium on Motivation*. Univ. of Nebraska Press.

PETERS, R. S. (1958) *The Concept of Motivation*. London: Routledge & Kegan Paul.

SEARS, R. R. (1957) *Patterns of Child Rearing*. New York: Harper & Row.

VERNON, M. D. (1969) *Human Motivation*. London: Cambridge Univ. Press.

ZIPF, G. K. (1949) *Human Behaviour and the Principle of Least Effort*. Cambridge, Mass.: Addison-Wesley.

CHAPTER 5

Skills

Nature of Skill

A sadly neglected area of research in education is the acquisition, development and measurement of sensori-motor skills in children. Compared with the highly specific investigations into actual and simulated skills employed in industry and the armed forces and research into verbal skills like reading, little progress has been made in the evaluation of techniques of teaching skills in school subjects such as athletics, games, art, handicrafts and domestic science. In the coaching and teaching of the advanced and more gifted performers there has been progress but not all children are so highly motivated or so physically well endowed that they profit from courses designed for the capable minority. At the lower and average levels of competence a great deal of long-term research needs to be completed, ranging from a clear statement of objectives to the detailed study of individual skills.

This highly undesirable situation possibly reflects an historical and cultural background to the academic versus practical dichotomy, to narrow and bigoted concepts of recreation and pleasure and to the supposition that because the process of learning is general it is not necessary to make a special case for the study of the acquisition of skilled behaviour. What little evidence there is at hand suggests that estimates of the number of children capable of achieving a competent level of performance, say in playing a musical instrument, learning to swim or in creative design, have been grossly pessimistic. From Japan one reads reports of the tremendous success of the Suzuki group method of learning to play the violin by masses of children, some so young they hardly have enough physical strength to hold their instruments.

Must the gulf between the skilled and the unskilled remain so impossibly unbridgeable, particularly in a technological age with increasing demands on finer and more complex skills and with an ever-expanding amount of time available for leisure and the pursuit of recreational activities and hobbies? Possibly the gulf is more apparent than real; unskilled perform-ance is immediately recognizable at all levels of competence, whereas differences in reasoning and thought processes between individuals are often well concealed. The end-product of skill is public and it is too frequently judged by its shortcomings rather than its virtues.

Research into effective methods of teaching skills in school is urgently needed. In the past there has been a tendency to rely on the reminiscences of the highly skilled themselves as a guide to basic general instruction and this has sometimes proved unsatisfactory because they do not always fully understand the complex nature of their own particular skill and seem unable to appreciate and fathom the limitations of others. This should not be taken to imply that the experts have little to contribute to the more generalized field of education, on the contrary their role is invaluable, provided they recognize hierarchies in the acquisition of skill from simple and gross movements to complex and fine coordinations.

It is difficult to attempt a concise definition of the concept "skill" other than to say that in this chapter emphasis will be placed on co-ordinated sensori-motor performance rather than social skill and status. At this stage it is sufficient to describe the characteristics of skilled performance which are common to a variety of tasks and these include: economy of movement, a sense of timing, fast responses, good anticipation and reliability of per-formance. Compare the ease and finesse of the accomplished batsman who smoothly dispatches a ball to the boundary without apparent physical effort with the thrashing and flailing of the beginner, or the compact rhythmical swing of the long-hitting golfer with the ungainly body lurchings of the rabbit who moves everything at his disposal in an attempt to propel the ball a few yards. The economy of effort, colloquially described by sportswriters in such phrases as "he makes it look so easy" and "he swings as if he had all the time in the world", results from perfect co-ordination, a good sense of balance and the elimination of unnecessary movements in a smooth continuous flow.

Despite the fact that some people appear to have a genuine aptitude for specific skills and natural or inborn talents it is nevertheless inescapable that a skilled performance is learned. Agreed some make faster progress than others; possibly because they have better facilities for practice and training and more experienced and gifted teachers, but they all acquire their competence by learning. It is to models of contemporary learning theory that the reader should turn for explanations of skill acquisition, in particular, to the feedback of information which provides knowledge of results and the theory of a channel of communication with a limited handling capacity.

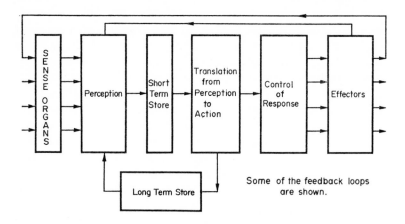

FIG. 20. Sensori-motor performance (after Welford, 1968).

Welford's Model of Sensori-motor Performance

Welford (1968) has summarized the mechanism of sensori-motor performance in a hypothetical diagram which is so clear as to be almost self-explanatory (Fig. 20).

This model has three principle and continuous stages and is sometimes referred to as a sensory reception–translation–effector sequence. Readers are familiar with the normal process of sensory reception or input from the sense organs, but remember this category also includes kinaesthetics and equilibrium as well as the better-known examples like sight and touch. It is by kinaesthetic sense that a person is made aware of his body movements.

At this point it is not necessary to go into a study of perception; this was mentioned in Chapter 3, in which reference was made to possible causes of distortion in perception. In a skilled performance danger not only arises from poor perceptual judgement but from a physical overloading of the sensory mechanism; too much information is received at one time and it becomes impossible to handle the load. Also in exactly the opposite way, too little sensory stimulation under conditions of monotony impairs vigilance and lowers standards of performance. An early stage in the model incorporates a filtering process, page 47, after Broadbent (1958), by which selective attention is paid to incoming signals and it also has a facility for the temporary and short-term retention of data.

Welford refers to the second stage as one of translation from perception to action and it incorporates a choice of response or a capability for weighing up possibilities before deciding on an appropriate motor action. This intermediate stage of decision-making is of dual significance, it acts in response to sensory input and stimulates the effector or motor processes.

From the earlier study of the regulation of human behaviour and references to work by Broadbent and Lunzer it is clear that many of the translation processes are almost spontaneous in character, demanding no more than a straightforward matching of sensory input against a ready built yet flexible schema, prior to running off the desired responses.

Bartlett's concept of a flexible schema will be recalled from Chapter 3 and it probably explains why there are often slight differences between standards and methods of performance under apparently identical circumstances. Every golfer aspires to possess a "grooved swing" which will automatically repeat itself under adverse playing conditions including personal stress, but it is seldom achieved, if ever. A master player of the calibre of Ben Hogan with an almost machine-like swing confessed that he rarely hit more than two or three perfect shots in a full round of golf.

With experience, practice and training a performer increases his capacity to absorb, assimilate and integrate progressively larger units into his schema and this leads to greater fluency and increased speed. A trained typist does not make a sequence of discrete responses to individual letters in typing commonplace words and phrases or a musician to individual notes in playing an arpeggio. Experienced pilots have learned to scan dozens of dials on an instrument panel and how to organize the essential interrelationships between separate readings into patterns so that they can respond to them in a smooth sequence of movements. The novice, on the other hand, tends to respond to individual readings and by a series of over-corrections proceeds on a more erratic course. To aid him, the most important instrument dials are grouped together in a logical and standardized position on the console, but even so it takes time to learn how to read them in an organized and meaningful pattern, particularly under blind flying conditions.

When a translation or response decision is made, electrical impulses travel down the motor nerve fibre and activates the necessary muscles and glands, the so-called "effectors." Skilled movements consist of many such sensory–translation–effector sequences and this necessarily requires the efficient functioning of a complex system of servo-mechanical or feedback loops. The complete process is virtually a restatement in slightly different terminology of a familiar cybernetic model of learning. As described above, the model seems basically simple but the same cannot be said about its complexities when put into practice. If a gifted gymnast thought about all the possible sources of error during a highly co-ordinated movement he would probably be reduced to a state of inactivity like the centipede:

> The Centipede was happy quite,
> Until the Toad in fun
> Said, "Pray which leg goes after which?"
> And worked her mind to such a pitch,
> She lay distracted in the ditch
> Considering how to run.
>
> (Craster—attrib.)

For simplicity of description the above model was divided into three stages: in practice, it would be unrealistic to think of it functioning other than as an integrated whole. Co-ordinated motor movements are not series of separate isolated or discrete actions but a continuous sequence of inter-related actions with complex feedback circuitry. Clearly in a cybernetic system of this kind time is required for the physical passage of signals, filtering and decision-making so there must inevitably be some delay between an initial stimulus and the actual response. This interval is called the reaction time and if it involves decision making it tends to be of longer duration and is known as "choice reaction time".

Reaction time in everyday usage implies speed of reaction like a sprinter to the starting gun, the motorist to a traffic signal or the machinist to a tracking line. It has been investigated for many years and probably the best explanation of CRT is due to Hick (1952) who maintains that it is the amount of information a signal carries which is crucial rather than the total possible number of choices available. In other words the more familiar the task the lower a person's CRT and the more difficult the task and sensory discrimination the higher the CRT.

Another form of built-in delay between discrete stimuli and response results from a "psychological refractory period" of about half a second between successive signals. For example, if the interval between the first and second stimulus is less than half a second, the interval between the first and second response will always be greater than half a second. Craik (1948) examined the corrections made by an operator as he continuously tracked a moving target and found them to be made at intervals of about half a second. The delay is not explained by physical or motor limitations in the movement of the hand or by the very short time of 0.15 second taken for the completion of feedback processes. Broadbent explains the phenomena by comparing the operator with a single-communication channel of limited capacity, physically incapable of dealing with two signals in rapid succession. At present there is no evidence to suggest that the delay can be reduced or eliminated with practice and training; yet there is reason to believe that there are individual differences in refractoriness. Welford asserts it is longer in older people.

Teachers of complex skilled activities need not be driven to despair and blame shortcomings on the refractory period because the human organism is capable of grouping and anticipating incoming signals. If the interval between two or more signals or stimuli is very short, say measured in milliseconds, then the signals are received as a grouped response. This would explain the skill of the musician in reading and playing an arpeggio. In playing a game in which a moving ball is required to be struck, like tennis, a player needs to anticipate a striking position in advance otherwise he would be so late in his response as to miss the ball completely. This kind of anticipatory mechanism is technically known as "perceptual anticipation" and Broadbent believes it is stored in the long-term section of the memory system. A good sense of anticipation is one of the facets of a skilled games player who learns through experience how to position himself correctly in a constantly changing situation and therefore expends less energy.

The Acquisition of Skill

Learning to co-ordinate movements in a skilled activity tends to be a fairly slow process of structuring meaningful patterns and deciding strategies and in a sense it differs from general learning only in emphasis rather than kind. Much of what has been said about learning theory including feedback principles, memory and motivation and what is to be discussed subsequently about transfer of training and thought processes is equally applicable to the narrower field of skill acquisition. This again emphasizes the need for a broad view of the concept of learning and it demonstrates the artificiality of attempting to divide the subject into arbitrary categories.

Motor skills are learned by training and practice; by training it is implied that desirable and successful movements for a skilled performance are acquired either through direct instruction and coaching or by knowledge of results, whereas practice means repetition of actions and includes undesirable and wrong movements. Practice without insight into technique and standard of performance is quite valueless, it is merely a form of exercise.

Hence the absolute desirability of a good teacher or model from the onset of skill learning; the initial instruction must reflect standards of excellence, there is no room for compromise on this point. Learning poor movements and bad habits to facilitate so-called ease of learning in the early stages is utterly condemned. Similarly, the adjustment of one basic fault by introducing another apparently compensatory fault must be totally rejected except in cases of physical handicap in which normal movements are impaired. Some individuals seem to have a great propensity for modelling themselves on skilled performers and successfully imitate their movements and actions, but for the majority there is no substitute for sound basic instruction under a trained teacher. The word trained is used purposely; the gifted craftsman and the star performer need to learn appropriate teaching techniques in order to impart their skills in a manner likely to be meaningful for beginners. Officially approved courses in methods of coaching have been designed for professional games players and already they have contributed towards raising standards of instruction in this country.

Assuming a young learner has been taught certain actions and movements correctly what are the most favourable conditions for practising the newly acquired skills? With a complex skill it is generally considered more profitable to divide the time available for learning into fairly short intervals with spaces or pauses for consolidation and rest, rather than practice an activity in one long continuous session until mastery is achieved. Fatigue cannot be overlooked as a factor in favour of spaced practice, but the most reasonable explanation is that it allows consolidation of memory traces and time for mental rehearsal during pauses. On the other hand, inhibition may cause interference between practice sessions and impede progress; it is known, for example, that some coaches dread pupils reading instruction books and articles in sports magazines between practical lessons.

It is impossible to make recommendations on the optimum length of time a person should spend in training; fatigue and lack of drive apart, there is sense in stopping the practice session when an acceptable level of performance has been achieved, that is, at a point slightly beyond first mastery. The feeling of progress which accompanies the conclusion of a successful practice period facilitates subsequent mental rehearsal and assists in building up self-confidence. For a more detailed study of this topic with particular reference to physical education, readers are urged to read Knapp's (1963) *Skill in Sport*.

A second question frequently raised by learners is whether it is advisable to learn a complex activity as a whole and unified movement or break it down into smaller units or to compromise and constantly integrate the part into the whole. The answer to this problem seems to depend on the structure of the task; if the activity demands a high degree of co-ordination like driving a vehicle, it is better to practice the co-ordinated movement as a whole. If the skill consists of a sequence and sum of discrete actions it does no harm to learn and practice each movement separately, provided the earlier parts are constantly revised and finally the whole is put together in a continuous performance. Probably the best advice for a learner is to aim for the largest possible unit he can reasonably grasp in a session and keep divisions of movement to a minimum, bearing in mind individual differences like age, intelligence, strength, speed and experience.

In the modification of a typical motor action involving, say, a change in the position of the hands in gripping a tool or bat it is no use teaching the new grip as a separate activity, it must be integrated into the total movement as a whole in order to facilitate kinaesthetic learning. A change of grip in a physical movement is usually resisted by the learner and is sometimes abandoned if it feels too uncomfortable and unnatural, but if the change is necessary then it has to be learned and constantly practised and this takes time. Poor techniques are not easily unlearned, hence the plea for sound basic training with correct movements co-ordinated into a fluent performance.

Another intriguing problem is whether in learning an easier and a more difficult task, should one always begin by learning the easier first? Paradoxically this is not as simple as it first appears; for example, from the hypothesis that it is better to work progressively from the known to the unknown it would seem that the easier task should be learned first, but in practice this does not always work out because it ignores the transfer effects of training. On the contrary, much experimental evidence with the exception of slow- and high-speed tracking of moving targets suggests that for a constant amount of time it is generally more efficient to learn the more difficult task first. Welford finds this view too sweeping and from a survey of relevant literature concludes that it is better to begin with the task which demands the greatest care and effort towards attaining a high standard of performance.

A common source of confusion lies in drawing a distinction between speed and timing in a movement. Many players generate tremendous speed in attempting to strike a ball but produce little power to propel it on its way. Disappointed at the lack of success they try to hit much harder at the next attempt and inevitably find it produces worse results. This not only happens to beginners but sometimes to skilled performers under pressure. How often does one read a statement in the press by the loser to the effect that his timing went astray? Timing is more closely allied to rhythm than gross speed; it is characterized by a fluent unhurried sequence of movements and it represents a very high degree of co-ordination. Possibly too much stress in the past has been laid on the role of smoothness in good timing. It is well known that a number of unorthodox sportsmen manage to time a stroke with the utmost precision in spite of a sequence of ungainly movements which lead up to the exact moment in time when maximum co-ordination is demanded for perfect execution of that stroke.

The relationship between speed of movement and thought processes, including decision-making, also poses problems for some learners. It is well known that in public speaking, particularly if it is intellectually demanding and has not been thoroughly rehearsed, thought lags behind the motor movements necessary for the production of speech. Similarly in playing games like tennis and golf, a last moment decision to hit the ball harder or to change the path of the clubhead often proves disastrous because it destroys a natural swing; once planned, in cybernetic terms, a programmed movement should be free to run its course with minimum hindrance and modification. Adjustments of this kind really represent indecision and reflect lack of confidence in a technique and they should be eliminated as quickly as possible otherwise progress will be retarded.

The optimistic golfer who attempts to modify his hit on feeling impact with the ball is probably unaware of the fact that by the time it has been registered in the brain and returned as a message to the grip the golf ball has flown at least 15 yards from the club head. A simple experiment in which a light is switched off at different points in a golfer's swing was carried out by a working party of the Golf Society of Great Britain (Cochran and Stobbs, 1968) to determine at what point the player was committed to his shot. The point of no return seemed to be early in the forward or downswing, although the golfers themselves were convinced it was immediately prior to impact.

However, in skills such as athletics, where speed is of fundamental importance, it is probably wiser to practice high-speed performances as soon as possible after the correct movements have been grasped.

Another question frequently raised in the acquisition of skill is the use and value of mechanical guidance. Is it worth while to literally take a person by the hand through a sequence of movements to reduce the possibility of making errors to a minimum? In verbal learning providing clues and prompts or instructing in the sense of directly telling the learner what is required have been found to be efficient methods of teaching, but mechanical guidance appears to be less effective possibly because of difficulties arising from kinaesthetic feedback and subsequent transfer to the non-guided activity. Guidance is probably only of general value in the initial stages of skill learning or in correcting a particular fault in a complex movement if the learner does not see or feel the source of error. Similarly, a visual mark for guidance proves helpful; golfers often find difficulty in lining up their shoulders correctly in taking up a stance. In a practice session lay a club on the ground pointing towards a target and mark the correct position for the feet with a couple of tee pegs. These artificial devices provide a frame of reference and act as cues. Physical supports such as a harness for practice on the trampoline or buoyancy aids in swimming perform other interrelated functions, promoting self-confidence and safety.

Teaching Skills

For the practical teaching of skills at least five basic requirements need to be borne in mind:

(i) state clear cut objectives,
(ii) make the task meaningful for the learner,
(iii) teach correct movements from the beginning,
(iv) provide feedback or knowledge of results,
(v) afford time for intelligent practice.

On objectives little further need be added to what has previously been said. In making a task meaningful audio-visual techniques and verbal instruction have a role to play, both in reinforcing practice and in eliminating much of the jargon which obscures true understanding of the nature of a skill. Coaches and instructors in a well-intentioned effort to put into simple language highly complex concepts like "hitting late" often only confuse the learner, so much so that they are often too inhibited and overwhelmed to ask for a clearer explanation or demonstration of the term. A short discussion and overview of general principles in a training session pause should help to clear such doubts and speed up the learning process. However, beware the glib theorist who finds more problems to raise and discuss than there are possible combinations of movements. The teaching of correct movements is absolutely essential both for reliability of performance and for progress towards a high level of competence—the foundations must be right. It takes time to build a skill, do not waste it by suggesting alternative easier but less effective processes which have later to be unlearned because they are impeding progress.

Throughout this book the central position of feedback of information and knowledge of results in learning has been maintained and nowhere is its significance more evident than in the acquisition of skill. It may prove helpful to think of two highly co-ordinated and interrelated feedback systems functioning in a skilled motor activity: one from within the learner involving the sensory organs, decision processes and motor responses in a closed circuit, the other external to the learner and conveying knowledge of the results of performance including discrepancies between aim and achievement. Should a reader be in any doubt as to the importance of this concept devise a simple experiment in which knowledge of results is withheld or interrupted. This also gives some insight into the nature of exaggerated movements in the limbs of people suffering from "tabes dorsalis".

Exciting advances have been made in the therapeutic use of feedback in lessening speech defects in the deaf and in controlling sub-vocalization in silent reading. A deaf person suffers from loss of auditory feedback, therefore if visual feedback in the form of sound patterns is substituted it is possible for him to draw comparisons between his personal patterns and normal sound patterns. He then has a frame of reference or standard against which he can judge and adjust his quality of speech. Similarly, a slow reader who over-engages in sub-vocal activity like whispering and lip movement can have his rate of reading increased as a result of feedback therapy (Hardyck *et al.*, 1966). A better known use of feedback principles in kinaesthetic learning is to introduce artificial feel into a control unit; for example, power-assisted steering in a motor car or by adding weight to a club head to give it more feel, although it is known that a lighter club is generally more desirable because it can be swung faster with less physical effort.

At the beginning of this chapter a plea was made for an expansion of research into the acquisition of skill in children. A great deal needs to be known about motivation and participation in skilled activities. Much woolly thinking and uncertainty has developed round concepts of readiness to learn and the so-called critical periods in learning. Are there dangers, physiological and psychological, in attempting to learn a skilled movement too early? If so, for how long should one delay? Possibly the answer to this will come from a more detailed study of physical growth including phases in the maturation and development of the central nervous system, as well as from more obvious factors like personal safety and availability of facilities for teaching young children.

The acquisition of skill is generally a long and difficult journey with few short-cuts. In the past it was fashionable to plot curves of progress with characteristic peaks and troughs showing a general upward trend and sometimes with plateaus denoting either a temporary limit or a period of consolidation in performance. It is no longer considered a particularly useful technique to plot these curves other than to demonstrate to the learner the uneven path he has traversed.

Fatigue

In colloquial usage the concept of "fatigue" presents little difficulty, it is usually experienced in a combination of three main forms: sensory, mental and physical. Psychological investigations into its nature are hindered in practice because it is very difficult to isolate, say, physiological from motivational factors. Who has not felt too blurred in the eyes to watch yet another television programme but has been stimulated by an intriguing opening into further viewing, or has felt too exhausted to work out a difficult mental problem but has suddenly seen a possible solution which has led to renewed effort, or has felt too tired to take another step up a mountain side but has been spurred on by the unfolding panoramic view ahead? Herein lies the core of the problem, differentiating between objective and subjective manifestations of fatigue. A person is normally very aware of the effects of fatigue but there are occasions when he does not feel fatigued and fails to recognize a cumulative and gradual fall-off in performance. Long-distance lorry drivers and observers maintaining vigilance for long periods like air-traffic controllers are susceptible to this phenomena which could prove highly dangerous. Quite often the subject believes he is sustaining or actually improving his performance or state of vigilance and is unaware that he is widening his standards of tolerance and shortcutting vital procedures.

It is probably the incentive effect which is so difficult to separate from genuine fatigue. This was very clearly demonstrated by Schwab (1953), who asked subject to hang on to a horizontal bar for (*a*) as long as possible (and they averaged about 1 minute); (*b*) as long as possible with encouragement (and they averaged just over 1 minute); (*c*) as long as possible for a monetary reward (they averaged nearer 2 minutes). In experiments involving intense physical effort like lifting heavy weights, work output due to fatigue can be decreased by suggestion that the weights have been made heavier and increased by suggestion that they have been made lighter. Environmental factors also have a considerable influence; for example, compare a 1-mile walk through a main thoroughfare in the West End of London with a walk of the same length in one of the more dreary residential suburbs.

A further problem in the study of fatigue is in differentiating it from the effects of anxiety and worry about standards of achievement, particularly when a performer becomes too conscious of his state of tiredness. In an effort to catch up, a tired person sometimes canalizes too much energy from the task in hand to wasteful distraction, falls further behind and ultimately succumbs to the disruptive effects of over-anxiety. A mild degree of emotional pressure such as caused by annoyance with a referee's decision or an opponent's antics or a crowd's partiality can revitalize a tired player or team with almost magical effects, but this is not to be confused with severe stress and breakdown.

Before examining some of the physiological aspects of fatigue and suggesting possible ways of preventing or delaying its onset, it is well to note that there are individual differences in the tolerance of mental and physical overloading. Highly intelligent and imaginative people who are said to be creative take less well to monotonous tasks and show early signs of fatigue, particularly if they know they can finish a job quickly but are prevented by poor working conditions and inefficient organization from doing so. Age tends to be another factor; with greater skill and experience the older person has learned how to adjust his output and conserve energy, but under greater or unexpected pressure his true upper limit will be revealed.

In training for athletic activities and competitive games great emphasis is nowadays placed on building up endurance, power, speed, strength and stamina. Moreover, it is necessary to have more than an adequate reserve to withstand overloading under pressure. Personality differences need to be considered too, including sensitivity to discomfort, physical pain and environmental distractions like undue noise. Broadbent (1958) describes distraction as competition from irrelevant stimuli. With the passage of time some unwanted signals tend to filter through gradually; for example, a feeling of discomfort caused by tense muscles resulting from sitting on hard seats will distract attention from a concert or play.

It is usual to draw a distinction between muscular and mental fatigue but clearly in practical circumstances the two are closely related. A craftsman might feel too mentally tired to maintain skilled movements and a scholar too physically exhausted to think further about a problem in spite of having been seated for a couple of hours. In this sense the feeling is possibly sub-jective but nevertheless it is very real to the person involved. The popular misconception about muscular fatigue which often stems from commercial advertisements is that certain by-products of a chemical nature are released into the bloodstream and circulate round the body, thus causing general fatigue of the nervous system. Physiological evidence suggests that fatigue tends to be specifically localized, unless of course the whole body is an extreme state of exhaustion. The fact that a muscle, which has ceased to contract due to fatigue, can be made to do so by electrical stimulation suggests that it is the appropriate neuronal system which ceases to function first.

Mental fatigue also tends to be limited to specific thought processes, after a brief pause a change to a different kind of activity is possible without too much discomfort. Reading a difficult textbook for a long period in the late evening often proves very exhausting, yet after a drink and preparation for bed it is not taxing to read something light like a magazine or a novel before sleeping. It probably does the world of good because it diverts the attention of the mind away from problems, so persistent, that they interrupt continuous sleep throughout the night. In this sense, running down a motor after activity is as beneficial as warming it up prior to exercise. Wherever the cause of fatigue lies, in sensory reception, in the central nervous system including decision making or in muscular response it would be folly to ignore its function as an early warning system and like a fuse in a circuit it is an important protective mechanism.

Bartlett (1943) has suggested that there is a progressive and sequential impairment of activity as a result of fatigue beginning with a loss of timing, followed by a disorganization of performance and co-ordination and finally to a reduction in motor efficiency. In other words the finer co-ordinations deteriorate before the gross motor movements. The observation that the onset of fatigue is more rapid in attempting to solve a novel problem compared with a familiar task supports the limited capacity hypothesis of information processing discussed in previous chapters. Familiar material is more readily processed and assimilated and is therefore less demanding on neural activity. In most forms of education, irrespective of levels of attainment, the pursuit of learning is the most common and fundamental aim; yet paradoxically, fatigue is rarely a problem encountered in schools and colleges. Its counterpart, boredom, on the other hand is often only too self-evident. Children not only seem to be naturally well protected against the effects of fatigue but also know how to protect themselves from its onset and development.

In the home and school environment it is relatively easy for a child to escape from undue pressure by switching off attention, by directing thought elsewhere and by changing an activity. As he grows older and takes employment he might find it less easy to take fatigue-avoidance measures therefore he has to learn how to protect himself from undue strain. One of the first techniques he learns is how to pace himself or how to offset length of working day against speed of output. Long hours of work, including overtime, do not necessarily imply greater total productivity; in fact it has often been shown that a reduction in the total number of hours leads to an overall increase in work output. Even when incentive bonuses are paid, workers will set themselves a realistic target and proceed at an appropriate pace in order to achieve it, bearing in mind their capacity for endurance.

The significance of regular rest periods, of changes in activity, of different rates of output at different times of the working day and of the need for sensory stimuli when engaged on monotonous and repetitive tasks is too well known from knowledge of industrial practices to warrant further comment. In schools the problem is somewhat different because the end-product is less tangible and individual output is less easily observed. Also the organization of the day into a variety of physical and mental activities, together with changing environmental stimuli, tends to preclude the more obvious manifestations of fatigue. Much of what has been written on this topic is directed towards the student and the older pupil, both of whom are at risk in highly competitive situations stemming either from the classroom with its heavy demands on the intellect or from the games and athletics field with greater demands on the body. The worst thing a student can do is to worry about the effects of fatigue; accept the concept of an optimum level of performance and rate of activity and work within self-imposed and realistic limits.

If fatigue is interpreted in terms of overloading, then boredom results from underloading of information especially at the sensory input stage. Welford makes a valid comment on this point when he refers to the classical bore as one who compels his hearer to listen to conversation that is insignificant in content. Does this occur too frequently in the classroom? Children are often compelled to sit rigidly and pay full attention to irrelevant information. It is irrelevant in the sense that the material is already known, it provokes no response and stimulates little thought or it is incomprehensible and therefore meaningless. Chronic boredom shows itself in the general tone of a school and is characterized by a drop in morale, sagging enthusiasm, assertions of futility and feeling of contempt for authority. Action, motivation and stimulation are the antidotes of boredom; inertia, helplessness and resignation serve only to sustain it.

Transfer of Training

When a child leaves school it is expected that some of the attitudes, standards and values as well as the knowledge and skills he has learned in a more formal educational environment will be carried over or transferred to later life in the home, in employment and in the pursuit of leisure activities. A thorough understanding of percentages in arithmetic will possibly prove useful in real-life problems including decisions on investment, hire purchase and mortgages. Whatever the long-term transfer effect of education may be in the broader perspective of life it is also necessary to examine some of the shorter-term effects and clear up the gross misconceptions which have arisen in the past. An historical approach to the subject shows how current thinking about transfer has evolved and it indicates why it has lost some prominence as a topic in educational psychology.

Some of the basic principles of transfer have already been encountered in the study of memory, more particularly in the experimental design for investigating proactive inhibition; also in the study of skill, in discussing whether it is better to move from a more difficult to an easy task or vice versa. In other words, the principle subject for study is the influence of prior learning on subsequent learning; if it has no effect then there is no transfer, if it significantly facilitates later learning then there is positive transfer and if it hinders or inhibits then it has a negative transfer effect. In practice it is sometimes difficult to separate the positive and negative effects. Clearly one anticipates positive transfer in geography between a plan of a school, an ordnance survey map and an air photograph or in rugby played according to union or league rules. In contrast, negative transfer between the initial learning of Spanish and Italian words with common roots, or between cricket and golf, is expected. However, many learning tasks although apparently alike in most respects exhibit both positive and negative transfer effects; for example, between learning to play a viola and a violin or between land-drill and water swimming. Certainly it must never be assumed that transfer inevitably occurs between similar activities and thought processes, if a high degree of prediction is required then it is essential to adopt simulation techniques. It is less expensive for pilots to train in a grounded simulator and less dangerous for medical students to practice initially on skeletons and cadavers than captive patients.

One of the traditions of the English educational system which is slow to die in spite of weighty evidence to the contrary is the doctrine of formal discipline which implies that certain subjects train the "mind" in the same way as exercise trains the muscles. By implication, mathematics facilitates logical thinking, the classics enhance the ability to reason, and history improves memory. Confusion which has arisen from attempts to evaluate the transfer effect of these subjects may be explained by the fact that they are commonly used as the basis of selection within schools with standards of excellence in academic achievement. The more highly intelligent children cope fairly easily with languages and mathematics; however, to say that the training which these subjects afford necessarily improves intelligence would be utterly wrong. Learning dates by heart in history and place names in geography does not improve capacity to retain data, and this is certainly not a valid aim in teaching these subjects nor a reasonable justification. The contemporary emphasis in education lies in the development of an historical attitude, a geographical approach and a scientific method of analysis.

Thorndike and Woodworth (1901) did much to clear up misconceptions about the training value of specific subjects and their findings considerably influenced the pattern of curriculum development in the United States in the inter-war period. The general conclusion that for transfer to be effective there must be identical elements in the two fields of training was widely accepted, even though it was derived from rather simple stimulus response experiments which reflect an atomistic view of psychology rather than a cognitive theory of transfer of principles and relationships.

Woodrow (1927) designed an experiment to investigate the nature of transfer in memory; it marked an improvement in technique because it differentiated between practice and training and it demonstrated that transfer involved more than a simple carry over of elements. The practice group who had learned material by rote displayed little or no evidence of transfer, the training group who were instructed in methods of memorizing showed the most significant transfer, and the control group none. In many ways this conclusion anticipated post-war experiments in which the emphasis changed from the study of S–R elements to the possibility of the transfer of the organization of a group of elements and the transfer of personal attitudes to learning. In his study of problem-solving, Katona (1940) not only demonstrated that material had to be meaningful to the learner but that the transfer of principles was more important than rote memory. Melton (1941) confirmed this finding and so did Hilgard *et al.* (1953), all of whom suggested that in learning by understanding it is the organization of material which is transferred rather than series of single responses. In an experiment to investigate transfer effects in the teaching of arithmetic, Swenson (1942) showed it was more profitable to teach the relationship between facts rather than drill children in learning facts alone by heart.

A novel interpretation of the whole subject came from Harlow's (1949) experiments on discrimination learning and concept development in monkeys and children. In his words, the child formed a learning set or simply learned how to learn. Subsequent work by Levinson and Reese (1963) on learning sets suggests that unless skills and concepts are over-learned there is unlikely to be a large transfer effect and that it tends to be restricted to specific or particular instances and problems. One of the earliest experiments in transfer was by Judd (1908) who examined the effectiveness of teaching the principles of refraction of light in water by having students throw darts at an underwater target. The experiment was not fully documented, so it was up-dated with three groups of boys shooting at targets at two different depths by Hendrickson and Schroeder (1941) with the following conclusions. At a depth of 6 inches the first experimental group, trained to understand the general theory of refraction of light in water, were slightly better than the untrained control group; however, they were not as good as the second experimental group who had learned general principles and a working rule on depth and apparent displacement. The target was then raised to a depth of 2 inches below the surface and the second experimental group who knew both the general principle and the working rule again proved themselves to be significantly better marksmen than the control group. Clearly, pupils who understood the principle and its relevance in practice and to whom the experiment was meaningful were placed at an advantage in solving the problem.

What are the implications of current findings on transfer of training for the work of the teacher in school? First, never assume that it is automatic like incidental learning; on the contrary, the learner should be aware and conscious of the process, and he must adopt a positive attitude towards transfer rather than a passive expectancy of it. Secondly, whenever possible teach by direct methods rather than simulated techniques, practise skills in a natural rather than an artificially imposed environment and realistically demonstrate techniques as they are to be used in actual practice. Thirdly, if transfer is considered desirable, point out identical properties, similarities in approach, common techniques and general principles. Fourthly, never expect any transfer effect from a concept which is not fully comprehended or from a skill which is not meaningful in practice. The danger of applying techniques and rules or sequences of computation without the learner really knowing what he is doing cannot be over-emphasized whatever the level of learning. This is of equal importance whether in the teaching of, say, the serial classification of articles with junior school children or the principle of "degrees of freedom" in testing for statistical significance to Advanced level pupils.

Transfer of training does not end with formal education in school. Think of the car driver and his probability of having to learn to drive vehicles with a normal floor-mounted gear lever, with a steering-column gear control or one with automatic transmission. Also consider the transfer of attitudes in society to ideals like justice and loyalty and how prejudice is spread in race, religion and politics.

Additional Reading

BILODEAU, E. A. (Ed.) (1966) *Acquisition of Skill*. London: Academic Press.
DIENES, Z. P. and JEEVES, M. A. (1970) *The Effects of Structural Relations on Transfer*. London: Hutchinson.
FITTS, P. M. and POSNER, M. I. (1967) *Human Performance*. Belmont, Calif.: Brooks Cole.
HASLERUD, G. M. (1973) *Transfer, Memory and Creativity*. London: Oxford Books.
HOLDING, D. H. (1965) *Principles of Training*. Oxford: Pergamon.
KANE, J. E. (Ed.) (1972) *Psychological Aspects of Physical Education*. London: Routledge & Kegan Paul.
LEGGE, D. (Ed.) (1970) *Skills: Selected Readings*. London: Penguin.
McGHIE, A. (1969) *Pathology of Attention*. London: Penguin.
SULLIVAN, A. M. and SKANES, G. R. (1971) Differential transfer of training in bright and dull subjects of the same mental age. *Brit. J. Educ. Psychol.* **41**, Pt. 3, 287–93.
WHITING, H. T. A. (1969) *Acquiring Ball Skill*. London: Bell.

CHAPTER 6

Language

Communication in Man and Animals

A conventional distinction is nowadays made between the acquisition of language and learning a language. Acquiring is used in the sense of attaining competence in the native or mother tongue and learning is normally applied to the study of a second or "foreign" language. Most of this chapter will be devoted to the psychology of language acquisition. For the greater part of this century psychologists have affirmed that the fundamental distinction between man and the remainder of the animal kingdom lies in the use of language, therefore it is surprising that deep and analytical studies of its acquisition are only of comparatively recent origin. Prior to the work of Chomsky (1957) which elevated the subject to a new level, research in this field tended to be descriptive, observational and too heavily reliant on ill-adapted general learning theory, for example, conditioning as a possible causal explanation.

Although it is true that some animals communicate with each other in a primitive vocal fashion, as for instance in giving warning calls when danger is imminent, it would be unreal to claim that this represents a genuine use of language. Similarly a parrot uttering a sequence of sounds like "pretty Polly" which is recognizable by most English speakers cannot be said to be talking in the sense that the bird is engaged in a simple conversation. There is no evidence to prove that an animal is capable of generating language and this tends to rule out any theory that human language has evolved from primitive sound patterns or elementary signal systems. Discontinuity in evolution is a theory strongly supported by Lenneberg (1967) and other distinguished ethologists who propose a theory of species-specific behaviour. Tinbergen (1951) uses the term sign stimulus to describe the release of a specific and stereotyped behaviour pattern and the process whereby other animals of the same species respond to that signal. Attempts to teach chimpanzees a primitive language have met with little or no success; this factor, together with the anthropological evidence that the language of the most primitive of peoples is technically complex, lends strong support to the suggestion that the biological mechanisms for the acquisition of language in human beings is unique.

Most scholars accept that there is a different brain structure in man compared with other animals and in particular, compared with other primates. It is also generally agreed that there is a common pattern of language acquisition in children of widely different cultural backgrounds and levels. Not all are in agreement that language is genetically determined in the sense that a child is born with a pre-wired biological mechanism or a printed circuit; in short, a ready-made schema capable of assimilating and modifying environmental data. Chomsky (1968) would go so far as to assert that children are born with a knowledge of the basic rules of grammar, a property which is said to be characteristic of a "linguistic universal". This kind of argument on the role of heredity and environment in child development is also central to the study of intelligence and it appears in other areas of psychological study including personality and temperament. Unfortunately, at present the genetic code has not been finally cracked and there is insufficient evidence at hand to support or refute an hypothesis of innate capacity.

Acquisition of Language

Language is a complex and difficult topic for study, partly on account of its rich and varied symbolism capable of expressing anything from a simple form of assent to an abstract or polymorphous concept, but also because it plays a role in human behaviour ranging from processes of thinking and reasoning to the cultivation of inter-personal relationships. This changing and interacting function is evident from a recording of the speech of two young children at play which might possibly reveal situations: (a) in which one child requires the other to do something for him or wants him to listen to some information and (b) in which social rapport is established with his friend through making comments to which a reply is not necessarily expected and by maintaining a running commentary on what he is doing. Lewis (1963) draws a distinction between these two forms of usage and calls them "manipulative" and "declarative". Piaget (1950) comments frequently on the "ego-centric" language of young children when they are merely thinking aloud rather than communicating information of specific interest to others.

The subject of language has so many facets that it attracts the full and serious attention of the linguist, philosopher, sociologist and psychologist alike; it is often difficult to state precisely their respective spheres of interest because they overlap considerably both in content and method of investigation. Between psychologists there is little universal agreement on the problem of how language is acquired, particularly as to how the earliest stages of speech emerge and develop and whether they are based on wholly innate propensities or not. However, all are in agreement that language is generated and flourishes in a social context and is sustained by environmental stimulation. One of the principal arguments in support of the theory that a child is born with an innate capacity for speech is based on a child's ability to respond to sounds from birth. Another reason is the speed with which language skill is acquired and, finally, the pattern and sequence of maturation is common to children of widely different cultures.

Lenneberg (1967) maintains that if the process of language maturation is impaired through illness or physical damage, recovery is possible up to the age of puberty. The sequence in which language develops in these children is not different, only later. His clinical observations suggest a theory of critical development, that is, a period when a child's language acquisition is said to be at an optimum. Research is needed into a detailed study of maturation as it might shed light on the problem of the initial stage of retardation in the linguistic development of children who are otherwise normal.

Behaviourist Theories

In the past too much emphasis has been placed on the imitation of adult language by children rather than on the study of children's speech as a system with its own linguistic conventions and phases of development. This possibly reflects the behaviourist approach to learning theory, based on conditioning and shaping, which gained wide acceptance before the publications of the linguistic-cognitive scholars like Chomsky.

It will be recalled that the classical conditioning model of Pavlov comprises two kinds of signal system; the first which is shared in common with the animal kingdom is concerned with sensory perception, and the second which symbolizes the first is speech: "Speech constitutes the second signalling system of reality which is peculiarly ours, being the signal of the first signals" (Pavlov, 1955). This second signal concept opened up a previously confined field of investigation into human behaviour for specialists in language and thinking like Luria (1961) and Vygotsky (1962).

The following sequence which demonstrates the simultaneous development of language and motor control in young children is derived from the work of the Pavlovian school of psychologists. In the opening experimental situation a child is verbally instructed to press a rubber ball whenever a coloured light is switched on. A very young child, say under $2\frac{1}{2}$ years of age, is unable to carry out the simple task on the first hearing but will succeed in doing so after receiving continuous verbal reinforcement. By about 3 years of age a child should have mastered this experiment quite easily and although he is specifically instructed not to squeeze the rubber ball on seeing a certain colour he cannot refrain from the activity. This is known as the inhibitory stage, the child is powerless to stop the motor excitation he has generated. In the next stage of the experiment the regulatory function of speech is demonstrated; the child will press the ball twice in response to self-repetition of a command, "go", "go". By about the age of 4 years a child, as a result of the development of internal speech, enters a stage of self-regulation of behaviour and motor control. This kind of process, in which thought becomes internalized, will be expanded in the context of Piaget's work on child development which is outlined in Chapter 7.

Skinner's view of language acquisition is set out in his book *Verbal Behaviour* (1957), but it has not been so well received as his contribution to programmed learning. The essence of his theory is that speech sounds emitted by a child are simply operants which are reinforced and that verbal behaviour is shaped by successive approximations to adult speech. Reinforcement occurs under a variety of circumstances: (i) as soon as a listener understands what a speaker is communicating and signifies this by a gesture or doing what is requested, (ii) in the process of thinking by engaging in sub-vocal activity and (iii) in physically writing down words or sentences on paper.

Skinner under-estimates the significance of semantics in language acquisition and holds the opinion that meaning is unimportant as it precedes the speech sound. Surely the meaning of a word must be taken in the context of the sentence or passage in which it appears? Again, he says little about imitation in children, thus denying much of what has been observed and recorded by linguists of initial utterances and their subsequent modification. Children not only imitate patterns of speech sound but also the system of their language. Further criticism of the behaviourist approach will be found in the section on psycholinguistics in which a cognitive theory of the generation of grammar is outlined.

Early Language Development

Mention of the technique "observe and record" in the previous paragraph serves as an introduction to the researches of many patient linguists who have faithfully noted every detail of young children's speech and have analysed masses of data in the search for common factors in language development. For a chronological account of this development read McCarthy (1954) or Lewis (1963). If possible, as a rewarding exercise confirm the sequence by actually recording sounds made by a young baby and observe his facial and other responses to specific situations, for example:

(i) when he first shows an active response like turning to the source of a sound;
(ii) when he first expresses pleasure on hearing certain words;
(iii) when he first responds to a negative command such as "don't";
(iv) when he utters his first recognizable word;
(v) when he constructs his first phrase or primitive sentence;
(vi) when he understands an instruction like "point to your face".

Up to about 6 months of age children, whatever their culture, engage in babbling; that is, practising a variety of vocal sounds for the pleasure it evokes. Congenitally deaf and dumb children are seriously impaired in their linguistic development because they cannot babble and imitate. The stage immediately following babbling and the utterance of first words causes controversy amongst psychologists because it is imperfectly explained by a single comprehensive theory. Behaviourists like Skinner point to the significance of processes like reinforcement and shaping. Others emphasize the part played by imitation but this presents difficulties because the child first has to learn how to imitate. A child's first attempt at imitation is so imperfect that it is virtually impossible to recognize the child's utterance as being the same word as that spoken by the parent. Whatever theoretical view of language acquisition one holds it is the interaction of child and environment, possibly in the sense of assimilation and accommodation as proposed by Piaget, that facilitates early speech.

From about the age of 18 months onwards a child begins to put words together. Suggestions as to how this is achieved have been put forward by Braine (1963) and his associates. All two- and three-word utterances of children of this age were recorded and analysed according to frequency of use and their relative position in a phrase. Analysis reveals that words commonly used in early speech fall into two classes: pivot and open. Pivot words usually occupy the same position in the utterance, either at the beginning or end; they are few in number, but are used most frequently. Open words are the common nouns and verbs, therefore they form a much larger class.

Pivot	Open	Examples
big	boat	big boat
gone	coat	big plane
more	Daddy	big toy
my	milk	my milk
pretty	Mummy	my Mummy
see	plane	my shoe
↓	shoe	coat gone
	sock	Daddy gone
	toy	sock gone
	↓	

In children's telegraphic speech, content words are frequently used and retained whereas function words are omitted and forgotten. Does this imply that the length of utterance is constrained by a young child's very short memory span, or is it simply a reflection of some aspect of normal maturational growth as suggested by Lenneberg (1967)?

Discussion of how normal 2-year-old children are capable of making speech sounds, words and simple phrases represents only a very limited and over-simplified concept of the expression and function of language. Children have to learn how: (i) grammatically acceptable sentences are generated, (ii) meaning is conveyed and interpreted, (iii) thinking and problem-solving is facilitated by verbal activity, (iv) feelings and words are communicated and (v) style and originality is added to verbal expression.

Most psychologists agree that the 2 years from $1\frac{1}{2}$ to $3\frac{1}{2}$ years of age are absolutely critical in language development; the infrastructure of grammar and vocabulary which is laid down in this pre-school period determines the whole future pattern of a child's linguistic competence. The sheer expansion in his vocabulary from under 50 to over 1,500 words is impressive enough, but to this must be added the acquisition of the fundamentals of a highly complex grammatical structure. Consequently the quality of linguistic communication between mother and child is of the utmost significance and indicates why a culturally impoverished social environment is so detrimental to disadvantaged children. This no doubt explains the relative retardation commonly shown in the linguistic growth of institutional children who lack free and frequent opportunities to engage in conversation with adults in an informal family group. Smaller family residential units like normal homes are probably more likely to facilitate language development in young children.

From the stage of construction of simple units of open and pivot words children expand their vocabulary in practising words and phrases to which they have paid attention in other children's or adult speech. In daily conversation with children, parents enlarge and elaborate simple utterances either by rephrasing them or restating them in different words which retain the same meaning. The research reported by Campbell and Wales (1970), based on observations in the experimental nursery of the Edinburgh S.S.R.C. unit, into the use of comparative expressions demonstrate the necessity for children to converse freely whilst playing together in social groups. From the analysis it was concluded that "comparative expressions occur much more frequently in 'comparative' situations where two or more children are vying with each other in various tasks—for example in threading strings of beads, building sandcastles, etc. Clearly, the language of a single child at home is less likely to show such structures."

Parents who take pleasure in simply repeating back the baby talk of infants without attempting to enrich their vocabulary or improve their syntax contribute little to the linguistic advancement of their children. Similarly in school, whatever the subject in the curriculum, a teacher has a responsibility and a duty to correct imperfections in language usage, spoken or written.

Assimilation, imitation and reinforcement is only a part of the story of the acquisition of language; it really begins to unfold with the more fascinating topic of how it is generated. This aspect is so important that a separate section has been allocated to it. The role of language in problem-solving and thinking is discussed in a later chapter.

Social Aspects

It is necessary to make brief reference to some of the social aspects of language acquisition, in particular to the work of Bernstein (1970). Psychologists and sociologists have recently taken greater interest in the form of language spoken in different social environments under a number of socially determined situations.

At a descriptive level readers are well aware of the social function of language, often as a greeting and prelude to conversation: "lovely day, today, isn't it?" There is also a superficial relationship between social class, word pronunciation and accent, which are in turn often coupled to a regional dialect. Liverpool supporters will confirm this by recognition of the phrase: "see yer savvy", meaning "I will see you this afternoon". The form of language used also varies with interpersonal relationships; between a child and other members of the peer group, a child and his parents and a child and his teachers. All this is at a very superficial level and it is to Bernstein that one turns for a more penetrating analysis of social-class differences in language development and use.

Bernstein's (1961) basic hypothesis is that the language heard and spoken by children from lower working-class homes is very different in content from that heard and spoken by children from a middle-class home background. This difference is reflected in their comparative educational progress and more particularly in their pattern of thought development. It is shown by comparing the performance of children from the two classes on verbal and non-verbal items in intelligence tests. The term "restricted code" is nowadays used instead of "public language" to describe the short, grammatically simple, often unfinished sentences with a poor syntactical form and stressing the active voice which are associated with the speech of working-class children. The term "elaborated code" replaces the original "formal language" to describe the more syntactically complex and logically related sentences with finer discriminations in the expression of meaning and a wider variety of speech organization which are associated with middle-class children.

The working-class child uses simple and repetitive conjunctions, few subordinate clauses, a limited number of adjectives and adverbs, statements like "you know?" which emphasize the previous speech sequence and an individual selection from a group of idiomatic phrases. The middle-class child is much less predictable in his use of language, he is more selective and he examines possibilities of expression. His grammar is more accurate and he makes greater use of prepositions and other parts of speech.

Bernstein takes care to stress that a child who uses the restricted code could not be described as non-verbal or linguistically deprived. Such a child has the same basic understanding of the rules of language as a child who more frequently uses an elaborated code. Neither does his model imply a perfect correlation between language and social class under all circumstances; for example, middle-class children in conversation with members of the peer group often use a restricted code. The important point is that they have access to the elaborated code which the majority of children have not. Restriction in linguistic competence impairs problem-solving and abstract thinking, it affects attitudes to learning, it diminishes curiosity and interest; in short, it influences all educational attainment and finally manifests itself in disruptive and anti-social conduct. Teachers have been educated in the use of an elaborated code and they are expected to put it into practice in the classroom: however, if what is being said by the teacher is not translated by the child to the restricted code, then there is little or no communication between them. Children who speak the restricted code reach a limit of learning which is associated with mechanical learning rather than conceptual thinking and the ability to generalize. The backwardness too often characterized by the lower-class child is culturally induced, and it is transmitted and sustained through the effects of linguistic processing. The gulf between speakers of the two codes widens over the years, particularly at the secondary school level where the educational process becomes more analytic and relatively abstract.

In a postscript to the above article, published in De Cecco (1967), Bernstein stresses "the two codes may be distinguished on the linguistic level in terms of the probabilities of predicting for any one speaker which structural elements will be used to organize meaning. In the case of an elaborated code, the speaker will select from a relatively extensive range of alternatives, therefore the probability of predicting the pattern of organizing elements is considerably reduced. . . . The codes themselves are functions of particular forms of social relationships, or more generally, qualities of social structures."

A more recent development in Bernstein's work is a consideration of the nature of social control in two different types of family (Bernstein and Henderson, 1969). Briefly, in a "positional family" social control is effected through imperatives and use is made of the restricted code; in a "person-oriented family" control is effected through personal appeals and greater use is made of the elaborated code. Readers who have not got access to the above article or to Gumperz and Hymes (1970) will find a summary of these and other aspects of sociolinguistics in Pride (1970).

Bernstein and his colleagues are continuing the development of the theory of a relationship between social structure and the generation of different patterns of speech. Teachers anxiously await guidance on possible methods of modifying or changing a child's form of speaking so that he moves away from the limitations imposed by a restricted code. Possibly it is all too deeply rooted in the environment, and it is this which is urgently in need of change. A point frequently raised in discussion is whether it would be more valid to think of a continuum rather than polarize linguistic codes into a clear-cut dichotomy. Possibly true, but it would not seriously alter the basic implications underlying Bernstein's hypothesis.

A unique account of the role of speech in the behaviour pattern and play of identical 5-year-old twins is described by Luria and Yudovitch (1960). The twins were retarded in speech development. They always played together and their pattern of play was abnormal. After separation and play with other children in a different environment their standards of speech improved and their play became more co-operative and creative. One of the twins was given special teaching in the use of language and speech training and later showed so much superiority in self-regulation over his brother that he assumed the role of the dominant twin whereas previously he had been the recessive of the pair.

A considerable amount of evidence is available to demonstrate the relationship between social class and linguistic development; unfortunately there have been few specific investigations into means and methods of solving the problem of poor language attainment in practice in school. Various suggestions have been put forward; for example, increased nursery school provision in the twilight urban areas, smaller classes with greater opportunity for inter-personal relationship between teacher and child and the use of trained auxiliaries to help individuals with special difficulties. Above all, teachers must accept greater responsibility in diagnosing and understanding the problems and limitations of children who exclusively use the restricted code. Through adaptation of the child's work, discussion and shaping rather than talking down or mechanically correcting, they must attempt to bridge the gulf between the language of the two codes. How boring it is for a normal intelligent adult to be forced to listen to a foreign tongue which is imperfectly understood; yet for some children this is the classroom norm, no wonder they want to talk to each other in their own code and take every possible opportunity of doing so in or out of school. The progressive disintegration of a lesson with its inevitable disciplinary troubles is often traced to the sheer boredom of children who are incapable of understanding what the teacher is saying and consequently what is required or expected of them other than passive attention.

Chomsky's Rule Generation Theory

In previous chapters some indication has been made of the rift between the behaviourist and cognitive schools in the study of learning and thought development; probably nowhere have arguments become so polarized as in the defence of their theories of language acquisition. According to Skinner (1957) the process is essentially no different from any other form of learning. By series of successive approximations a child emits and modifies the sound of a word until it makes a sound pattern similar to that of adults in speech. In other words, as a result of feedback a child's speech is progressively modified by reinforcement until he succeeds in getting it right.

A theory of this kind is attractive for its simplicity and seems to fit into "established" schools of thought with little difficulty, but as Chomsky (1959) in his review of Skinner's *Verbal Behaviour* points out it leaves far too many questions unanswered. It is not too difficult to visualize how simple sound patterns and individual words are acquired through conditioning; however, it is in applying it to larger units of study like sentence construction and the generation of semantically complex passages that problems arise. Miller (1967) has estimated from calculations that a child could not possibly have heard all the sentences he uses or is capable of using in everyday speech. In conversation children produce many sentences which have not been previously heard, therefore they must generate them according to rules which are learned. The core of the objection to conditioning processes in language acquisition is that children create language which is not necessarily an imitation of parental speech. Problems also arise as soon as semantics, or the study of meaning, is investigated. A sentence is not merely a chain or sequence of words but a planned unit and the meaning of a word is affected by the structure of the sentence in which it occurs.

Chomsky has opened up new frontiers in the scientific study of language and his seminal work has pioneered research into a fascinating variety of topics ranging from logical analysis to communication theory. In terms of bonuses or by-products for the advancement of techniques in language teaching the results of current research may seem disappointing. In comparison with other disciplines linguistics is still in its infancy and many investigations are needed before firm recommendations are made as to how best to teach native and foreign tongues in school.

Before examining Chomsky's work, it might prove helpful to make reference to some of the earlier contributions to linguistics, beginning with de Saussere's (1915) distinction between "langue" and "parole". The basic structural organization of language and the rules whereby the system is governed is approximately "langue", its imperfect expression in day to day speech is "parole". Chomsky has adopted this dichotomy and distinguishes between "competence" which is equivalent to "langue" and "performance" which is similar to "parole". Linguists tend to study structural models of competence rather than models of speech performance because the latter are too full of complexities and irregularities. A useful but not wholly accurate analogy by de Saussere was between the structure or score of a piece of music and its performance on several occasions. As any collector of gramophone records knows too well from instant comparison no two performances of, say, a Mahler symphony are identical. The structure of the music is immediately recognizable from a score and although each performance, technically speaking, possibly marks the highest standards of excellence in achievement, it is unique.

A second concept needs to be grasped before examining Chomsky's theory of generating grammatical sentences by the use of transformational rules. Harris (1957) pointed out that a simple declarative sentence, called a "kernel sentence", may be rewritten and a number of sentences derived from it by merely transforming or reordering a number of words. For example, the phrase "David opened the door for Jane" uses a verb in the active voice and is identical in meaning to "The door was opened for Jane by David" which is in the passive voice. In the same way: "Philip swims well", "Philip is swimming well" and "Philip does swim well" are tranformations of a simple kernel sentence. Hockett (1958) used the terms "surface" and "deep" to demonstrate sentences with different structures. The arrangement of words in the phrase "That boy will read the chapter" is not identical to "The chapter will be read by that boy". The surface structure has been changed yet both sentences retain the same meaning and there is no ambiguity about them. However, and with gratitude to Lord Butler (1971), if one writes: "My wife makes good soup. So said the cannibal chief at dinner" the deep structure or semantic meaning of the sentence is not entirely clear. It is imperative to know more of the context of the comment in the story before the deep structure or full meaning of the statement is revealed.

Chomsky initially accepted the derivation of transformations from kernel sentences but in his latest publication, *Aspects of the Theory of Syntax* (1965), he argues that language is generated by the syntactic component; namely, the arrangement and relationship of words to each other in a sentence. It is necessary to go back to his *Syntactic Structure* (1957) for a critical evaluation of what is technically known as "finite state grammar" and its inadequacy as an explanation of the generation of language. It is a fairly simple exercise to construct a number of grammatical sentences in a left to right sequence by means of a finite set of rules:

The boy plays rugby.
The boys play rugby on Saturday.
The Old Boys play rugby on Saturday afternoon.

The grammar of each sentence is in the finite state, yet it is capable of generating many hundreds or an infinite number of simple sentences. Language is not structured in such a straightforward fashion; on the contrary, it is highly complex with embedded phrases within phrases and it often contains alternative hypotheses. It is too limited a concept to think in terms of a simple generative sequence of grammar, the whole sentence has to be conceived as a total plan.

Chomsky has suggested that two sets of rules are required to generate language, phrase-structure and structural transformations. To illustrate the meaning of the term, "phrase-structure grammar", a sentence will be constructed or generated according to sets of rules:

(i)	Sentence	Noun phrase	+ Verb phrase
(ii)	Noun phrase	Determiner	+ Noun
(iii)	Verb phrase	Verb	+ Noun phrase
(iv)	Verb	Auxiliary	+ Verb
(v)	Determiner	That........the	
(vi)	Noun	Boy..........chapter	
(vii)	Auxiliary	Will	
(viii)	Verb	Read	

"That boy will read the chapter."

The constituent parts of the same sentence may be shown in the form of a tree diagram which will illustrate its total plan rather than a sequence of words (Fig. 21). School children are more familiar with the opposite process known as parsing in which sentences are broken down into constituent parts.

Chomsky's second set of rules incorporates the transformations previously referred to in the definition of surface and deep structures and includes the reorganization of sentences from active to passive, negative, interrogative and compound forms. He not only confirmed the relation-

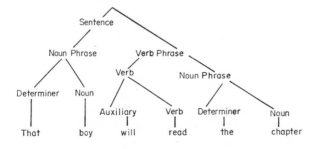

FIG. 21.

ship between deep and surface structures but showed how they can be added to the rules of phrase-structure. A brief reference to an ambiguous sentence will more clearly illustrate the point: "they are cooking apples" has two forms of surface structure and different deep structures. Using a phrase marker tree the two surface structures may be set out according to whether the word cooking is used as a verb or as an adjective (Fig. 22). However, some ambiguous sentences are so structured that it is impossible for a phrase marker tree to differentiate between the separate deep structures: "The driving of the golfers was erratic."

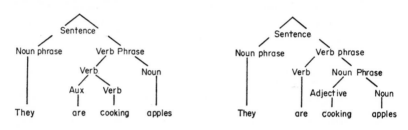

Fig. 22.

From the foregoing it is evident that deep structure is closely related to meaning; to understand what is implied by the above sentence, it is essential to know the context in which it is used. Does it mean that they were hooking and slicing golf balls all over the course instead of hitting them straight down the fairway, or that the golfers were driving their cars unsteadily after spending too long drinking at the nineteenth?

One might validly question the relevance of Chomsky's study of a generative grammar and other semantic theories for educational practice. The models appear to have little direct value particularly as they are applicable to linguistic competence rather than performance. To students of learning theory they are important because they suggest how a child might possibly acquire language in a relatively short period of time by learning sets of rules. Miller, who pointed out the mathematical improbability of a child mastering a working vocabulary and grammar under techniques of conditioning, estimates that English could be learned in 10 to 15 years with less than 100 rules of formation, with less than 100 transformations and with about 100,000 rules for pronunciation and vocabulary.

A rule generation theory of this kind is not quite so simple as it appears at first sight, it leaves important questions to be answered. Here is one frequently asked by teachers: "why does a very young child commonly express an irregular form such as 'buy/bought' correctly, but soon after he has learned rules he might possibly utter an incorrect form such as 'buy/buyed'?" The learning of rules creates opportunities for over-generalization and increases the probability of making mistakes in grammatical usage. Does this suggest that a child goes through three gradually changing and sometimes simultaneous phases in acquiring language: (i) an initial and more clearly defined period of imitation in which a restricted and limited grammar is often correctly used, (ii) a rule-learning period in which mistakes are most probably made because of the rather sudden yet enormous expansion in grammatical usage and (iii) a life-long period in which most errors are gradually eliminated as a result of speaking socially in school, at home and in employment?

One way of dealing with the paradox of the child who makes mistakes after learning rules for say the formation of the past tense or the plurals of a noun is to compliment him for learning the general rule, but at the same time bring to his attention the existence of irregular forms by quoting examples. In the early stages of learning, certain errors must be considered part of the normal process of development and not a sign of linguistic incompetence. Only when they become persistent and their source is not understood by the speaker are they seriously indicative of poor linguistic skill. This view in no way suggests that passive acceptance of grammatical errors is desirable, on the contrary, every opportunity must be taken by parent and teacher alike to modify and eliminate them by demonstration and explanation.

In 1965 Chomsky published *Aspects of the Theory of Syntax* and a modification of the earlier transformational grammar. Figure 23 is based on one drawn by Lyons (1970); for a clear and brief description of Chomsky's more recent theory readers are recommended to his excellent account.

The three components or sets of rules of the grammar of a language are SYNTACTIC (correct relationship of words), SEMANTIC (meaning) and PHONOLOGICAL (speech sounds). Sentences are generated by syntactic rules with an underlying phrase marker or deep structure and a derived phrase marker or surface structure. Whereas the deep structure of a sentence is generative in the sense that it is the creative or productive aspect of language,

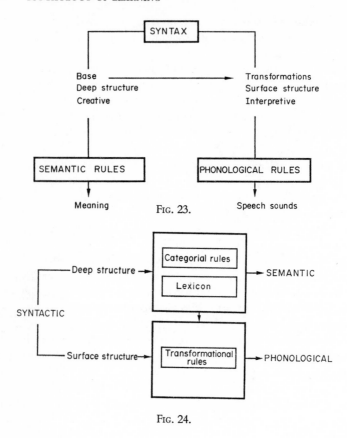

FIG. 23.

FIG. 24.

the surface structure is interpretive of the abstract structure which has been generated.

Figure 24 suggests how deep structure is derived from a base with two sub-components, categorial rules and the lexicon. In many ways the categorial rules are similar to the phrase-structure rules of the original model. The lexicon consists of all the meaningful elements or words, as opposed to purely grammatical elements, which are essential for the correct operation of the rules. Transformational rules convert surface structures into the phonological component, the speech sounds of language.

that working–class children have less exposure to the structure of passive voice sentences in parental speech.

Miller (1962), and in conjunction with McKean (1968), measured times taken in seconds to perform transformations of sentences, hypothesizing that the variations in time would indicate the relative ease or difficulty of making a transformation. An earlier experimental design utilized a simple paper and pencil test. The second design was more sophisticated as it required a subject to search for a required transformation from an illuminated display of eighteen possible sentences formed by taking:

—— John, Jane or Joe as the first word of a sentence,
—— liked or warned as the second word, and
—— the small boy, the old woman or the young man as the final phrase.

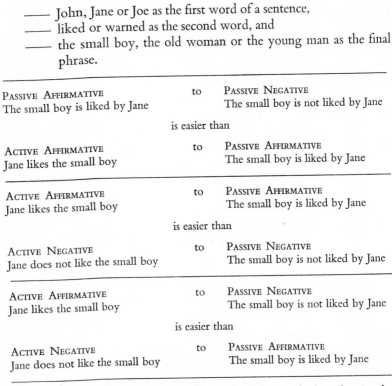

PASSIVE AFFIRMATIVE The small boy is liked by Jane	to	PASSIVE NEGATIVE The small boy is not liked by Jane
	is easier than	
ACTIVE AFFIRMATIVE Jane likes the small boy	to	PASSIVE AFFIRMATIVE The small boy is liked by Jane

ACTIVE AFFIRMATIVE Jane likes the small boy	to	PASSIVE AFFIRMATIVE The small boy is liked by Jane
	is easier than	
ACTIVE NEGATIVE Jane does not like the small boy	to	PASSIVE NEGATIVE The small boy is not liked by Jane

ACTIVE AFFIRMATIVE Jane likes the small boy	to	PASSIVE NEGATIVE The small boy is not liked by Jane
	is easier than	
ACTIVE NEGATIVE Jane does not like the small boy	to	PASSIVE AFFIRMATIVE The small boy is liked by Jane

In a discussion of the results, Miller and McKean calculate that it takes an additional 0.41 second to deal with an affirmative–negative difference, compared with an additional 0.91 second to deal with an active–passive

Chomsky's model is idealistic and not all would agree with
of linguistic competence as defined in the *Aspects* (1965):
theory is concerned with an ideal speaker–listener, in a complete
geneous speech community, who knows its language perfect\
unaffected by such grammatically irrelevant conditions as \
limitations, distractions, shifts of attention and interest, and errors (\
or characteristic) in applying his knowledge of the language in actu
formance."

Some Psycholinguistic Experiments

Many psychologists have found Chomsky's work a useful base fr\
which to explore linguistic problems impinging on their own fields \
study; for example, the analysis of difficulties encountered in learnin\
transformations, estimates of the capacity and possible methods of memor\
storage and the relationship between language acquisition and communi–
cation theory.

An investigation into children's understanding of deep structure in
sentences by Hezlett Dewart (1972) suggests that there are social class
differences in the rate at which mastery of the syntactic rule system of
language is acquired. It is well known to teachers that children tend to vary
in their understanding and comprehension of active and passive voice
sentences in which deep and surface structure differ considerably. Children
from two contrasting social groups were asked to manipulate objects
which correspond to sentences spoken by the experimenter:

"The red car is pushing the blue car"
"The blue car is pulled by the red car" } using toy model cars.
"The wolf bites the duck—Show me that" } using hand
"The wolf is bitten by the duck—Show me that" } puppets.

Results of the experiment clearly showed that middle-class children
made fewer errors than working-class children. Does the investigation also
suggest that linguistic competence is more clearly reflected in the comprehension and understanding of sentences rather than in their production or
generation? This in many ways confirms the findings of Lawton (1968),
based on Bernstein's earlier work, that the frequency of using passive
voice sentences varies with social class. A point made by Cazden (1965) is

difference and an additional 1.53 seconds when both differences are involved. From the experiment it is clear that times are always shorter when active–affirmative sentences are matched and one wonders if this has any special significance?

The longer time spent on certain transformations might possibly include additional time for semantic rather than syntactic operations. Miller's general impression is that syntactic operations are performed automatically and any deliberate control over them is exercised at the semantic level. This substantiates the findings of Slobin (1966) who spoke true and false sentences about pictures presented to subjects and found it took them longer to evaluate affirmative to negative than active to passive sentences. The difficulties encountered with reversible passive sentences could be explained by the necessity to remember which noun-phrase is the actor in the sentence. This can prove a fairly troublesome operation:

"The teacher spoke to the boy."
"The boy was spoken to by the teacher."

Another method of measuring the relative difficulty of sentences has been suggested by Yngve (1962) and is termed depth hypothesis. Take a simple phrase marker tree and count the number of left branches leading to a given word and call this the depth of the word. The depth of the sentence is the sum of the depths of all individual words it contains and its mean depth is this total divided by the number of words in the sentence (Fig. 25).

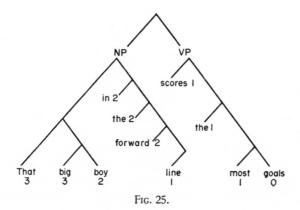

FIG. 25.

"That big boy in the forward line scores the most goals"

$$\text{Total depth of sentence} = 18$$
$$\text{No. of words in sentence} = 11$$
$$\text{Mean depth of sentence} = \frac{18}{11} = 1.64$$

The left branch is taken as the criterion of complexity because a speaker has to retain this in his memory when he constructs a sentence in a normal left to right sequence. Presumably a sentence with considerable depth is less easily recalled without error because of limitations imposed by the handling capacity of short-term memory.

Few teachers of language would disagree with the general hypothesis that in learning a second or third tongue, individual capacity to recall words, phrases, structures, irregularities, generalizations and the like is highly variable; yet possession of this kind of ability is a tremendous asset to a student in facilitating more rapid progress towards language mastery. Two kinds of memory process appear to be involved in recalling sentences and these are related to surface and deep structure respectively. It is much more difficult to recall the exact sequence of words or surface structure of a sentence than its underlying meaning or deep structure. In attempting to repeat back a sentence immediately after hearing it a subject has to rely on his short-term memory, which we already know has a relatively limited capacity. By contrast, in expressing the meaning or interpreting a sentence one draws from a ready-formed schemata or long-term memory storage of infinitely greater capacity. Short-term memory traces, associated with the surface or phonological component, are more subject to immediate decay or extinction than coded material associated with the deep or semantic component.

Miller, McKean, Yngve and others have clearly demonstrated experimentally how the complexity of syntactic structure of sentences is directly related to the loading of the short-term or immediate memory system. Certain transformations are troublesome in this respect, so are embedded clauses and physically distant separations between related verbs and nouns in a sentence. In the private reading of a complex sentence one normally has time to unravel or restructure its sub-components to make it meaningful, but in listening to the same sentence spoken by a teacher (who may be imperfect in his delivery) a student neither has the time nor the handling capacity to deal with it correctly. Lecturers who literally read word for word "carefully" prepared but intellectually demanding statements rather than series of clear, concise and logically structured notes often fall into this trap and lose an audience through fatigue, and not as they may imagine due to loss of interest.

The lecturer who abandons a prepared text and talks round a topic or headings is placed on a more equal footing with his audience because he too is forced to make use of his immediate memory in generating intelligible sentences. Students often comment that a certain teacher only makes a subject come alive when he gets down from his dais, approaches the front bench and quietly discusses a point, narrates a story, explains a problem or provides an example. Of course, factors other than the linguistic skill of the teacher, such as psychological distance, enters this kind of teaching situation.

Reference to memory brings readers full circle back to problems of perception, information storage and retrieval and the role of feedback. Practically nothing is known about the processes involved in decoding speech messages and their physical storage. The theoretical models by Broadbent (1958) and Lunzer (1968) of selective attention, cue reception, scanning and matching are highly relevant to the problem and possibly also is an information theory proposed by Shannon and Weaver (1949). According to this theory the probability of the comprehension of a sentence increases as each unit of information is revealed. In other words, the listener probably knows what is likely to follow whilst listening to a spoken sentence because the speaker is constrained by rules of grammar and the need to make his utterance meaningful. The context of the whole conversation is assimilated and difficulty arises only if there is conflict in the listener between incoming and anticipated information.

An ingenious attempt to examine the role and measure space taken by syntactic structures in memory storage was made by Savin and Perchonock (1965). A subject would be asked to recall a sentence and a list of eight unrelated words. He is given sentences of different grammatical structure including active, passive, negative and interrogative forms. Provided the sentence has been recalled correctly he is asked to recall the word list. The investigators worked on the assumption that the more words correctly recalled, less space had been taken up by that particular kind of sentence in the memory. Passives took up more space than actives, interrogatives than declaratives and emphatics more than words not emphasized. The general conclusion was that the amount of space taken up was a function of the transformations in the deep structure of a sentence and not the number of words it contained.

Johnson-Laird (1970) suggests that the result does not hold good if a subject is not told beforehand that the sentence and words are to be subsequently recalled. From this he concludes that people adopt a strategy to store and retrieve detail. At present there is no evidence to show that syntax is a prerequisite for the storage of meaning, yet it is in communicating meaningful information to others. About the process of recall there is little that can be profitably added at present to knowledge of the way subjects actively reconstruct sentences to make them more meaningful.

A number of investigations have been made into the function of syntactic analysis, for example, phrase units in the perception of sentences. The technique of listening to a "click" in the middle of a word and asking a person to recall where the click sound had occurred in the sentence is attributed to Ladefoged and Broadbent (1960); it was developed by Fodor and Bever (1965) and again by Garrett et al. (1966). The latter constructed pairs of sentences with identical endings and different beginnings, but each sentence had a different surface structure or grammar:

"From a good pass Tom *scored the goal.*"
"The player who passed the ball to Tom *scored the goal.*"

Read the sentences aloud and in the first the natural pause occurs before "Tom"; in the second, after "Tom". Subjects in the experiment heard a click simultaneously with the word "Tom" in each sentence and were subsequently requested to locate its position. The tendency was for them to locate the click not in its original position but at the syntactic or grammatical boundary. From this it is concluded that phrase structure is of significance in the perception of messages and that grammatical analysis has genuine psychological reality. A listener actively searches for grammatical structure and does not passively perceive sound patterns. The importance of this "active" process of perception, together with a prediction as to what is likely to follow, say, an article or a verb phrase in a sentence, can be demonstrated by relatively simple experiments using either meaningful or nonsense words.

Epstein (1961) constructed strings of nonsense words, then added function words like "the, and, with" and finally inflections like "-by, -ed, -s" to make a "sentence" such as: "The erenstany cates eleudied the edom eptly with ledear and aris". Subjects found it was easier to recall the complete nonsense string than nonsense and function words without inflections. Most difficult of all was the recall of isolated nonsense words. As a result of using inflections and function words the "sentence" is given a series of markers, thus short sequences of words become conveniently grouped into phrase units and these are more readily remembered.

Semantics

It would be wholly unrealistic to examine problems of perception and storage without reference to semantics and the role of prediction in sentence construction. It is difficult and tedious to try and hold a conversation with a speaker who constantly and rapidly changes his subject matter. Trouble arises in trying to anticipate or predict what he is going to say next; in a more common idiom, the conversationalists are not tuned to the same wavelength. Conversation becomes wellnigh impossible when a speaker resorts to the use of clipped sentences or if he has an imperfect knowledge of grammar. Intelligent conversation degenerates into a sequence of decoding cryptic messages until it ultimately becomes impossible to keep pace. This commonly occurs at cocktail parties where a person tries to hear a conversation and only grasps part of it against background noise. The listener has to rely on prediction to make sense of what is heard. On the whole, under these conditions sentences between speakers are made progressively shorter in order to lessen the predictive load and there is also a tendency to avoid inversions in word order and other complex constructions, including negative forms. Forster (1966) has shown that it is more difficult to make up a suitable beginning to an incomplete sentence than an appropriate ending.

In education generally, insufficient attention is paid to semantics, particularly as to why some teachers possess the gift of generating sentences which are grammatically correct, aesthetically attractive and yet wholly meaningful to children, whereas others seem to wallow in ambiguity, uncertainty and vagueness of expression.

From the beginnings of formal experimental psychology, word associations have been studied mainly in the expectation that they would throw light on the problem of learning theory. As Clark (1970) has rightly pointed out, word associations are a *consequence* of linguistic competence and do not show how language is generated. He divides responses into two major groups: paradigmatic and syntagmatic. A paradigmatic response is from the same syntactic category as the stimulus word; for example, tree-flower. A syntagmatic response is from other categories; for example, tree-green or a non-reversible idiomatic phrase like whistle-stop. Young children tend to give more syntagmatic responses but as their vocabulary builds up at about the age of 8 years they gradually change and give more paradigmatic responses.

Moran *et al.* (1964) identified three groups of subjects in word association: (i) those who gave contrasts: light–dark; (ii) those who gave synonyms: quick–fast and superordinates: table–furniture; and (iii) those who gave functional associations: screw-driver. The first group tended to respond very rapidly, the second group took slightly longer and the third were the slowest. However, there are so many possible classifications of words that it is impossible to categorize them objectively or analyse them into easily recognizable factors. It is more profitable to study networks of words, chains of responses and patterns of relationships than isolated words subjectively chosen by an investigator on the basis of intuition.

Word associations are currently used in a different context; namely, in assessments of creativity and in general interest and personality tests like the Brook Reaction Test. These are open-ended in the sense that the testee creates an answer without the usual constraints of a single correct/incorrect response. For example, "write down the first word that comes into mind when I say—POST", or "suggest some normal or unusual uses for a SAFETY PIN".

A technique to investigate the particular meaning a word has for an individual has been devised by Osgood (1952) and is known as the semantic differential. People usually give the same response to common words but the meaning of some words for one individual may be different to another. In debates and summaries of speeches remarks to the effect that a certain word or term had a different connotation to the listener are commonly reported. Differences in shades of meaning and in the emotive force of words are often highly personal. It is this personal connotation of a word which is Osgood's "semantic differential" and it is measured on eight bipolar rating scales (Fig. 26).

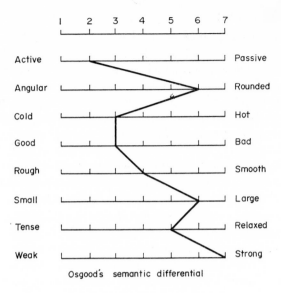

Osgood's semantic differential

FIG. 26. One person's ratings of the word—MATRON.

In rating what he feels about a word, a person is making an emotional or affective response. From the analysis of responses using factorial methods, Osgood isolated three basic dimensions of affective meaning:

(i) Activity: fast–slow   sharp–dull   excitable–calm
(ii) Potency: strong–weak   heavy–light   hard–soft
(iii) Evaluation: good–bad   clean–dirty   kind–cruel

The three basic dimensions are not only found in English cultures but in widely different cultures throughout the world.

The term "semantic satiation" used by Lambert and Jakobovits (1960) describes how a word may lose its meaning if it is continually repeated or stared at for a prolonged period of time. Children are known to suffer from this phenomena when they are forced to study a phrase or a simple set of figures on a blackboard prior to translation or computation and literally see nothing.

Language Learning

Discussion of the relative effectiveness of various methods of teaching foreign languages in school lies beyond the scope of this book. Suffice to say at present that students should be exceedingly cautious in evaluating small-scale researches. It is essential to take a large number of linguistic, psychological and sociological variables and their interaction into consideration for a period of at least 5 years before arriving at tentative conclusions or making generalizations about techniques and sequences of teaching languages. Results from longitudinal studies of children drawn from a wide cross-section of primary, secondary and further education are urgently needed. There are so many topics for investigation on the psychological side alone that it is difficult to know how to begin:

(i) *Motivation*—how does a teacher sustain an initial interest in a foreign language, why does this interest often decay rapidly, what is the point of learning another tongue—to increase the prospect of better employment, for cultural insight and the promotion of international understanding or for social communication on holiday abroad?

(ii) *Transfer of training*—to what extent is learning inhibited or facilitated by possession of a working knowledge of one or more languages including the native tongue? Do some children have a specific ability or gift in linguistic competence?

(iii) *Skills*—is there a definite hierarchy or particular sequence in which language skills should be learned, say oral before written or colloquial usage before grammatical precision, and should these skills be acquired against background knowledge of the contemporary environment of a country including its historical, cultural, political, economic and geographical development? What is the purpose of studying errors in feedback processes. How does a learner promote self-confidence in oral expression and under what conditions of practice?

(iv) *Learning theory*—what factors affect attention to sound patterns and the perceptual recognition of structures, rules and irregularities? Is level of maturation directly related to stage of cognitive development? How does one best utilize and evaluate the effectiveness of teaching aids and modern technology?

Even this selection would not cover all possible variables because differences would certainly arise which reflect the competence and personality of the teacher, the attitude of parents to language learning, previous knowledge of the child and how much he acquires through genuine ego-involvement in activities and through contacts outside the formal school setting. Also textbooks, syllabuses and methods of examination, assessment and testing (including their backwash effect) would have to be evaluated.

Assuming all these investigations have been made there is still no guarantee that an ideal syllabus could be produced or that standards of language teaching would radically improve in a relatively short period of time. In many ways learning a language shares much in common with learning a motor skill and many of the characteristics and problems of the learner are similar in nature. Perfect performance is probably unattainable and linguistic incompetence is too easily displayed in public. Errors and shortcomings are rarely concealed from the teacher. However, it is the attitude of the teacher and the manner in which he makes use of errors that often determines progress and increases a child's confidence in his ability to acquire skill. Errors must be anticipated and expected; progress in learning is rhythmical, cyclic and variable in pace.

Finally, has the study of theoretical models of language acquisition and generation or of the findings from psycholinguistic experimentation contributed towards greater efficiency in language learning? Unfortunately, at present, evidence to support any such bonus is minimal. For a detailed account of the relationship between linguistic theory and language teaching, readers are referred to Corder (1973), who discusses a number of practical psychological difficulties and conflicts which would inevitably arise in attempting to teach a foreign language on the basis of models and theories of native language acquisition. To quote one example; if a pupil were required to learn mastery of motor-perceptual skills like sound recognition and production before learning linguistic skills like oral communication, his interest and motivation would be killed off: "like practising golf swings without ever playing golf".

Corder also examines the possibility of relating the known deep structure of the native tongue to the unknown surface structures of a foreign language by acquiring a new set of transformational rules (Fig. 27). Such a relationship would depend on the possession of common properties in the deep structure or base of all languages. In fact, languages are not universal in

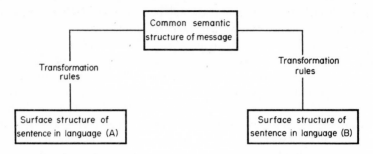

Fig. 27. The relation between message structure and surface structure in two languages (Corder, S. Pit, 1973).

this sense, and this includes genetically related languages. The discovery of a workable set of semantic rules or a reliable model of meaning would be of paramount importance; whatever else is said about learning foreign languages, communication of meaning in an accurate form is the principle objective of language learning for most individuals.

Additional Reading

BARNES, D. and BRITTON, J. (1969) *Language, the Learner and the School*. London: Penguin.

BATEMAN, B. (1965) *The Illinois Test of Psycholinguistic Abilities in Current Research*. Urbana, Illinois: Institute for Research on Exceptional Children.

BOYLE, D. G. (1971) *Language and Thinking in Human Development*. London: Hutchinson.

BROWN, R. (1972) *A First Language*. Cambridge, Mass.: Harvard Univ. Press.

BROWN, R. and BELLUGI, U. (1964) Three processes in the child's acquisition of syntax. *Harvard Educ. Rev.* **34**, 133–51.

CARROLL, J. B. (1963) Research on teaching foreign languages. In GAGE, N. L. (Ed.).

CRYSTAL, D. (1971) *Linguistics*. London: Penguin.

DAKIN, J. (1973) *The Language Laboratory and Language Teaching*. London: Longman.

ERVIN-TRIPP, S. M. and SLOBIN, D. I. (1966) Psycholinguistics. *Ann. Rev. Psychol.* **17**, 435–74.

GAGE, N. L. (Ed.) (1963) *Handbook of Research on Teaching*. Chicago: Rand McNally.

GREENE, J. (1972) *Psycholinguistics*. London: Penguin.

HALLIDAY, M. A. K. *et al.* (1964) *The Linguistic Sciences and Language Teaching*. London: Longman.

HERRIOT, P. (1970) *An Introduction to the Psychology of Language.* London: Methuen.
HERRIOT, P. (1971) *Language and Teaching: A Psychological View.* London: Methuen.
OLDFIELD, R. C. and MARSHALL, J. C. (Eds.) (1968) *Language.* London: Penguin.
ROBINS, R. H. (1964) *General Linguistics.* London: Longmans.
SLOBIN, D. I. (1971) *Psycholinguistics.* Glenview, Illinois: Scott, Foresman; and London: Open University Set Book.
SLOBIN, D. I. (1972) Seven questions about language development. In DODWELL, P. C. (Ed.).
SNIDER, J. G. and OSGOOD, C. E. (Eds.) (1969) *Semantic Differential Technique.* Chicago: Aldine.
STERN, H. H. (1965) Modern linguistics and the teaching of foreign languages. *Educ. Res.* **VII**, No. 1, 37–54.
WATTS, A. F. (1944) *The Language and Mental Development of Children.* London: Harrap.
WHORF, B. L. (1956) *Language, Thought and Reality.* New York: Wiley.
WILKINSON, A. (1971) *The Foundations of Language.* London: Oxford Univ. Press.
WOLFF, J. G. (1973) *Language, Brain and Hearing.* London: Methuen.

CHAPTER 7

Thinking and Problem-solving

Concepts

The nature of the interrelationship between the acquisition and use of language, concepts, problem-solving processes and principle learning is so subtle and intricate that it practically defies definition and logical analysis. No one will deny the importance of acquiring an ability to form and utilize simple and abstract concepts in the development of thought processes in the attainment of intellectual maturity and in the communication of the product of purposeful thinking. An introductory working definition of a concept is a generalized notion of an object, event or idea; it implies a classification and naming of attributes which assist in its subsequent identification. In that they enable a person to relate present experience to past or existing schemata and to interpret and communicate these experiences to others, except for the most simple examples, they must by definition be highly personal and unique to each individual.

How and at what age do children form various categories of concepts and can the process be promoted and accelerated by certain teaching techniques? What is the function of language in concept attainment? Why are concepts of the negative and disjunctive type more difficult to manage, yet they play a vital role in elimination strategies? Answers to these and a host of other questions are not yet fully known in spite of the amount of research which has gone into their investigation, ranging from a myriad of highly specific inquiries to Piaget's monumental study of the mental development of the child.

Piaget's Theory

The first half of this chapter is devoted to a description and discussion of the observations and theories of Piaget and his colleagues working with children at the Rousseau Institute in Geneva. Readers must not assume from the prominence given Piaget in this text that he is the only well-known investigator in this field or that his contribution is absolutely definitive. His work is discussed before that of other researchers like Bruner *et al.* (1956) for chronological reasons and because some of the concepts Piaget develops, such as schema, should by now be familiar to readers and fairly straightforward to grasp. Unfortunately one cannot generalize and say that all his work, in the original tongue or in translation, is quickly comprehensible, hence the proliferation of guides to reading Piaget in which technical terms are simplified and illustrated by descriptions of children engaged in problem-solving experiments and recordings of their conversations.

Students are strongly recommended to read one or more of Piaget's works, say *The Origin of Intelligence*, to obtain experience of his methods of investigation into children's thinking and to gain insight into his hierarchical approach to child development. Fundamentally he differs from many contemporary psychologists in that he adopts a "clinical" approach to child observation rather than the "empirical" method which demands carefully designed experiments capable of rigid statistical analysis. Piaget claims that an "open"-ended investigation into methods of thinking, irrespective of whether a child gets the problem right, partially correct or completely wrong, is far more revealing than a simple yes/no response to a set question. For Piaget it is the process of thinking through a problem which is of far greater significance than the actual solution given by the child, therefore his work is not always quantifiable because responses to a simple test situation are not necessarily comparable.

The lack of rigour in design and "proof" in conclusion is taken by some critics to be a serious limitation in his methodology but it has not prevented later experimenters from adapting Piaget's experimental methods to a format which is more capable of analysis in the statistical sense of the word. Many such researchers, using valid psychometric techniques, have tended to substantiate much of what was originally discovered clinically but exceptions are reported occasionally. Differences in cultural patterns, educational systems and methods of bringing-up children are understandably reflected in slight variations in intellectual growth; it would be highly surprising if it were otherwise.

A further point to bear in mind in reading one of Piaget's texts is that no single book provides a satisfactory account of his dynamic theory which is constantly expanding into newer realms of thought development. His investigations currently encompass the Growth of Intelligence; concepts of Physical Causality, Space, the World, Number and Geometry, Language, Judgement and Reasoning, Moral Judgement, Logic, Construction of Reality and Play, Dreams and Imitation in Childhood. Each volume is part of an hierarchical structure of massive and complex design.

Piaget was strongly influenced, particularly in his early years, by his training as a biologist. This is self-apparent in his writings for he makes constant reference to the interaction between an active organism and its natural environment. The process of biological adaptation of a living organism to its physical world is universally observable whatever rank it holds on the phylogenetic scale from the most primitive amoeba to man himself. Piaget describes adaptation as a balance between assimilation and accommodation, the dual process determines intellectual growth throughout life.

The concept of assimilation is basically similar to the intake of food by the human body and the normal functioning of the digestive system. Substitute perceptual experience or "environmental input" for food and "schemata" for the process of digestion and a generalized but fairly sound analogy emerges. Assimilation is the effective incorporation and organization of environmental experience into existing schemata; for example, when something new is conceived in terms of a past experience with which he is familiar. A young child at play, say in the act of catching a ball, assimilates the ball to his grasping schema. In the classroom the child who follows and understands what the teacher is saying is assimilating or absorbing the incoming information to his current state of schematic development. To a certain extent the process of assimilation is close to that of recognition, just as there are errors in recognition so there are distortions in assimilation; in over-generalizing a rule learned in the language laboratory, or in accepting an unsubstantiated claim in an advertisement at face value. Assimilation shares much in common with the behaviourist concept of generalization.

Clearly if assimilation was the only process of adaptation then mental development would remain at a very low level of functioning. For mental development and the growth of intelligence an organism must be capable of adapting its schemata to accommodate perceptions, stimuli and inputs which were previously impossible to assimilate.

Accommodation involves the modification and combination of existing schemata and the formation of new schemata. Give a young child a number of different balls, say a tennis ball, a beach ball and a football and in the act of catching note how he accommodates to the flight, size, texture and weight of each ball. In the lecture hall a student concentrating on the explanation of a new theory accommodates existing schemata to information which is novel either in itself or in combination with known data. Accommodating activities such as discovery, experimentation, imitation, trial-and-error and rote learning are examples of the active search for new and successful lines of behaviour when existing schemata are unable to cope.

Piaget has said little about how accommodation is achieved but he recognizes the significance of adaptation as a human propensity or motivational force. In the world of Olympic athletes, standards are continually and systematically pushed higher and higher as the runners, throwers and jumpers strive to attain something slightly beyond their reach. Man similarly grasps for new intellectual standards and progressively develops his intelligence.

The concept of a dynamic balance or state of equilibrium between assimilation and accommodation is central to Piaget's theory of adaptation. This is probably most effectively illustrated by drawing a crude analogy with a domestic central heating installation or a cooling system in a motor vehicle. Whereas the radiator, pipes and pump have a static structure, the circulation of water within the system is dynamic yet stable in the sense that any loss of water is automatically compensated in the heating system, or delayed until the radiator is topped up in a vehicle. Without taking the analogy too far, mental ·equilibrium is dynamic but not necessarily in perfect balance. On the contrary, an oscillation between under- and over-compensation is essential for mental development. In solving a problem a child blindly applies a learned "rule" and makes an error (disequilibrium) ; as a result reorganizing his approach he solves the problem correctly (restored equilibrium) and learns another technique or "rule" which may or may not apply under different circumstances. The cycle of loss and restoration of equilibrium is life-long.

Assimilation and accommodation are complementary to each other; the force which makes one want to act and think in terms of past experience (assimilation) is opposed by a force which makes one want to modify action and thought to meet the demands of a new or changed situation (accommodation).

Schematic development is another process which continues throughout life. The simplest kinds of schemata are the early sensori-motor activities of young children such as sucking and grasping; they are characterized by ease of recognition, a well-defined sequence of action and frequency of repetition. Schemata are not inflexible structures. As a result of modification, expansion and co-ordination, schemata progressively become more complex and elaborate in structure. Intelligence is therefore capable of definition in terms of speed and state of development of schematic structure, which in turn is dependent upon the balance between assimilation and accommodation. A child's accommodation is limited by the complexity of his existing schematic structure and the range of alternative schemata he has at hand.

Finally, Piaget's theory is both genetic and hierarchical in that all stages of development subsequent to the initial stage incorporate all previous stages. He uses the term stage and period in a wide sense and for ease of recognition, they are not fixed boundaries or dimensions and the ages he quotes are blurred approximations. Not every child reaches the final stage of development, many find difficulty in accommodating to abstract concepts and logical deductions. Similarly not all adults are freed from the ties of earlier levels of thinking; a person capable of an advanced general level of thought development quite commonly reverts to a very low level of reasoning in an attempt to impress or make a point in an argument.

In the generalized summary of stages of development in the growth of intelligence which follow, it is the sequence of events which is important rather than the ages which are suggested. Possibly it might prove more helpful if readers with knowledge of intelligence test terminology think in terms of "mental" age rather than "chronological" age. To gain some indication of the magnitude of the task Piaget set himself, ask yourself the following questions then consider the possible range of replies to them. What picture of the external world have I composed in my mind? How did I construct it? Does it really correspond to the world around me; if not, how and why has it changed? Do others see it as I do? How did I see the world when I was transferred to a secondary school or when I began formal education? In fact, how did it all begin?

(a) *Sensori-motor* (from birth to between 18 months and 2 years)

Piaget uses the term "sensori-motor" to describe this period because it is characterized by an increasing co-ordination of sensory perceptions and motor movements. A child is born with a limited capacity for reflex actions like grasping or sucking and possibly two or three drives such as food seeking. In repeating and extending these actions; say to sucking a thumb or sheet, albeit in a seemingly restricted environment, the infant assimilates a variety of perceptions and learns to make elementary discriminations. He would gain more satisfaction from sucking a sheet than a woolly blanket.

The short stage of about 1 month, in which an infant's motor responses are largely innate reflex actions, is followed by an ability to make simple co-ordinated movements such as between hand and mouth. These are voluntary movements and simple in the sense that the co-ordinated actions are not related to each other in a structural pattern but remain independent. An infant's use of sight to explore the environment is a predominant activity in this sub-stage, he will spend hours gazing at his surroundings and assimilating visual perceptions not as a means to an end but purely as an activity for its own sake.

After about 4 months of age an infant begins to make purposeful movements to achieve a simple aim and actions like grasping are extended to shaking and pulling. Previously unrelated co-ordinations are integrated into single schematic activities; for example, movements of eye, hand and mouth. Imitation is sustained and this implies that the child has learned to differentiate and to select events and actions from an established repertoire.

Between 6 and 12 months of age an infant consolidates all that has gone before but his actions are more deliberate and purposeful. An object such as a new toy is positively explored and as a result of experimentation he discovers new means and ends. More significant, however, is the emergence of the concept of a permanent object at about 8 months. Prior to this stage an infant would take no further interest in an object with which he had previously been playing and is now hidden from sight behind his mother's hand or under a cushion. To him the object no longer exists. Learning that an object continues to exist in space even if it cannot be seen marks an important step forward in mental development as it shows the beginning of reasoning and it indicates an ability to dissociate objects from himself and his physical actions. He also learns how to anticipate events and to recognize signs, a sprinkling of refreshing powder is followed by a warm dry nappy and a sharp pin-prick if Dad is in charge.

In the early months of his second year of life an infant engages in active experimentation and exploration and the balance shifts from assimilation to accommodation. Actions are not repeated exactly as before; accommodations are made to novel situations such as dropping various objects with different hand and arm movements and in turn, he assimilates the results of his experiments. Elementary problem-solving is observed in the manipulations of a baby when he draws the pram cover towards himself in order to bring a required object within reach. The recognition of spatial relationships is demonstrated by an infant at play with an educational toy of the kind which necessitates placing blocks into appropriate spaces or hollow containers one inside the other.

Towards the latter part of his second year an infant shows evidence of symbolic or representational behaviour; in a very elementary fashion he begins to represent sensori-motor movements in mental models, free from physical actions. By now he is clearly aware of the independence of objects and consequently acquires the capacity of forming a mental image of an object and some of its properties including shape, size and colour. Although he is now capable of forming images and engaging in symbolic play, he is not yet advanced enough to make use of imagery in problem-solving because the images he forms are independent and isolated. In the same way past events are recalled as separate and unique occasions. Concepts of causality, time and space begin to develop; he learns to differentiate between the actual physical movement of an object away from his body, compared with the apparent movement of an object as he moves his body away from it.

(b) *Pre-conceptual Thought* (from 2 to 4 years)

This stage is sometimes also referred to as either "pre-operational" or the "beginnings of symbolization" in thinking. At the end of the previous stage of development it was implied that the internal imitation of activities gave rise to sensori-motor thinking. As soon as an infant re-creates in his mind imitations of sensori-motor activities he must also be capable of producing mental images. This is important in the enrichment of a child's life because he now begins to think symbolically in the sense that he is able to visualize the "image" of an action prior to performing it. The evolution of imagery from imitation is termed by Piaget, "internalized imitation" and the re-creation of a past activity in the present is "deferred imitation". Growth of an awareness that an object continues to exist even though it is no longer visible suggests that it is represented symbolically as an image in the mind. The acquisition and growth of symbolic function opens the way for the development of another symbolic form, the use of words and language. Images and words free the mind from dependence on the physical presence of objects. No matter how many times an object appears, disappears and reappears its existence continues in the mind as an image and as language. In the early period of an infant's acquisition of language words are not used as a substitute for the image of an action but rather as an accompaniment to that action. Only when language evokes a past action does it mark the beginning of representation and words begin to function as symbols.

The term "preconceptual" was adopted to describe this stage of development because an infant is only capable of forming a concept of a single object rather than a class of objects. The fact that "Mother" belongs to the classes, woman, human and animal, has no meaning for a young child whatsoever because he is unable to generalize or specify and name by word the various classes and their properties. Instead he inconsistently assigns an image or symbol not only to the appearance, characteristics and actions of his mother but to all women. Male adults in the shopping queue know only too well the feeling of embarrassment suffered as a result of being the victim of an infant's attention, particularly if it is accompanied by loud repetitions of the word "Dadda".

Clearly if a child is unable to achieve consistency in the classification of objects then his thought processes will not be logical. Piaget uses the term transductive to describe a process of reasoning which fluctuates from the particular to the particular without generalization and logical sequence; "I haven't had my nap, so it isn't afternoon". This kind of thinking frequently leads to the right answer or conclusion but not necessarily so: that Mother is putting on her hat and looking at the mirror in the hall probably indicates to the child that she is going out but these actions could possibly lead to other consequences. In this case the child argues by implication that event a is necessarily followed by event b even though the two events are not related. Another form of transductive thinking is in the use of false analogies; for example, *x* and *y* are common in one respect therefore *x* and *x* are common in other respects. At this age children are blissfully unaware of the inconsistencies in their thinking, particularly when they attempt to make explanations of daily happenings in their lives.

Two common forms of transductive thought identified by Piaget are juxtaposition and syncretism. The former occurs when a child gathers together observations or judgements and fails to relate them to a consistent whole. For example, an aeroplane flies because it has an engine and is heavy, a bird flies because it has wings and is light and a kite flies because it is on the end of a string and is very light. Similarly in drawing a sketch of a bicycle many children find it difficult to relate the moving parts to each other, they draw the wheel, chain, cog and pedals either as separate entities or place them in an impossible functioning relationship. The opposite form of reasoning in which the child gathers together unrelated parts or makes indiscriminate connections between one event and another is syncretism.

Other common examples of errors at the stage of preconceptual thinking include the attribution of lifelike characteristics to inanimate objects and conversely, the attribution of natural physical phenomena to human activity; "The stairs are horrid, they hit me" and "Clouds are moved by men". The world around a child is personal to that child, his outlook is purely egocentric and he is unaware of the possible existence of other points of view. No wonder they are often thought to be selfish and difficult at this age.

(c) *Intuitive Thought* (from 4 to 7 years)

In many ways the stage of intuitive thought shares much in common with the previous period of symbolic thought and may therefore be regarded as an extension of it, but with a marked reduction in the absurdity of gross errors in reasoning. Intuition is characterized by immediate perception and judgement; in other words, children's thinking is so dominated by perceptual processes that objects and events *are* what they *appear to be*. An oft-quoted experiment to illustrate intuitive thinking involves the observation by children of beads being poured from a normal glass or container to a much narrower and taller glass, none being added or removed. When asked if there are more or fewer beads in the second

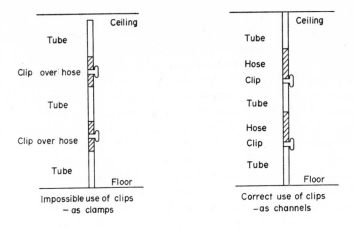

FIG. 28.

glass than the first, the most common response is "more" because the level of beads in the narrow glass has risen and occasionally "fewer" because it is a narrower glass. Piaget argues that the child's reasoning is dominated by one perceptual feature, say the height of the glass to the exclusion of width. His thoughts are focused or centred on one element at a time and he is unable to compensate the decrease in width of the glass by an increase in height.

Adults normally take into account several aspects of an object or situation at once; but not always, it is well known that part of the advertiser's armoury is to package goods in shaped containers which appear to offer greater value for money but in fact they contain less than is first perceived. In problem-solving experiments it is frequently the unusual use of a familiar tool or piece of apparatus which leads to the correct solution. Take, for example, the classic problem of the construction of a continuous channel from ceiling to floor using tubes, rubber hose and bulldog clips (Fig. 28).

It is not possible to solve it correctly if the bulldog clip is used as a clamping device rather than as a channel. Thoughts tend to be centred round the normal use of a bulldog clip. The solution is facilitated by going back to first principles and taking up fresh points of view of the total problem situation. Young children are incapable of this mental strategy, their perception is so intensely focused or centred that they cannot go back over their thoughts or compare judgements without being aware of their inconsistencies. In other words, their thought is irreversible.

A young child's inability to make mental comparisons and compensations or to distinguish between cause and effect severely handicaps and colours a whole range of thought processes from simple problem-solving experiments to making judgements. For him, moral laws are absolute, obedience to adults is synonymous with good behaviour and punishment is retributive justice. As a result of social activity, especially sharing and playing with other children and linguistic development, the child slowly gains awareness of alternative points of views, of differences in opinions held by other children and of conflicts between expectancies and subsequent events. Gradually the child's thought processes are liberated from perceptual dominance and become less centred: "It is by a constant interchange of thought with others that we are able to decentralize ourselves in this way, to co-ordinate internally relations deriving from different viewpoints" (*Psychology of Intelligence*, 1950).

(d) *Concrete Operations* (from 8 to 11 years)

The transition to a genuine reasoning process and the beginnings of logical thought slowly evolves as soon as a child acquires the capability of making an internalized mental action or an operation with concepts. It is not the final stage in thought development because the child is still restricted to concrete as opposed to abstract thinking. To make clear what Piaget means by this stage it is necessary to define more precisely some of the terms he uses and to describe typical experiments he conducted with children of primary-school age.

Piaget uses the word concept in the sense of a classification by similarities of objects and ideas in a logical or an ordered system. Think of classes, groups and catalogues but at this stage of development confine the process to relationships between common objects, do not expand it to include abstract ideas like justice. Normal young children find it great fun and easy to sort counters into various colour groups and wooden rods into different lengths, or to manipulate "educational toys" such as Russian dolls into appropriate containers and fit nesting boxes together; yet adult patients with severe brain damage sometimes find difficulty in making the simplest of physical classifications with common objects. The ability to form concepts is not only essential for progress in thought development, it also serves as a protective mechanism against fatigue of the nervous system in the act of recognition and increases the handling capacity of the short-term memory store. Up to about the age of 7 years a child quite easily picks out all the red counters from a set of counters of different colours; in doing so he performs an external action with concrete objects. The time arrives when he is able to think about a set of red counters without having any counters physically in front of him, or in Piaget's words he internalizes a mental operation with a concept.

The most important systems of concepts or operational classifications a child is capable of handling at this stage of development are:

(i) *Classification*—the formation of classes and sub-classes beginning with very simple examples like odd and even numbers through to more complex biological examples such as animals and plants. "In modern mathematics" young children are nowadays taught sets and Venn diagrams at what might at first seem a surprisingly early age, yet many 8-year-old children successfully cope with the kind of classification of all things that fly seen in Fig. 29.

(ii) *Seriation*—placing related objects in their correct order or succession; alphabetically like names on the register, or by increasing size when lining up teams in physical education or in a logical plan such as a family tree. In primary school much time is devoted to the comparison of measurements not only in formal arithmetic periods but also in History (sequence of dates), Geography (weather recordings) and Nature Study (growth). The more practical the exercise and active pupil involvement so much the better.

(iii) *The construction of a number system*—this necessitates an understanding of both classification and seriation in the sense that 9 is placed between 4 and 16 in a sequence of squares of whole numbers, as opposed to a parrot-like learning of 1, 2, 3, *et seq.* which is purely verbal counting.

Concrete operations are co-ordinated into structures which are weak in the sense they only permit limited logical reasoning of the step-by-step kind rather than an ability to generalize. Piaget calls these structures, "groupings"; for consistency in thought, five properties or combinations

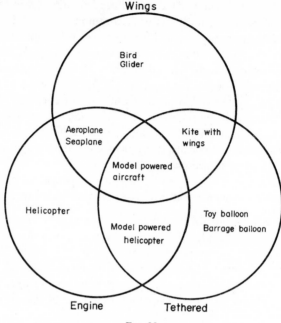

FIG. 29.

of operations are necessary and these obey logical laws:

(1) *Law of combination, composition or closure*—two distinct classes may be combined to form a comprehensive class which includes both the previously distinct classes, e.g. all boys and all girls = all children,

$$\text{or} \quad A + A^1 = B$$

(2) *Law of reversibility or inversion*—for each operation there is an opposite operation which annuls it, or two classes combined to form a comprehensive class may be separated, e.g. all children, except all boys = all girls:

$$A = B - A^1$$

(3) *Law of associativity*—if several operations are to be combined, the order in which they are combined is of no consequence, e.g.

$$A + (B + C) = (A + B) + C$$

(4) *Law of identity*—when the operation is combined with its opposite it is annulled, e.g. travel 5 miles due north then 5 miles due south and one is back at the starting point,

$$\text{or} \quad A - A = 0$$

(5) *Law of tautology*—with the exception of combination of numbers, e.g. $3 + 2 = 5$, whenever a class is combined with the same class it remains the same class, e.g. all girls plus all girls = all girls. Or, in other words, a classification which is repeated is not changed; for example, repetition of the same point adds nothing to an argument.

Piaget devised many simple but ingenious experiments to demonstrate how children perform operations. From observation of the sequence and nature of approaches to the set problems by different age groups he concluded that thought gradually becomes reversible and the concept of conservation slowly emerges after the age of 7. A child's thinking is said to be "reversible" when he can go back in his operations to the point of origin and find it unchanged; he then changes his approach or outlook and begins again. Conservation emerges when he compensates one judgement, say length by another judgement breadth to give conservation of area. Experimental evidence suggests that in conservation, shape precedes weight and weight precedes volume.

The difference in approach between children at the intuitive and operational stages may be demonstrated by asking them to place a number of coloured rods of unequal length in serial order of increasing length. At the intuitive stage a child tends to compare successive pairs of rods, but at the stage of operational thought he works more systematically and quickly places the smallest on the left and the longest on the right without making physical comparisons. But remember, at the stage of concrete operations some children continually find verbal reasoning difficult and even at the age of 11 cannot cope with a problem of the kind: Jack runs faster than Tom, Jack runs slower than Harry—who runs the fastest of the three boys?

(e) *Formal Operations* (over 11 years)

An alternative title sometimes given to this sub-stage is the rise of propositional thinking. Both "formal" and "propositional" are taken from the vocabulary of the logician, more particularly from the logical inference rules which are normally expressed in formulae. The system of mathematical logic in which variables like p, q and r are combined with logical consonants—*and* &, *not* $\sim$, *or* $\vee$—to form valid logical formulae is called propositional calculus:

$p \,\&\, q =$ proposition is true if both p and q are each true (conjunction),
$p \vee q =$ proposition is true if either p or q is true (disjunction).

Readers wanting a more detailed account of the binary propositions of p and q are recommended to read Piaget and Inhelder (1966) or Peel (1960). However, an exceedingly lucid explanation is to be found in Ward (1972), where the propositions are fully set out and discussed in the context of the construction of a logical reasoning item for the new British Intelligence Scale. An excellent introduction to the principles of logic, particularly the syllogism and its relation to Boolean algebra and Venn diagrams, is Basson and O'Connor (1959).

Educational Implications of Piaget's Work

So much for technical definition. Much of the above seems very academic compared with the real world of the developing adolescent as he struggles to free himself from the limitations of concrete levels of thinking. Tragically very many school-leavers never get anywhere near the final stage of thought development; the apex demands a capacity for genuinely logical reasoning and an ability to master and handle complex abstract concepts.

A child at the previous stage of development tends to be restricted in thought to problems with a large practical component and to the combination of objects into classes. The next stage demands an ability to think in terms of combinations of classes and, by implication, an ability to form complex concepts of an abstract kind. Through social interchange as well as formal education an adolescent gradually grows aware of inconsistencies in arguing at the concrete level. He begins to make generalizations, to form and test hypotheses, to examine variables, to hold factors constant whilst investigating combinations, to explore many possibilities and to suspend judgement until further evidence is available.

A young person's exploration of combinations and permutations is illustrated by Inhelder's (1958) classical experiment with one small and four large bottles of colourless liquid. A certain combination of liquids produces a yellow-coloured liquid and another liquid can be added to remove the colour. Children are asked to attempt to reproduce the demonstration they had just observed and to arrive at a general law. Whereas children at the concrete level tended to make random combinations of liquids, older children planned their approach more systematically and more thoroughly. They also tested the general principles of laws which they had proposed about the properties of the liquids. The beauty of the experiment is that it does not simply require the testing of an hypothesis but the combinatorial testing of hypotheses in a systematic manner. The use of colourless liquids debars a lower level of reasoning based on purely perceptual factors.

Similar experiments may be devised to demonstrate proportion; for example, by the use of weights and a balance or the projection of shadows at varying distances. Proportion in turn serves as an introduction to probability and the laws of chance. Place 32 coloured balls into a bag; say 14 green, 10 red, 7 yellow and 1 blue and ask a pupil to predict the colour or colours of two balls most likely to be drawn from the bag, then repeat. Children of primary-school age give almost random combinations, but adolescents see the significance of the greater probability of drawing two green balls despite repetition and the colour combinations which were drawn in previous trials. The concept of correlation is understood quite easily by the older adolescent, particularly the fact that variables may be compared without an implication of causation. Complex causation is not necessarily restricted to the field of science and mathematics but applies equally in the humanities in the study of historical events and in the geographical distribution of settlement patterns.

A willingness to appreciate alternative points of view, a growing skill in the systematic examination of possibilities and the capacity for proposing and testing hypotheses all develop in a social context through discussion, debate and argument with peers and adults. Sixth-formers are renowned for their deeply held convictions, they show a sincere awareness of limitations and shortcomings in their immediate social environment and in the world generally. The broadening of horizons in thinking modifies their views on moral issues, conventions and institutions. Inhelder and Piaget (1958) attribute much of the adolescent's idealism and critical outlook to his constant formulation of hypotheses about society and its values. No wonder student teachers feel some trepidation before opening a contro-versial topic for discussion with sixth-formers.

Inevitably a comprehensive study of child development of such monu-mental proportions does not escape criticism, particularly if the replication of the Geneva experiments either produces conflicting results or opens up alternative possible explanations. It would be a gross injustice to Piaget and his co-workers if their contribution to thinking and learning were dismissed as literary speculation on relatively minor points of technical detail. Teachers in primary schools will recognize in Piaget what they already feel by intuition and experience to be right and profitable in educational practice.

In the past, secondary-school teachers have tended to remain more conservative in their approach to methodology and have also resisted change in curriculum content with equal tenacity. The undesirable conse-quences of this traditionalism for the average child are self-evident when one observes that the demarcation between primary and secondary types of school is anything but clearly defined if judged by the criterion of stage of intellectual development. In the independent-school sector head teachers have recognized the value of a break in type of school at the age of 13 rather than 11. The Plowden Committee (1967) came nearer to this in their recommendations of transfer at the age of 12, but financial expediency outweighed logic when they arrived at a compromise.

Activity methods in primary schools lay stress on the importance of children manipulating objects with widely differing properties of texture, colour and shape. This, together with the discovery, collection, classification, construction and analysis of materials, is essential for the natural develop-ment of concrete reasoning. Concepts are developed not only in the basic disciplines Arithmetic and English, but in a whole range of studies including map-drawing, chart-making and recording in Geography, History and Science; model-making which includes measuring, cutting and assembling in Craftwork; and movement, imagination, co-operation and creative activity in Music and Drama. Out of school, too, the young child continues to build and reconstruct schema, assimilating and accommodating as the need arises. To an outside observer progress at times seems painfully slow because adaptation is a gradual process; a child moves forward by small incremental steps when previous experience is assimilated.

Inappropriate teaching techniques which lead to rote learning without true understanding, the acquisition of rules of thumb without genuine insight and the passive observation of events and experiments without an opportunity for personal discovery and exploration are utterly condemned by educationalists, yet so much sterile work of this kind is frequently observed in Secondary schools irrespective of the age and intellectual development of children. For some pupils, including school-leavers, the only method of teaching which is considered appropriate to their stage of thought development is at the concrete level with constant and specific reference to related objects and events. Teachers should take every opportunity to point out similarities, equivalents, opposites, relationships and other group structures if they want their pupils to acquire the art of generalization and skill in handling concepts of increasing complexity. Only when foundations are firmly laid by teachers who are prepared to devote time to the growth of children's thinking rather than pouring out inert facts can one reasonably expect the majority of school-leavers to begin to think logically.

It is not simply a question of maturation, namely that standards of thinking will improve naturally as pupils approach the sixteenth year of age. On the contrary, it is a slow structural process and not confined to the development of thinking within narrow curriculum studies; it is interdisciplinary with transfer and interchange across *all* subjects. One frequently hears expressions to the effect that a child should be taught to think historically, geographically and scientifically; worthy aims no doubt, provided the child is already capable of reasoning accurately at the concrete level.

The extent to which the ability to think is capable of being taught by some direct method is open to question, therefore it is essential for each and every teacher to provide a structure or framework within which thinking will develop. This is best achieved not only by the handling and classification of materials and objects, but by developing a sound technique of analytical questioning and setting individual work in the form of carefully graded exercises and thought-provoking problems. Kalmykova (1962) on the teaching of arithmetic writes: "Experienced teachers, therefore, organize the explanation of new materials in such a way that the pupils as if by themselves (though, of course, on the basis of the teacher's questions) find the necessary relations between the facts and the questions posed."

Problem-solving need not be as difficult or dull as first imagined particularly if it is incorporated into group activity, for example. role playing, games and simulation techniques. Geographical games have been well received for they effectively promote co-operation in thinking and reasoning, in a format which children find both stimulating and entertaining (Walford, 1969; Taylor and Walford, 1972). Piaget stresses the educational significance of learning in a social context. Group discussion of a common problem, provided pupils have some experience or factual knowledge of the topic, is invaluable in the development of formal reasoning and logical argument and it should not be reserved solely for the sixth form. Never adopt an authoritarian manner in discussion; however bizarre or senseless one regards certain lines of argument do not provoke outright hostility through direct confrontation but listen patiently, suggest alternative approaches and points of view and draw attention to gross examples of illogical or crooked thinking.

Experimental work in science, geography and history should evoke a genuine feeling of discovery in the child. Too often field-work exercises are a mere confirmation of facts and laws learned in the classroom. First, prepare in advance of the meeting an outline map or framework, a traverse or a transect; secondly, ensure that each child makes a personal record of his observations, draws sketches and takes measurements in the field, then finally collate and synthesize all the available information into an integrated study. Encourage them to make and verify hypotheses, to theorize and to examine possible causes and consequences. In the sixth form, pupils are expected to analyse, compare, criticize, discuss and evaluate factual material and with practice and experience they should also be capable of establishing relationships between abstract mental constructs. Lunzer (1965) defines genuine formal reasoning in terms of second-order relations; namely, an ability to handle relations between relations as opposed to relations between material things.

Replication of Piaget's experiments as reported in Beard (1969), Lovell (1961), Lunzer (1968), Peel (1960) and (1971) indicate that his theory of child development is basically valid; however, some of his techniques and conclusions have been challenged by research workers along the following lines:

1. His structural model of environmental adaptation and growth of thinking is essentially an eclectic learning theory which borrows from both the behaviourist and cognitive schools of psychology.

2. The hypothesis of schematic development implies the existence of a

concept of readiness or maturation, otherwise a child equipped with a limited mental schema will almost find it impossible to assimilate new stimuli and to reorganize existing schema to accommodate novel inputs. It is only when schemata are sufficiently mature enough to receive certain stimuli that the perceptual input will prove meaningful and intelligible to the child. Maturation theories, particularly if they are considered to be a psychological counterpart of physical growth, are fairly speculative and open to misinterpretation. Before general acceptance of a theory of readiness one needs to know a lot more detail about its application to specific topics in a given subject. With what age groups (mental and chronological) should a teacher attempt Ordnance Survey map interpretation? The teacher who waits passively for a child to show overt signs of readiness before actively motivating him to make progress in learning is doing as much, if not more, harm than the so-called pusher or driver. Provide a stimulating environment for growth, if necessary change and modify it time and time again, but never sit in a cultural desert hopefully expecting raindrops from above. To be absolutely fair to both Piaget and his colleague Inhelder (1964) they do recognize that maturation alone is not all-significant: "the maturation of the nervous system can do no more than create the conditions for a continual expansion of the field of possibilities. The realization of these possibilities demands not only the action of the physical environment . . ., but also the educational influence of a favourable social environment."

3. The various stages of development and chronological ages associated with them are considered by some critics to be too rigid and that a concept of mental age would prove more helpful. Obviously there are individual differences in general intellectual development and these manifest themselves according to the specific demands of the immediate problem-solving situation, including familiarity with the task in hand and cultural and social factors. Piaget recognizes this to be true and repeatedly stresses that it is the *sequence* of development which is important and not the median age he assigns to it.

4. From the voluminous literature published by Piaget one gleans little direct information about teaching techniques and conditions which are most conducive to the development of intellectual capacity in the child. A little may be inferred from the ingenious experiments he designed, but even so it would be more than helpful to know if the process could be

accelerated by teaching. For example, Mays (1965) and Allen (1965) have investigated the effects of teaching elementary logic to young children. Unfortunately the results are rather inconclusive because it is so terribly difficult to assess the transfer value of this kind of instruction; however, they can aptly be described as promising, no more. Lunzer (1968) makes a good point when he observes "that what the child is learning is not a logic as such, but certain ways of thinking (i.e. of symbolic action) which conform to a logic".

5. The lack of statistical rigour in estimating the significance of his experimental work is not quite as serious a shortcoming as was first believed. Piaget's hypotheses can be tested under controlled conditions by researchers working with children of widely different cultural backgrounds from the primitive to the educationally sophisticated. It is known that many of the theories and conclusions about the sensori-motor period of development are based on Piaget's observation of his own intelligent children, yet this is in many ways the most productive and least provocative section of all his writing.

There is a paramount obligation for every practising teacher, whatever his subject, in or out of school, directly or indirectly, to promote and develop standards of thinking and reasoning. If both school and home fail in this, the young adolescent is left defenceless against the onslaught of subtle deceptors and persuaders with powerful channels of mass communication at their disposal.

Learning Concepts, Rules and Principles

It would be grossly misleading if readers were to gain the impression that the study of concept growth is in any way exclusive to Piaget and his colleagues, or that it is a relatively fresh field for investigation by contemporary research workers. The function of language in the development of a conceptual system has long been a controversial topic. Evidence from experiments of the kind devised by Harlow (1949) to study "learning set" suggests that simple concepts like colour, number and shape of objects are learned by animals without recourse to language.

A monkey given a class of objects, say three up-turned beakers, two red and one blue, quickly learns to pick out the "odd" colour and obtain a reward hidden beneath it. Repetition of the experiment with successive changes in the attributes of objects indicates that the primate has learned how to generalize a common property, the concept of oddity. Findings from deaf-mute children facing a similar kind of problem are also consistent with the premise that language is not essential in the discrimination of simple concepts.

The Russian school of psychologists, including Liublinskaya (1957) and Luria (1961), stress the importance of "verbal signals" in the formation of concepts; or, more particularly, the function of language in the establishment of relationships between concepts, which is a characteristic of higher-order abstract thinking. In Pavlovian terminology a word functions as part of the second signal system only when it becomes a concept; or, alternatively, the concept of an object, event or idea continues to be signalled regardless of minor changes in its attributes.

Luria (1961) traced a sequence in the development of behaviour from early childhood when it is regulated externally by the mother, to the time it is internally regulated by imageless thought. One of the difficulties in studying the beginnings of conceptual development is attributed to the fact that concepts are formed for the young child by parents who name and label objects.

Liublinskaya (1957) convincingly demonstrated that language not only speeds up concept attainment but also more readily facilitates their subsequent transfer and longer retention. She used control and experimental groups to investigate the acquisition of the concept of smallness. To the control group nothing was said as children searched for a sweet hidden under the smallest of a group of objects, but to the experimental group she said "small". The latter learned the concept three times more quickly. Similar experiments with different age groups suggest that for efficiency in learning children need to be told directly or by cues the attributes which define a required concept.

A number of researches into transposition learning, notably one by Kuenne (1946), showed that children with the ability to verbalize a rule such as "the smaller one is correct" were more capable of handling similar and more difficult problems than were children less competent in the use of language.

Many investigations into the relationship between language and thought share a common weakness when compared with Piaget and other cognitive theorists; namely, they are intrinscially simple and isolated laboratory experiments into the more accessible concepts and therefore exclude the higher flights of thought development which man is capable of attaining.

The adequacy of a single term like concept to cover both elementary relational properties and complex interrelated abstractions is open to question. Gagné (1965) has proposed a structural model of learning in which he identifies eight types and arranges them in a hierarchy from simple responses to complex problem-solving activity:

Type 1. *Signal Learning*

Equivalent to Pavlov's conditioned response. A diffuse response an individual makes to a signal such as a baby turning its head towards mother and showing signs of pleasure and excitement as she approaches the play-pen before lifting him out. The facial gesture of a teacher can communicate a generalized feeling of disapproval and without comment or specific action it normally acts as an effective early-warning signal.

Type 2. *Stimulus–Response Learning*

Equivalent to a Thorndike S–R bond or Skinner's discriminated operant. It differs from Type 1 in that an individual makes a definite and precise response to a discriminated stimulus. A baby responds to the sight of his milk bottle by raising his arms in anticipation and exclaiming "Madda" or some other isolated "baby-word". The child has learned to make a connection at a very elementary level. Learning sounds and simple words falls into this category, including the beginnings of learning a foreign language in primary school.

Type 3. *Chaining*

Establishing a chain of two or more stimulus–response connections. It could include a sequence of motor actions like placing a piece of paper in a typewriter, or the joining of words together in telegraphic speech by a young child—"my coat dirty". In a chain the response to one stimulus is in itself the stimulus to the next response and so on in sequence.

Type 4. *Verbal Association*

Learning verbal chains, for instance, at an early stage of learning to read when a child is beginning to recognize printed words. Teachers using published reading schemes will be familiar with the short phrases and often repeated words characteristic of those brightly illustrated publications often accompanied by work cards and other visual material. Learning material by heart, with an awareness of cross-connections, is another example.

Type 5. *Multiple Discrimination*

An individual learns to discriminate between stimuli which resemble each other and make a correct response. Similarity of stimuli sometimes causes interference in recalling a required spelling:

WERE, WHERE, WEAR and WARE.

"We were gazing through the window of the hardware shop where Evelyn was born, appropriately she was wearing her Mother's broach at the time."

It also causes humour:

"the comedian who obliged a fan's request by sending a *singed* photograph of himself".

Type 6. *Concept Learning*

The response to stimuli, attributes, objects and events which although individually different make up a recognizable class in concrete or abstract form.

Type 7. *Principle Learning*

A chain of two or more concepts, implying a thorough understanding of the underlying concepts, their interrelationships and if necessary their application.

Type 8. *Problem-solving*

Solving problems by the use of principles. This category would also include creative thinking and inventiveness.

He uses the word principle to describe the relationship between two or more concepts provided it also demands demonstration as opposed to straightforward identification. The simple act of identification of a concept like triangular involves a process close to stimulus generalization; however, a principle needs to be demonstrated to be fully understood. He quotes the example "work" which requires the identification of at least three concepts: force, distance and product, together with a demonstration of the sequence in which they are related.

Simple concepts are learned by the observation and differentiation of positive and negative instances of stimuli. For genuine principle learning there must be evidence of complete mastery of all the component concepts, together with a demonstration, usually by verbal communication, of the correct sequence of these components. Teaching children the concept of a number such as "two" by the identification of pairs of objects is very different from teaching the principle that $(a + b)^2 = a^2 + 2ab + b^2$, or more basically that eight divided by four is equal to two.

For the practising teacher this raises a question; what are the most effective methods of teaching general principles and rules, by definition with examples or by guided discovery? Many contemporary theorists point out the merits of the latter, the inductive approach, because it is more likely to motivate learning with understanding, to have greater transfer effect and to be retained longer in memory. Against this must be set the highly practical argument that discovery methods are not always easily organized and they tend to be time-consuming. Most teachers, on the grounds that the superiority of one method over the other is not proven, tend to rely on common sense and vary techniques according to how essential the concept is considered either immediately or in the future development of the subject. Others are inhibited against discovery techniques partly by lack of confidence and experience and partly by lack of access to the teaching materials which are necessary for its success. So much also depends on individual differences in the ability of children, the organization of classes in streams and sets and on the nature of the time-table that it is exceedingly difficult to generalize about the most effective methods of teaching principles.

In higher education the teaching of principles is normally by definition and broad discussion of examples in the lecture, followed up and subsequently reinforced in the laboratory, library, seminar and tutorial. The defence of this method is that principles taught to the point of overlearning facilitates their subsequent transfer and application to allied problems and disciplines. A principle thoroughly mastered is most resistant to extinction.

Problem-solving

Whereas Piaget studied the origin and development of concepts from childhood to adolescence in a wide range of topics, Bruner *et al.* (1956) investigated strategies adopted by students in the attainment of concepts under highly controlled experimental conditions demanding systematic search and elimination. The Harvard team were primarily interested in the overall plan or strategy of thinking and the order or sequence in which intelligent individuals carry it out.

The experimenter shows a student an array of eighty-one cards, each card is different because it represents a varied combination of four attributes, namely: colour (black, green, red); shape (circle, cross, square); number of figures (one, two, three) and number of borders (one, two, three).

The student is asked to identify a concept predetermined by the experimenter in as few questions or choices as possible, something like the parlour game—Twenty Questions. He is first shown a positive example of the required concept and then proceeds to ask the experimenter if the next card and subsequent cards are positive or negative instances of the concept. He carries on choosing cards one at a time until he identifies the concept which is one of a sub-set of attributes; for example, of a particular shape, say a circle, there are twenty-seven possible examples, of a particular coloured shape, say a red circle, there are nine possible examples, and of a specified number of shapes with a specified number of borders say two circles with three borders there are three possible examples.

In searching for concepts students tend to formulate hypotheses or strategies using either scanning or focusing techniques. A scanner makes an hypothesis, looks for positive instances of it, then abandons it as soon as he discovers it is unworkable. He formulates a new hypothesis and repeats the sequence. A focuser selects a positive attribute and stays with the example until he arrives at the correct concept. Bruner identified four main approaches to problem-solving:

(i) *Simultaneous Scanning*

The student holds in memory all possible hypotheses and for each card he decides which are tenable and which should be eliminated. From accumulative information he reduces the number of possibilities until the required concept is discovered. It is a logical but exacting process of deductive reasoning which makes heavy demands on memory, particularly if an array of increased complexity is presented. Assume that a student chooses three black circles with two borders and is informed that this is a positive instance, he automatically eliminates crosses and squares and circles with one or three borders. With each repetition of this kind of reasoning process in a logical sequence he constantly rejects all untenable hypotheses. At the same time he tries to ensure that each subsequent choice does not reveal redundant information. A perfect plan guarantees useful information, provided, of course, the subject has sufficient time to formulate the correct strategy.

(ii) *Successive Scanning*

The student tests one hypothesis at a time. He seeks instances which directly test the chosen hypothesis, as soon as one proves negative he revises it. This is a form of guesswork like playing a hunch, wasteful in that it throws up much redundant information yet it makes little strain on the intellect. Taking the previous example, if he is informed that three black circles with two borders is a positive instance, he might next pick a card with a black cross and two borders. If this proves negative he changes his hypothesis from colour to number of borders and so on until he arrives at the predetermined concept. This approach is particularly wasteful if the required concept is a single attribute, say a colour, and the student opens by choosing a card with a multi-attribute, say two squares with three borders.

(iii) *Conservative Focusing*

Instead of making an hypothesis the student focuses on one attribute. When he makes a sequence of choices he changes one attribute only at a time and notes whether it reveals a positive or negative instance. If the changed attribute still yields a positive instance then it is not part of the concept, if it yields a negative instance then it *is* part of the concept. Take again the example of three black circles with two borders, which is known to be positive, and note how the concept may be deduced in four choices by varying one attribute at a time:

3 B ○ 2 b (+) positive
1st choice   2 B   ○   2 b   (+) :   inference, eliminate three figures
2nd choice   3 R   ○   2 b   (−) :   inference, black is relevant
3rd choice   3 B   □   2 b   (−) :   inference, circle is relevant
4th choice   3 B   ○   1 b   (+) :   inference, eliminate two borders
∴ the concept is black circles.

The approach may at first sight appear tedious but it does guarantee that each choice will reveal some new information. Mentally it is less exacting because the focus card is a permanent reference point to return to after each choice.

(iv) *Focus Gambling*

In many ways similar to the previous approach except that the student changes two of three attribute values at a time. It can prove quicker than conservative focusing provided the next instance is always positive, but in this, there is an element of risk. If the next choice proves negative it will take longer and demand additional trials before the concept is discovered.

The benefits of using some kind of strategy or plan as opposed to random choice are fairly obvious, particularly if the problem is highly complex and consists of many variables. A sound plan minimizes cognitive strain, maximizes usable information and calculates a risk.

In the experimental situation outlined above, the subject selected his card and inquired whether it was a positive or negative instance of the required concept—an example of a selection strategy. A variation on this is to present the subject with a number of cards and inform him which are positive and which are negative instances—an example of a reception strategy. In many ways this is a less artificial or abstract method of experimentation because research frequently raises problems of this kind; namely, the investigator has to arrive at a conclusion from the evidence available to him at a given time. This evidence probably represents only a part of the total possible information which would otherwise be revealed by further costly and time-consuming research.

Without going into detail the ingenuity behind the basic Bruner design becomes apparent when one looks at some other variations on the original experiment. If subjects do not have the total array of cards visually in front of them the experiment becomes more abstract and therefore increases work-load on the mental processes. This in turn affects the strategy adopted, under conditions of strain it is more appropriate and generally more successful to use a focusing strategy.

All the Bruner experimental designs considered so far utilize examples of the "conjunctive" category of concept, namely the joint presence of more than one attribute. The category emphasizes the word *and*; square *and* single border. A "disjunctive" category is much more difficult to handle because it necessitates consideration of the word *or*; three green circles *or* any sub-set. Finally there is the "relational" category in which specific relationships between attributes are required; fewer borders than figures. For a more detailed discussion of these and other terms interested readers are recommended to read Thomson (1959); and for subsequent developments in the study of concept attainment, Wason (1966).

Prior to Bruner's masterly and objective demonstration of the variety of strategies adopted in the process of problem-solving, experimenters like Wertheimer (1945) and Duncker (1945) had almost wholly relied upon techniques of introspection and observation. The earlier methods of investigation were of limited validity, because no matter how ingenious the problem or experimental design, the subject's comments on his approach to the problem were as subjective as the recordings of the external observer. Could a method be found which would incorporate the best available design and methodology, speeden up the process of investigation and possibly provide a generalized model of human problem-solving? This is the ambitious aim of Newell *et al.* (1958) in their search for a General Problem-solving (GPS) model. They have designed computer programs to simulate human strategies in the solution of complex problems of the logical theorem and games-playing kind.

Methods of problem-solving are either algorithmic or heuristic, the former is also sometimes referred to as the "exhaustive" method as it examines every possible transposition and sub-goal in its movement towards a guaranteed solution. Inevitably this method is both tedious and time-consuming and is not characteristic of human thinking which is more economic in its search for promising routes. The heuristic or selective approach does not guarantee a solution to a problem.

In the GPS program two basic routines are run off in cycles until the problem is solved or rejected; the first routine decides which of the possible sub-goals looks most promising and the second attempts a direct solution of the chosen sub-goal by heuristic methods. If this sub-goal proves un-rewarding, the first routine selects another sub-goal for analysis and so on until the problem is solved. Evidence from programs computed to date is most impressive; for example, the simulation of human strategies in solving some of Whitehead and Russell's theorems in *Principia Mathematica* (1925). However, theorem-solving typifies a fairly narrow range of human thinking and this raises two questions; how general is GPS and is artificial comparable with human intelligence?

The main criticism is that no matter how sophisticated the program, it is still devised by human beings and the computer ultimately does only what it is told, no more. In terms of the self-generation of a problem and innovation of ideas, computer or information processing techniques are sterile. Computers have a more accurate memory and greater speed of computation than human beings and they are not so easily distracted by boredom and lack of motivation. On the other hand, an error does not throw a human problem-solver completely out of action as it does a computer, unless of course it incorporates a specially designed program to deal with particular errors.

In spite of the obvious and fundamental differences between man and machine, information processing techniques are proving helpful because they demonstrate in practice how a complex problem may be broken down into logical series of precise sub-goals, capable of straightforward analysis. Basic assumptions are never ignored by the computer and no detail of the problem-solving routine is ever overlooked. Man knows the secret of the storage of symbols in the memory bank of a machine, for he invented the coding procedures; but, as yet, he knows virtually nothing about the physiological storage of stimuli in his own memory.

Principles of Problem-solving

From a number of investigations into the general principles involved in problem-solving, the following may prove helpful:

A. *Comprehension of the problem:*
  (i) Avoid jumping to a hasty conclusion.
  (ii) Make certain it is thoroughly understood in every particular and detail.
  (iii) Ask questions about it.

B. *Possible methods of approach to the problem:*
  (i) Recall and select all apparently relevant facts, ideas, rules and principles.
  (ii) Combine and reorganize them.
  (iii) Generate ideas, look for unusual usages, novel applications and extensions beyond common or past experience even if they seem implausible.

C. *Specific approach to the problem:*
  (i) Formulate a detailed plan of solution, if necessary break it down into a sequence of sub-goals.
  (ii) Verify the solution, for example, by substitution or confirm it by a re-run with alternative data.

The recommendation in B (iii) above possibly needs some clarification. Classical problem-solving experiments of the kind devised by Duncker and Wertheimer clearly demonstrate how intelligent subjects become so bound by narrow and familiar hypotheses that it is impossible for them to break out and discover correct solutions. Gestalt psychologists interpret this in terms of a person's inability to reorganize his perceptual field, he therefore blocks out cues which would have otherwise emerged from different spatial rearrangements. In everyday life, at work or play, the rhetorical question, "why didn't I think of that", is commonplace. That this blindness in thinking should occur in meaningful, real-life and concrete situations is rather puzzling until one is made aware of the powerful yet stultifying effect of habituated behaviour in many problem-solving situations. Man has the potential to master his environment through the use of intellect or become its slave through narrowness, bigotry and obsession.

Failure to think clearly and correctly at the abstract level is not necessarily a consequence of reverting back to concrete levels of reasoning. Galton (1869) produced convincing evidence to prove that many eminent scientists and inventors came to their greatest discoveries through concrete imagery. Few present-day scholars could honestly deny having translated abstract concepts into concrete terms in a search for meaning or in confirmation of a result. Intelligent school-children are quick to learn the trick of substitution in working-back algebraic equations.

In similar vein, the practice of thinking aloud or engaging in sub-vocal activity is often a useful device in solving difficult problems. Student teachers find that during lesson preparation, teaching an imaginary class helps them to clear up vague ideas and overcome difficult steps in logical progressions. Much more needs to be discovered about human thinking; but one fact has certainly emerged from all past research, complex concepts and principles are consolidated slowly and gradually. This is because their structure is hierarchical and sequential. A skilled teacher has a vital role to play in this development; partly by effectively using many of the technical aids at his disposal and employing analytical questioning techniques, but also by the direct identification of the common attributes of concepts and discussion of marginal examples.

In the sixth form, particularly, breadth of concept is equally as important as principle learning; a principle cannot be properly demonstrated if it is based on a hazy or limited grasp of its component parts. Schematic structure is slow to change and become reorganized despite repeated exposure to novel ideas and changed stimuli. Many children have seen films, pictures and television broadcasts about the Southern States of the U.S.A., all of them emphasizing the changing social and economic background of the region. However, asked to write impressions of the South, pupils tend to describe a cultural pattern more appropriate to the nineteenth than the present century.

Two factors which affect a child's capacity for thinking, problem-solving and creative activity have barely been touched upon, yet they are so vitally important they warrant separate and careful consideration: namely intellectual and emotional development.

Additional Reading

ADAMS, P. (1972) *Language in Thinking*. London: Penguin.

ATHEY, I. J. and RUBADEAU, D. O. (Eds.) (1970) *Educational Implications of Piaget's Theory*. London: Ginn-Blaisdell.

BARTLETT, F. C. (1958) *Thinking: An Experimental and Social Study*. London: Allen & Unwin.

BERLYNE, D. E. (1965) *Structure and Direction in Thinking*. New York: Wiley.

BOLTON, N. (1972) *The Psychology of Thinking*. London: Methuen.

BOYLE, D. G. (1969) *A Student's Guide to Piaget*. Oxford: Pergamon.

BREARLEY, M. and HITCHFIELD, E. (1966) *A Teacher's Guide to Reading Piaget*. London: Routledge & Kegan Paul.

BRUNER, J. S. *et al.* (1966) *Studies in Cognitive Growth*. New York: Wiley.

ELKIND, D. (1970) *Children and Adolescents: Interpretive Essays on Jean Piaget*. London: Oxford Univ. Press.

ELKIND, D. and FLAVELL, J. H. (Eds.) (1969) *Studies in Cognitive Development*. London: Oxford Univ. Press.

FEIGENBAUM, E. A. and BRUNER, J. S. (1956) *A Study of Thinking*. New York: Wiley.

FEIGENBAUM, E. A. and FELDMAN, J. (Eds.) (1963) *Computers and Thought*. New York: McGraw-Hill.

FLAVELL, J. H. (1963) *The Developmental Psychology of Jean Piaget*. Princeton, New Jersey: Van Nostrand.

FURTH, H. G. (1970) *Piaget for Teachers*. Englewood Cliffs: Prentice Hall.

GINSBURG, H. and OPPER, S. (1969) *Piaget's Theory of Intellectual Development: An Introduction*. Englewood Cliffs: Prentice Hall.

HALFORD, G. S. (1972) The impact of Piaget on psychology in the seventies. In DODWELL, P. C. (Ed.).

HUMPHREY, G. (1951) *Thinking*. London: Methuen.

LOVELL, K. (1961) *The Growth of Basic Mathematical and Scientific Concepts in Children*. London: Univ. of London Press.

LOVELL, K. (1968) *An Introduction to Human Development*. London: Macmillan.

MODGIL, S. (1974) *Piagetian Research: A Handbook of Recent Studies*. London: N.F.E.R.

NEWELL, A. and SIMON, M. A. (1963) GPS, a program that simulates human thought. In FEIGENBAUM, E. A. and FELDMAN, J. (Eds.).

PHILLIPS, J. L. Jr. (1969) *The Origins of Intellect: Piaget's Theory*. San Francisco: Freeman.

PIAGET, J. (1952) *The Child's Conception of Number*. London: Routledge & Kegan Paul.

PIAGET, J. (1953) *The Origin of Intelligence in the Child*. London: Routledge & Kegan Paul.

PIAGET, J. (1964) *The Early Growth of Logic in the Child*. London: Routledge & Kegan Paul.

PIAGET, J. (1965) *Logic and Psychology*. Manchester: Manchester Univ. Press.

PIAGET, J. (1970) *The Child's Conception of Movement and Speed*. London: Routledge & Kegan Paul.

PIAGET, J. (1971) *Biology and Knowledge*. Edinburgh: Edinburgh Univ. Press.

PIAGET, J. (1972) *Play, Dreams and Imitation in Childhood*. London: Routledge & Kegan Paul.

PIAGET, J. (1972) *The Principles of Genetic Epistemology*. London: Routledge & Kegan Paul.

PIAGET, J. (1973) *Psychology and Epistemology*. London: Allen Lane, Penguin Press.

PIAGET, J. and INHELDER, B. (1969) *The Psychology of the Child*. London: Routledge & Kegan Paul.

RICHMOND, P. G. (1970) *An Introduction to Piaget*. London: Routledge & Kegan Paul.

SIME, M. (1973) *A Child's Eye View: Piaget for Young Parents and Teachers*. London: Thames & Hudson.

SKEMP, R. R. (1971) *The Psychology of Learning Mathematics*. London: Penguin.

SMART, P. (1972) *Thinking and Reasoning*. London: Macmillan.

WALLACE, J. G. (1965) *Concept Growth and the Education of the Child*. London: N.F.E.R.

WASON, P. C. and JOHNSON-LAIRD, P. N. (Eds.) (1968) *Thinking and Reasoning: Selected Readings*. London: Penguin.

CHAPTER 8

Intelligence and Ability

Concept of Intelligence

Intelligence is a perfect example of a multi-definable concept with so many facets that it has been appropriately described as "polymorphous". Listing its attributes like a mini-Thesaurus does not necessarily help identify it. For an attempt to distinguish six possible senses in which the term intelligence may be defined readers are recommended to the paper by Miles (1957).

A Variety of Comments on the Nature of Intelligence

AUSUBEL		A general level of cognitive functioning, as reflected in the ability to understand ideas and to utilize abstract symbols (verbal, mathematical, or spatial) in the solution of intellectual problems.
BINET		To judge well, to comprehend well, to reason well. Practical sense, initiative, the faculty of adapting oneself to circumstances.
BORTELMANN		The patterns of behaviour comprising intelligence are accumulative, acquired, maintained and elaborated by sequential learning experiences.
BURT		Innate general cognitive ability.
HEBB	A.	Inherited potentiality for growth (genotype).
	B.	Everyday intelligent behaviour (product of nature and nurture).
(VERNON)	C.	As measured by tests—an inadequate sampling of B. Possibly A sets a limit to the development of B.
HEIM		Intelligent activity consists in grasping the essentials in a given situation and responding appropriately to them.
KNIGHT		It is the capacity for relational constructive thinking, directed to the attainment of some end.
PIAGET		. . . behaviour becomes more intelligent as the pathways between the subject and the objects on which it acts cease to be simple and become progressively more complex.

RAVEN — In order to act intelligently in any situation, a person needs both the necessary information and the capacity to form comparisons and reason by analogy.

TERMAN — The ability to carry on abstract thinking.

THOULESS — General intellectual capacity.

WECHSLER — Intelligence cannot be separated from the rest of the personality. The global capacity of the individual to act purposefully, to think rationally, and to deal effectively with his environment.

Working definitions of intelligence have tended to reflect either the rigid assertions of those engaged in specific empirical research into the nature of human ability, or the largely unsubstantiated views of political commentators who are exceedingly sensitive to any suggestion that there are inequalities in the distribution of intelligence and that they are in part due to innate factors. A more middle-of-the-road course is generally taken by practising teachers and educational psychologists. For them, the important question is not what proportion of *measured intelligence** is attributable to heredity or environment; rather, how do they interact, what is the nature of the interaction and what are its implications for planning work in the classroom and in various kinds of guidance?

The argument about the relative contribution of heredity and environment to intelligence, sometimes expressed as "nature and nurture", centres round the interpretation of results from the testing of identical (monozygotic) and non-identical (dizygotic) twins:

APPROXIMATE CORRELATIONS BETWEEN I.Q.S OF CHILDREN

	Reared together	Reared apart
Siblings	.50	.45
Dizygotic twins	.55	
Monozygotic twins	.90	.85

Note: Samples for monozygotic twins reared apart are small —below 55 pairs.

---

* One must not infer from this expression that intelligence is an object which exists and that it is accurately quantifiable.

Champions of the role of heredity in determining intelligence like the late Sir Cyril Burt (1970) and Jensen (1973) derive support from the statistical interpretation of test results and even go so far as to suggest approximate percentages which might be apportioned to environmental and heredity factors and their interaction. Such figures need to be treated with caution because they apply to general populations rather than specific individuals, the underlying statistical assumptions are not universally accepted and the discriminatory function and validity of the measuring instrument (type of intelligence test) is by no means perfect. Studies of the test performances of foster children can be taken to support either the hereditary point of view or that of the environmentalists. The higher correlations reported between foster children and their biological parents compared with their foster parents suggests an hereditary influence. However, the tendency for an increase in the I.Q. of children selectively placed in good homes by social and welfare agencies and of deprived children under improved living conditions both indicate the importance of environmental factors.

Obviously this kind of argument about nature and nurture is spurious and of little practical interest to the teacher who is more likely to ask, "is the concept of intelligence worth retaining and for what purpose?" Talking about intelligence as an isolated mental attribute is a potentially hazardous exercise because it is only one of an interwoven complex of traits that make up an individual's total personality. Possibly the notion of an attribute is in itself misleading. Ryle (1949) argues that intelligence is a "disposition-word" and not an attribute; it is preferable to say a person may be disposed to behave or perform intelligently rather than boldly state he is intelligent. Traditionally it is treated as a separate topic for functional reasons, particularly in educational practice where an estimate of a child's intelligence is considered necessary for planning courses of study and in guidance.

The word "selection" has been avoided deliberately, partly because of its past and sometimes emotional connotation with intelligence *per se*, but mainly because attitudes have moved away from the narrower confines of allocation and selection to the broader possibilities of choice and guidance. Despite certain imperfections and limitations a test of general ability is still the best single indicator of a child's potential educational development and a powerful diagnostic tool provided it is used skilfully and in conjunction with other assessments.

If intelligence is to be discarded as a redundant concept, what replaces it in the cognitive process? The two contenders commonly quoted for promotion are previously acquired knowledge and motivation, but on what evidence other than literary speculation? Nearly a century of empirical research is unlikely to be superseded by something which bears a pseudo-psychological label, remains ill-defined, is possibly more elusive and is born out of political prejudice and social idealism. In a problem-solving situation demanding resourcefulness and foresight most teachers would back the so-called intelligent and possibly indolent child against a factual storehouse rated highly in intrinsic motivation. To suggest that the concept of intelligence should be abandoned is quite unhelpful compared with the less radical view that it should be modified, restructured and if necessary expanded in the light of genuine advances in research. Butcher (1968) summarizes it: "few would maintain that concepts of ability have thereby been superseded. So far they have at best been supplemented."

This was also the view of several distinguished psychologists who met in Toronto in 1969: "The crucial unresolved question before the symposium was whether the intelligence variable should be retained in the model. (Husén's model of learning 1967—the interaction of previous knowledge, motivation and intelligence.) . . . In view of the wide range of human activities, where ability independent of previous experience and motivation seems to be important, the hypothesis that there is an ability component in human learning seemed plausible and worth the consideration of a symposium" (Dockrell, 1970).

Research workers in many fields of psychology, educational and otherwise, have found intelligence a useful control, reference or yardstick against which other aspects of behaviour and performance may be compared. For practising teachers the important issue should not be the possible future existence of the concept of intelligence, but how its potential may be developed and utilized by individual children. So much misconception about the nature of intelligence is still prevalent today that it is worth spending time in getting rid of some of the old wives' tales which have grown up with it.

Falacies about Intelligence

(a) That Intelligence is Innate and Fixed

From what has been said previously, intelligence is the product of endowment at birth and subsequent environment; in each individual the two are inseparable and their proportions are not really amenable to rigorous statistical analysis. The environment of an organism is subject to both major changes and minor fluctuations; the world of man is never constant, therefore as a product, it cannot possibly remain fixed. An estimated intelligence quotient of a child at best is only a sampling of a cross-section in time of cognitive growth and development. No parent or teacher can escape the implication of this fact and all that it demands from those responsible for providing the kind of environment in which human potential is likely to develop and flourish. Belief in the doctrine of fixed intelligence and the permanent stereotype is a confession of abdication from this responsibility. It is far more rewarding to visualize Piaget's concept of a flexible schemata rather than a rigid structure of predetermined capacity.

(b) *That Intellectual Development reaches a Peak in Adolescence then Gradually Declines*

In the past, attainment of the chronological age of 15 years was normally taken to represent the upper limit of mental development, followed by a plateau then a gradual decline with age. However, this has since been shown to be mainly an artefact of test construction. With the specific design of mental tests for young adults and their proven validity, it is now considered reasonable to expect a continuation of growth through the mid-teens to the early twenties. The problem of intelligence test score and ageing is well summarized by Heim (1970), an acknowledged expert in the practical construction and interpretation of tests for those over 15 years of age. The changing attitude towards the idea of an early peak of development has also been brought about by improved educational standards resulting from a gradual extension of formal schooling, wider educational opportunities out of school and the impact of mass media. Neither can one ignore the intellectual demands made by certain courses of study, the chosen vocation and other individual interests, on cognitive processes like discrimination, judgement and thought. Most psychologists, experienced in testing students, cite evidence of continuing general mental development in young adults provided they remain receptive to intellectual stimulation and challenge.

The decline in speed of calculation and reasoning which in part reflects an attenuation of short-term memory capacity and loss of perceptual acuity cannot be denied as people grow older. Reasons for this are probably both physiological and psychological; fortunately the balance is to some extent maintained by growth in wisdom, expansion of knowledge and effective use of past experience. Much of the research into the intelligence and abilities of adults has been confined to student populations and specific vocational groups. Results from a broader cross-section of the general public would prove theoretically informative and of practical value in re-training schemes in an industrial society where job mobility lags behind changes in technological development.

(c) That the Nation's Intelligence is Declining

This old chestnut is based on the fallacious argument that because the more intelligent tend to have smaller families and the less intelligent have larger families; according to the law of averages, the national intelligence level must necessarily decline. Without recourse to evidence from published national surveys, for example in Scotland (1949 and in 1953) which shows the exact opposite to be true, its fallacy can be exposed by what is already known about the inseparability of hereditary and environmental factors in measured intelligence. Obviously changes in nutrition, length of education and test sophistication have also to be considered, but even if these are held constant, the argument is nullified by the fact that the earlier calculations did not take into account the fairly substantial number of people of low I.Q. who have not produced families. In any case the problem is now largely academic because recent census returns suggest a trend to families of about equal size irrespective of class or ability, estimated according to occupational categories. The classic negative correlation of -0.25 between intelligence and family size often quoted in pre-Second World War days might by now have dropped below the level required for statistical significance.

In addition to the three fallacies discussed above some would add: (d) that intelligence is normally distributed throughout the population and (e) that there is a compensatory element in human ability.

The answer to the first is not easy because it has something of the chicken and egg controversy about it; namely, is the distribution natural in the sense that physical measurements often conform to the Gaussian curve (Fig. 30) or does it reflect a design policy artificially imposed by testing agencies to facilitate subsequent standardization and analysis? It is safer to say that in the total population intelligence approximates to a normal distribution with a slightly greater number than expected at both the higher and lower extremities.

Compensation implies that if an individual is weak in, say, verbal reasoning he counter-balances this by his strengths in other abilities, or that another person makes up, say, his lack of mechanical ability by being highly creative. There is no evidence to support this theory whatsoever as most mental ability test scores tend to intercorrelate positively. Vernon (1950) criticizes the theory forcefully and, more particularly, those who think they can make a genuine distinction between the so-called academic and practical child.

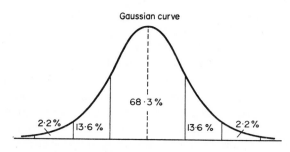

FIG. 30. The normal distribution curve showing per cent of area at various points on a base line.

Types of Intelligence Test

A convenient method of classification is to divide tests into those taken by individuals in group sessions and those by an individual in the presence of the test administrator alone. It is common practice to further subdivide the former into verbal, non-verbal and composite types, and the latter into performance and composite types:

	Examples
(i) Group Verbal	N.F.E.R. and Moray House Group Tests
(ii) Group Non-verbal	Progressive Matrices (Raven)
(iii) Group Composite	A. Heim (A H 4 to A H 6) Tests
(iv) Individual Performance	Porteus Maze
(v) Individual Composite	Wechsler Intelligence Scale

This purely arbitrary classification has weaknesses common to all taxonomies and is offered as a rough working guide. Broadly speaking the main difference is between testing an individual in what is sometimes referred to as a "clinical situation" with only one tester and one testee present and testing a group by what is commonly called the "paper and pencil" method.

Teachers are most likely to be called upon to administer group rather than individual tests in school; what are the advantages and limitations of each?

1. The introduction to a group test, its supervision and marking is generally a straightforward routine exercise requiring little more than implicit obedience of a few common-sense instructions. Prepare in advance so there is no shadow of doubt about administration procedures, provide the group with materials required for the test and hold spares in reserve. In contrast, the administration of an individual test calls for special training and its assessment and interpretation requires expertise.

2. Probably the most obvious difference in testing large groups compared with individuals is in time-saving, but whether this is necessarily an advantage or not depends on the ultimate objective; for instance, using a test as a diagnostic instrument. It is generally far more valuable to observe a child's method of approach or strategy and its step-by-step implementation than to record the end product, which may or may not be the correct solution to the problem. Time spent with individual children under these circumstances is more than worth while in eliciting valuable information which would not have otherwise been revealed in a group testing situation.

3. The marking or scoring of group tests should be a model of objectivity, answers are either correct or incorrect and without ambiguity. This dreary exercise has been alleviated by the provision of overlapping answer stencils with cut-out holes to show the correct responses and by a more sophisticated technology called machine scoring.

4. Personal relationships and attitudes do not enter group testing situations as they do between tester and testee in a face to face confrontation. Subjects in groups working under personal pressures and at speed are normally unaware of the presence of a supervisor whose function is totally different from that of a trained psychologist slowly progressing through a Stanford–Binet scale with a poorly motivated child, a boy with sensory deprivation or an emotionally upset girl. Individual tests frequently reveal significant aspects of personality development, temperamental disposition,

deep-set attitudes and other qualities like creativity, imagination and adaptability.

5. The strict and generally parsimonious timing of group tests is often criticized for introducing the factor of speed into an individual's perform-ance. It is not uncommon to hear teachers equate a high test score with the quick-witted, smart-aleck speed merchant rather than the reliable, steady and thoughtful boy. This, of course, is quite an erroneous point of view because speed correlates positively with accuracy and the grading of test items in order of difficulty gives an advantage to the more thorough-going and penalizes the careless. A time limit is often imposed purely for adminis-trative expediency and it is not generally expected that all the testees will complete the test in the set period. The need for greater flexibility in the timing of individual tests is fairly obvious.

6. For young children of about 9 years of age and under, an individual test with oral as opposed to written instructions is far more appropriate. Group tests for the very young child have many inescapable design limita-tions, they are not very reliable and only a limited amount of confidence should be placed in them. Attempts to restandardize well-known tests like the Stanford–Binet by extending the scale downwards have not proved entirely successful and their subsequent predictive value is unquestionably poor.

7. The generally free availability of mock tests of intelligence in "educa-tional crammers" and test extracts which appear from time to time in newspapers, magazines and television quiz games together with familiarity, coaching and practice have all exerted an influence on the average level of test sophistication of children and students. As these so-called I.Q. tests more nearly approximate group than individual tests it is not surprising that the former are less reliable than composite examples of the latter with their greater breadth of assessment including performance items.

Problems of test reliability and validity are discussed more fully later in this book (p. 264); however one or two words of caution are not out of place at this point. Do not attempt to design, construct and administer an intelli-gence test without professional guidance: it is downright harmful to put together original, modified or copied test items from a variety of sources and think you have designed something new. Good intentions are no compensation for psychometric inadequacy. If a test is required consult your Local Authority who will recommend a tried and trusted example appropriate to the age and ability of the children to be assessed. When it is received do not tamper with the test itself like shortening it, do not alter marking procedures and do not meddle with the age and raw score conversion tables. This warning may seem trite but it is so often ignored that it can stand frequent repetition. The misuse of a reputable test in any kind of educational assessment or research is utterly indefensible.

In the simple classification of tests into five types the difference between group verbal and group non-verbal is self-explanatory. Non-verbal group tests, of which Raven's Progressive Matrices is probably the best known example are claimed to have special advantages over verbal tests for they are said to be largely independent of educational and other learning factors. A similar claim may also be made for performance tests and because they are free of many of the limitations imposed by verbal competence they are therefore suitable for testing people from widely different social and cultural backgrounds. For this reason they are sometimes referred to as "culture-fair". At face value the argument that non-verbal and certain performance tests are superior in assessing the intelligence of culturally disadvantaged groups or primitive peoples appears reasonably plausible. However, research workers with great experience in widely contrasting cultures have begun to doubt the hypothesis and even deny the existence of a test which is universally applicable to all cultures. Moreover, between populations broadly classified as "primitive" there are such enormous cultural and environmental differences that the design of a genuinely universal culture-fair test must remain a remote possibility. Setting aside important factors like differences in personality, tempo of life and motivation there is no evidence to show that lines, shapes and figures are perceived in exactly the same way by social groups irrespective of mode of living and cultural heritage. Patterns which are freely recognized in a sophisticated European society possibly have little meaning in other parts of the world, certainly no more or no less than if patterns and shapes from oriental scripts were adapted for testing children in this country.

In the psychological journals there are reports to the effect that in comparison with performance on verbal tests cultured children are more favourably advantaged in some non-verbal tests. Vernon (1969) who has spent much time on this problem in field testing urges caution and avoidance of such sweeping generalizations.

Non-verbal items and tests supplement information obtainable from the traditional type of verbal test used in classroom assessment and are a requisite part of the composite tests which are most frequently used in individual or clinical testing. It would be wrong to argue that they are equally as good or that they are better in their assessment of general ability than verbal tests. The more culture-fair a test is claimed to be the less well does it predict subsequent achievement because it excludes use of language, an essential component without which no method of evaluation would be complete. Non-verbal tests such as the Porteus maze are not only useful in general assessment but in the specific diagnosis of types of brain-damage.

Performance tests like Kohs Block Design are much less frequently used in clinical practice than the composite tests which to some extent incorporate their principle characteristics. Possibly the word "performance" to describe a type of test is misleading because it is apt to be confused with physical dexterity or with an aptitude test like that of mechanical ability.

Composite tests include the well-known Stanford–Binet and Wechsler Intelligence Scales and the British Intelligence Scale which is currently undergoing development trials and statistical analysis. The Stanford–Binet test dates back to the work of Binet and Simon in France in 1905 who utilized a set of thirty items taken from everyday problems in an order of increasing difficulty. From time to time it has been revised, modified, and renamed to mark its association with either Stanford University or the co-workers in its development, Terman and Merrill. The present (1960) revision is based almost wholly on the 1937 version and is obtainable in two main forms: Form L for standard use and Form M for retesting. There is also a shortened version which gives a fairly accurate assessment of a child's I.Q. but is sometimes inclined to slightly under-estimate it.

A summary of the test's content suggests a fairly heavy verbal loading, particularly in the following items: comprehension, vocabulary, sentence completion and arrangement, analogies and abstractions. It also takes into consideration perception, memory, spatial organization, number, co-ordination and manipulation. The total score for all the items is presented in a single global measurement of I.Q. and this to many psychologists is its principal weakness. Other criticisms are often unfairly levelled against its age-range suitability, but what test of reasonable length accurately and reliably measures the I.Q. of very young children at one extreme and the gifted young adolescent at the other?

Of the Wechsler series of intelligence tests, the scale devised for children from 5 to 16 years of age (WISC) is probably the most widely used today in clinical practice. British psychologists find the grouping of sub-tests into verbal and performance scales more informative than a single assessment of I.Q., it correlates significantly with other intelligence tests, it is both reliable and efficient, children find it stimulating and enjoyable and its administration is uncomplicated. The five basic sub-tests in each scale, together with options (in brackets) are:

Verbal	Performance
General information	Picture completion
General comprehension	Picture arrangement
Arithmetic	Block design
Similarities	Object assembly
Vocabulary	Coding
(Digit span)	(Mazes)

Other tests in the series are the Wechsler Adult Intelligence Scale (WAIS) and the more recent Wechsler Pre-school and Primary School Intelligence Scale (WPPSI) for children from 4 to $6\frac{1}{2}$ years of age. A short form of the WISC has been devised by Maxwell (1959) and is proving helpful in practice. Widespread acceptance of the WISC in clinics does not imply it is a perfect test instrument which can be recommended without reservation because, like all tests, it has some weakness in its theoretical basis and a few limitations in practice. Test profiles are not always easy to interpret objectively, they cannot always be employed in diagnosis and prediction with absolute confidence because the nature of the inter-relationships between scores on the various sub-tests has not been clearly defined and to the inexperienced could prove highly speculative.

It is well known that the test was meticulously standardized in the United States for the white population only, therefore in this country is it an appropriate instrument for assessing the I.Q.'s of immigrant children from widely different social, cultural and educational backgrounds? Finally and on a theoretical note, workers like Littell (1966) want to know exactly what the test measures and request an explanation of its rationale. This is difficult to answer, even after consideration of Wechsler's (1944) definition of intelligence which on inspection seems to cover a broader spectrum of ability than, say, the Stanford–Binet test yet correlates very highly with it.

Readers will have noted that neither of the two major composite scales of intelligence discussed so far are of British origin and that caution has been advocated in adapting and modifying tests for use in different cultural backgrounds. A project to develop and publish a general ability test known as "The British Intelligence Scale" was launched by the late Professor F. W. Warburton at Manchester University and should fairly soon be in clinical use in this country. It is of modern concept incorporating ideas on children's thinking from Piaget and curriculum development in mathematics; yet it owes much to the Stanford–Binet in administration and to Thurstone in its classification of specialized abilities:

Specialized ability	Sub-scale
R (Reasoning)	Matrices, Induction and Operational Thinking
V (Verbal)	Vocabulary, Information and Comprehension
S (Spatial)	Kohs Blocks and Visual Spatial
N (Number)	Numerical
M (Memory)	Visual Memory and Auditory Memory
F (Fluency)	Creativity

Each sub-scale is likely to contain twenty-five items or scorable points and the final score will be given on a nine-unit scale: 64 and under, 65-74, 75-84, 85-94, 95-104, 105-114, 115-124, 125-134, 135 and over. There will be some flexibility in the administration of the scale with permissible omission of occasional items and eventually it is expected that longer forms of some of the sub-scales will be constructed for specialist use. For a fuller introductory account of The British Intelligence Scale and progress reports interested readers are referred to Warburton (1966) and to his chapter in Dockrell (1970) which details the purpose and method of a try-out sample and also provides a lucid exposition of the theoretical basis for the selection of items in its construction. Test rationale has been stated too broadly or vaguely in the past and has relied heavily on empirical evidence rather than cognitive functioning. The British Scale draws evidence from three principal sources:

(i) Factorial studies of the structure of human ability.
(ii) The nature of cognitive development.
(iii) Clinical and research experience of individual testing.

As an example of the assessment of a child's cognitive skill against Piaget's theory and model of development, Table 1 has been reproduced from Warburton's chapter in Dockrell (1970); it clearly shows how test content may be classified by development level and sub-scale of ability.

TABLE 1. *Test content classified by sub-scale and development level*

Stage	Reasoning	Number	Verbal	Fluency (Creativity)	Memory	Spatial
2. (i) Preoperational (conceptual)	Simple classifications Tactile testing Pattern completion	Counting Matching tasks	Picture vocabulary	Naming objects (fluency) Creative play with blocks	Recognition of toys Imitation (digit span) Object memory	Imitation Matching shapes
2. (ii) Preoperational (intuitive)	Simple matrices Inclusion classes Inductive problems Sorting	Conservation Various	Verbal classification Differences Similarities General knowledge	Controlled word association Pattern meaning Unusual uses Consequences	Recognition of designs Recall designs Object memory Sentence memory Sense of passage	Block designs Matching involving reversals Copying tasks
3. Concrete operational	Sorting (several attributes) Logical multiplication (matrices) Inference problems Induction (several variables)	Shapes	Definitions Social reasoning Similarities	Number of synonyms Meanings	As above	Block designs Visualization of cubes Reversal and rotation of shapes
4. Formal operational	Matrices (sets and operators) Hypothesis testing (induction) Inference problems Propositional logic	Number bases Practical calculations	Abstract definitions Proverbs	As above	As above	Block designs (three-dimensional) Cube development

FIG. 31.

An unreservedly recommendable account of the development of a series of reasoning items for the "operational thinking" sub-scale of the new British Intelligence Scale has been written by Ward (1972). The test is in the form of a logical game, "The Saga of Butch and Slim", and is played with four cards on each of which is drawn a picture of two imaginary criminals. Under each criminal is written, "Yes, I did rob the bank" or "No, I did not rob the bank" as his response to the question: "Did you commit the robbery?" (see Fig. 31).

The subject is given a number of statements Butch might have made to the police and is asked to look for cards which could agree with what Butch said. After the first set of statements has been presented the subject is told that whatever Butch says is a lie and is asked which of the cards could be true when Butch is telling a lie. In the second or negation condition the previously false answers are now correct.

Experimenter should emphasize that Butch is speaking.
ANSWERS:
Cards:

True	False	
1	2, 3, 4	(1) "Slim and I robbed the bank together." If the subject responds wrongly or does not understand, point to Card 1 and say, "This is the only one which can be true because this is the only one which both admit to the robbery." "Now try this one. Butch said"—
2	1, 3, 4	(2) "I robbed the bank on my own." In case of error or misunderstanding, point to Card 2. "This is the only one which can be true because this is the only card where Butch is saying 'Yes' on his own." "Try this one. Butch said"—
2, 4	1, 3	(3) "I am certain Slim did not rob the bank." In case of error, point to Cards 2 and 4 and say, "These could both be true because Slim says 'No'." Administer rest of Item. The experimenter may repeat statement if requested. The experimenter should precede each statement with the words "Butch said"— N.B.—Where the subject appears to be guessing, it is desirable to ask him why he made his choices. If he cannot explain, mark as a fail.

Sixteen different statements or binary propositions are presented to the subject in the first condition, and a further sixteen in the second or negation condition:

NEGATION   "Now let us play the game a different way. Let us suppose that whatever Butch says is a lie. Which of the cards could be true when Butch is telling a lie?"
N.B.—For Negation, the "False" answers now become "Correct".

Statement (1)   If the subject does not appear to understand, point to Card 1, and say, "It cannot be true because what Butch says is a lie, but all these could be true"—(point to Cards 2, 3 and 4).

Statement (2)   If the subject fails or does not understand, point to Card 2, and say, "This was true but cannot be true now because Butch is telling a lie."

The experimenter points to Cards 1, 3 and 4: "These could now be true then, couldn't they?" Give no further help with rest of statements. N.B.—Before each statement say, "Remember, Butch is telling a lie."

The provision of a third example in the introductory procedure was absolutely necessary since, without it, subjects tended to view the task as a sort of multiple choice situation in which only one of the four cards was correct. Despite example 3 this initial "set" persisted in many cases: for instance, on item 4 Card 2 would be chosen and the subject would sit back considering the task accomplished. The convention was therefore adopted of asking the subject "Could any more of the cards be true?" irrespective of whether the full range of correct cards was chosen or not.

A revised form of the sub-scale will be published, incorporating recommendations by professional testers who have used the test in practice. The paper by Ward is one of the most fascinating of its kind to have emerged for many years; it gives insight into problems of test-scale construction, it demonstrates how a typical Piaget hypothesis may be adapted for psychometric purposes and it also touches upon the elements of propositional logic and psycho-linguistic aspects of reasoning.

It would not be appropriate or ethical to reproduce sample test items in a textbook of this kind. In any case students and teachers are reminded that the new scale is designed for individual use by professional testers in clinics and will not be available for general use in schools.

The Structure of Abilities and Factor Analysis

Throughout the present century fiercely contested arguments have centred round the nature and structure of human ability. The better known hypothetical models or structures shown diagrammatically below give some indication of differences in thinking about an unresolved problem. They also serve as a basis to introduce a discussion on the existence and characteristics of factors and the technique of factor analysis (See Fig. 32).

The historical sequence in which they are presented covers a period from 1904, when Spearman published his important paper on general intelligence, to the present-day systematic search by Guilford (1956) for specific factors to complete a structure of intellect model. Spearman's model is frequently called a two-factor theory of ability with general (g) and specific (s) factors. However, if general intelligence is common to all abilities then it is in a sense a one-factor theory or "monarchic" in structure. Spearman likened "g" to general mental energy, equivalent to physical energy and therefore dominant. By implication it is innate and unchangeable; but "s" which is energized by "g" is capable of modification under different environmental conditions such as formal education. The extent to which tests differ in their saturation of "g" is considerable, being very high in the case of verbal reasoning compared with say music or mechanical ability.

Spearman's theory was simple and elegant, it pioneered advances in

Test	General g	Specific factors				
		S1	S2	S3	S4	S5
1	+		+			
2	+	+				
3	+			+		
4	+					+
5	+				+	

Spearman's Two Factors

Test	Primary mental abilities							Specific factors	
	P1	P2	P3	P4	P5	P6	P7	S1	S2...
1		+	+				+		
2	+			+		+		+	
3	+			+	+				+
4		+			+		+		+
5	+		+				+	+	

Thurstone's Multiple Factors

Test	General g	Group factors			Specific factors	
		1	2	3...	S1	S2...
1	+	+		+	+	
2	+		+		+	
3	+	+	+			+
4	+		+	+		+
5	+	+			+	+

Burt's Group Factors

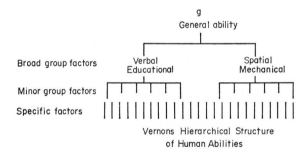

Vernons Hierarchical Structure
of Human Abilities

FIG. 32. Vernon's hierarchical structure of human abilities.

psychometric techniques and it firmly established the concept of general intelligence in psychological literature for half a century, but it had serious limitations which did not go unchallenged. His early denial of the existence of group factors was so tenacious he drove contemporaries, especially in the U.S.A., towards "oligarchic" structures of ability in which several factors assumed broadly equal importance. In this country, research workers like

Thomson (1951) mathematically demonstrated evidence to support a theory of overlapping group factors, and others like Vernon (1950) have pointed out the impracticality of designing a single test of, say, mechanical aptitude according to Spearman's hypothesis. A test of general ability together with a series of tests of specific mechanical skills would be required in practice.

In the U.S.A. the construction of a battery of tests by Thurstone (1924) and his development of new techniques of factorial analysis have influenced theories about the structure of ability and test design more profoundly than any other psychologist with the possible exception of Guilford. His model of ability is oligarchic and is presented in a multiple factor pattern which completely excludes a general factor. Thurstone is well known for his proposal that there are seven primary abilities, which in alphabetical order are:

M —	Memory	(recalling pairs of items)
N —	Number	(simple arithmetical calculations)
P —	Perceptual speed	(visual details, differences and similarities)
R —	Reasoning	(series and generation of rules)
S —	Space	(spatial forms and designs)
V —	Verbal	(vocabulary and comprehension)
W —	Word fluency	(speed in thinking of words)

His use of the word primary has proved misleading because the factors are in no sense psychologically basic or are they physiologically established. Indeed, they have appeared in modified and revised forms with amendments and omissions at various times. In diagnostic work and practical guidance they are useful because scores are not reported in a global measurement like an I.Q. but in profile form. However, Thurstone's tests have not proved superior in prediction to others, mainly because the primary abilities are not independent. They are intercorrelated. Also, different testing programmes would produce additional factors which would be equally acceptable. Naturally Spearman (1927) did not approve his model—"the new operation (Centroid technique of factor analysis) consisted essentially in scattering 'g' among such numerous group factors, that the fragment assigned to each separately became too small to be noticeable".

From a point of origin somewhere between the two extremes of the major protagonists emerged an hierarchical structure of ability which owes much to the work of Burt (1940). It is still generally considered acceptable

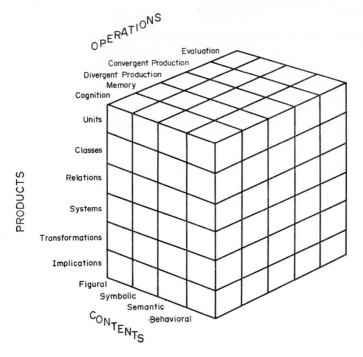

FIG. 33. Guilford's Structure of Intellect model.

in this country and it has recently become better known abroad after a period of relative neglect. The model caters for Spearman's concept of general and specific abilities together with group factors such as those shown to exist by research workers like El Kousey (1935) in an investigation into spatial ability. It is hierarchical in that it shows an orderly progression in generality of ability from a single general factor to a multiplicity of specific factors. Vernon (1950) warns readers against taking the structure too literally; for example, minor group factors have not always been found to be direct descendants of the two broad group factors: verbal—educational and spatial—mechanical. Science ability seems to cut across this dichotomy. Again note the retention and pre-eminence of "g" in the model and consider its implication for the prediction of educational attainment, provided it is assessed accurately.

Of all the possible approaches to the study of ability, without doubt that of Guilford (1967) and his "Structure of Intellect" model is the most unique and controversial. Instead of analysing batteries of test performances in a search for common factors or attempting to establish the existence of single factors, he first constructed a model on logical principles and then set out to discover factors which would meet his theoretical concept. The model, illustrated by the cube in Fig. 33, is three-dimensional.

OPERATIONS

The type of operation performed or five kinds of mental processes:

Cognition	C	Discovery, rediscovery or recognition of information.
Memory	M	Recalling information—retention.
Divergent production	D	Searching for possible solutions and varieties of thinking—broadening out and opening up.
Convergent production	N	Single correct answer as in conventional thinking.
Evaluation	E	Making decisions about the adequacy of information.

PRODUCTS

The resultant form into which information is processed or six products of the above operations:

Units	U	Varying from a simple product.
Classes	C	
Relations	R	
Systems	S	
Transformations	T	
Implications	I	To a complex product.

CONTENT

The material on which the mental operations are performed or four kinds of content in which mental processes operate:

Figural	F	Concrete material perceived through the senses. Spatial and linear relationships.
Symbolic	S	Letters, digits and conventional signs.
Semantic	M	Meaning of words and ideas.
Behavioral (hypothesized)	B	Non-verbal understanding of human behaviour and interaction or "social intelligence".

This cellular model generates a total of $5 \times 4 \times 6 = 120$ possible independent abilities; one of them, for example, is coded C M U, it could be tested by a multiple-choice vocabulary test. An enormous amount of empirical research is required before the specification of each and every ability is satisfied and a factor positively identified. To date it is claimed that tests have been designed and factorial techniques developed to identify seventy-seven abilities. In some areas progress is slow and difficulties inevitably arise with the identification of a behavioral content.

The total number of factors will come as a surprise; it reflects the breadth of Guilford's concept of intellect, particularly with regard to divergent production and its association with creativity. It is certainly a much wider view than that connotated with general intellectual ability and I.Q.s; it unites cognitive with other psychological processes like personality development. The superiority of Guilford's technique in the practice of mental measurement has yet to be convincingly demonstrated because it is generally understood that the more specific the nature of a test the lower is its predictive value. For up-to-date accounts of progress on the structure-of-intellect factors and their tests read the Reports from the Psychological Laboratory of the University of Southern California.

From what has been said so far about differences between the structural models of human ability it should not be implied that the factorial techniques in the analysis of data are of dubious mathematical pedigree. Without exception the statistical techniques are eminently respectable. The problem is in deciding which method of analysis is the most appropriate. Not only is the choice of method subjective but more seriously is the identification and naming of factors as they appear on a computer print-out. At this stage of the operation it is too easy to draw ready conclusions from false assumptions, particularly if the pattern of results seem to confirm an original hypothesis.

Psychologists have possibly expected too much from factorial methods: at its zenith it diverted too many minds from alternative research methods including the investigation of underlying rationale, hypothesis formation, test design and administration and the development of appropriate statistical techniques, particularly testing for significance. Sophisticated factorial analyses in no way compensate for poor experimental designs and techniques, they can hide weaknesses and even highlight obsessions and prejudices. To practice this knowingly in the pursuit of psychological "status" is utterly deplorable. Like any tool used correctly, factor analysis serves a useful but limited function. As an indicator of principles of test classification it is almost indispensable, but in the interpretation of factors or more specifically what they actually represent it is sometimes a less than helpful aid.

Creativity and its Assessment

In the discussion of Guilford's structure-of-intellect model attention was drawn to the breadth of his concept of ability and the inclusion of divergent production or thinking as a mental process. The creative aspect of development has been too often neglected or by-passed in the search for "pure" abilities, yet its place in the cognitive domain is undeniable not only on its own merit but as a sector in the whole area of psychology known as personality study. Looking at the history of mental testing in this country in retrospect and the predominance of the concept of general mental ability, as shown by the number of intelligence tests with high "g" saturations, inevitably explains why the measurement of convergent thinking was considered the more desirable and profitable pursuit. Divergence did not fit comfortably into a restricted concept of ability and the educational system was unready and unwilling to accept it at that time. Early studies of men of genius by Galton (1869) and Terman (1925) stressed the importance of the recognition and cultivation of talent, but it was Guilford in his famous presidential address to the American Psychological Association in 1950 who opened the floodgates for a torrent of literature on creativity.

Like many other topics in psychology it is far easier to discuss in broad generalizations than to define precisely. Some of the senses in which the term creativity is used, include:

(i) Cultural and aesthetic talent including original, artistic, literary and musical composition.
(ii) Scientific inventiveness including a facility for the generation of novel ideas.
(iii) Divergence of thought, fertile imagination and spontaneous reactions.
(iv) Unconventional personality, independence and radical attitude.
(v) Superior performance on open-ended as opposed to closed methods of assessment.

Obviously some senses of usage subsume others; therefore, is a unitary concept of creativity valid or should one think of kinds and degrees of originality? This is not an easy question to answer because on the one hand factors of originality and self-expression are common to creative acts like "g" in intelligent behaviour; yet on the other hand is it right to equate the scientific genius of a Newton with the musical fertility of a Beethoven or the practical inventiveness of a Brunel? Possibly confusion arises, as was found in the acquisition of skill, by the artificial limitations necessarily imposed by the restriction of studies to the gifted and the outstanding. For this reason it is helpful to envisage creativity as a continuum and to think of certain people as being more likely to behave creatively. Consistency of behaviour is an important attribute otherwise an isolated flash of insight, ingenuity or imagination may be taken as a general characteristic. With some caution and reservation arising from specific-situation behaviour the generality of creativity will be accepted as reasonable.

As to the origin of creativity there is no universally acceptable theory; in fact, there are as many theories of creativity as there are so-called schools of learning, each offering an explanation which neatly fits into an existing theoretical framework. The rewarding of behaviour for a creative act is consistent with instrumental conditioning, the active organization of ideas and objects into novel but recognizable patterns is postulated by the cognitive theorists and the elaboration of imaginery wishes from the unconscious level is characteristic of the Freudian school. Or again, in the current language of information theory, creativity may be described in terms of data coding, organization and method of storage. Bruner, it will have been noted, differentiates between narrow and broad categorizers, a logical outcome of his work on focusing and scanning in problem-solving situations. Whereas the focuser adops a more rigid and less risky approach by concentrating on a narrower field and a logical sequence, the scanner is more flexible in approach and is prepared to gamble.

Similarly creativity and theories of motivation are inextricably linked; the association has been neatly summarized by Maslow (1968) and (1970) who described it in a term borrowed from Jung—"self-actualization". Most people have a desire or urge to create and when these potentialities are expressed in an active form feelings of well-being and great self-satisfaction are experienced as a result of the release of inner tendencies. The intensity of drive varies from one individual to the next and its overt expression is an important trait in the study of the total personality.

Other than self-fulfilment why is the discovery and promotion of creativity an important issue for the classroom teacher; with what accuracy can it be assessed and subsequently fostered? Advanced societies are currently undergoing rapid changes as a result of technological innovation and to meet the voracious demands of a dynamic age no country can afford to neglect potential ability. The existing educational system and its different forms of examination is fairly successful in identifying and developing abilities associated with convergent thinking, but is it at the expense of the more divergent thinker? It is too easy to become emotionally involved in this kind of problem and to falsely accuse the system or institution of gross neglect and of failure to recognize and unearth talent. The problem is not as straightforward as this because, first, a great deal more specific and conclusive evidence is needed to prove the stultifying effects of formal education; secondly, how closely is creativity correlated with intelligence, and thirdly, how quickly is the worthless day-dreamer, who uses glibness of tongue and eccentricity of behaviour as a cover for idleness, detected?

Clearly then, it must be the genuinely productive mind with which the teacher is concerned and not the superficial and transient. Again it is worth repeating the warning that it is too easy to look at extremes rather than a continuum of creativity with the more personable divergent thinker euphimistically described as liberal, open-minded, questioning and imaginative; whereas the convergent thinker in contrast is labelled conventional, conformist and closed. Perhaps it would be more fruitful to forget about identifying stereotypes and to give more thought to a child's disposition towards creative action and behaviour. Not all the attributes of the creative person are necessarily and wholly desirable; the wizard ball-artist on the football field who does not fit into a team pattern is of limited value, so is the artist who fails to communicate with an audience because his unique personal style obscures the message and the scientist who develops yet another invention with even greater destructive potential than the hydrogen bomb.

Is creativity a particular kind of intelligence, a specific ability factor or is it independent in the cognitive domain? Research into this problem tends to produce conflicting results. From the mass of papers published to date no firm conclusion may be drawn on the relationship between creativity and intelligence. One of the most widely quoted researches by Getzels and Jackson (1962) showed a clear dichotomy between I.Q. and creativity, but the experimental design and analysis was so fundamentally weak as to make it almost unacceptable. Replication of the experiment by Hassan and Butcher (1966) with Scottish children and a much improved design failed to establish the dichotomy, in fact it suggested exactly the opposite, a positive correlation between I.Q. and creativity.

Whereas Hasan and Butcher tested children of a wide range of ability Getzels and Jackson only included children of high ability in their experiment, therefore is there an upper level or area where creativity assumes progressively greater significance over general intelligence? Were all the tests sufficiently discriminatory and to what extent were the conditions of testing appropriate? Wallach and Kogan (1965) saw weaknesses in the normal methods of testing and adopted a much more open and informal approach to their assessment of creativity and included non-verbal items. For a sample of 151 children between 10 and 11 years of age the following average correlation coefficients were reported:

Intercorrelation among creativity items	+ .41
Intercorrelation among intelligence sub-tests	+ .51
Correlation between creativity and intelligence	+ .09

these figures suggest independent measurements.

Tests of creativity are normally of the "open-ended" kind, that is, for a particular question there is not necessarily a single correct and specific answer. Responses are individual, multi-faceted and often highly personal to the testee. The items below are typical of those used in the assessment of creativity:

CREATIVITY ASSESSMENT: TYPICAL ITEMS

1. Unusual Uses:
   List as many uses as you can think of for the following objects:

   a brick,   a barrel,   a paper clip,   a bed sheet

2. Imaginative Drawing:
   Draw a picture without words or symbols to illustrate the title "Some Like It Hot".

3. Product Improvement:
   Think of the cleverest, most unusual and most interesting ways of changing this toy so that children will have more fun playing with it.

4. Incomplete Figures:
   Sketch an object or make an original design from the following figure:

5. Consequences:
   Imagine what might possibly happen if all laws were suddenly abolished.
6. Word Associations:
   List as many meanings you can think of for the following words:

   FAIR   DUCK   CANVAS

7. Controversial Statements:
   Comment on the following statements:
   (a) Raising the standards of television means taking away what people do enjoy and substituting what they don't.
   (b) Modern Americans like Hemingway make English novelists of the nineteenth century seem tedious.
   (c) Fox-hunting, the unspeakable in full pursuit of the uneatable.
8. Story Writing:
   Look at this picture of a nursery rhyme story then:
   (a) think of as many possible causes for the events which are shown in it;
   (b) think of as many possible endings or consequences of the events or actions shown in it.

A perusal of the various attempts to assess creativity by open-ended techniques inevitably raises the question not only of reliability and validity but of objectivity in marking. Assessment must be more subjective compared with a convergent test of intelligence or a standardized test of attainment because personal judgements have to be made as to what is considered the more original of a given number of responses. Even so, it is possible to achieve a fair amount of consistency between markers, provided they are given some guide-lines to form the basis of a fairly broad marking scheme. Items involving verbal fluency are marked more objectively than free drawings which are often difficult to judge by standards of originality, excluding artistic skill. Given a widely contrasting battery of sub-tests the problem of marking is not completely unacceptable from the point of view of subjectivity.

Similarly, the reliability of creativity tests with average test retest coefficients ranging from $+.4$ to $+.7$ is reasonable considering its susceptibility on certain verbal items to coaching and practice. However, the same cannot be said about the validity of these tests, particularly when test performance is correlated against children who are judged as being creative by teachers. In the armed forces and industry the predictive validity of creativity tests has also proved disappointingly low. It is therefore reasonable to assert that no universally acceptable test of creativity has so far been constructed for assessing children in schools or adults said to be divergent

and of original turn of mind; such tests as exist are at best only broad indi-
cators, not precise instruments. It is doubtful whether a test of high predictive value will ever be developed because personality factors exert too
great an influence in the expression of creativity to be ignored.

In this country the work of Hudson (1966) on a possible relationship
between convergent thinking and specialization in science, and divergent
thinking and specialization in arts subjects, is well known but his arguments
are not entirely convincing and need to be confirmed with different groups.
Students reading for the Graduate Certificate in Education at King's College, London University, were given creativity tests and no significant
differences were found between the mean scores of science and arts
graduates (see Fig. 34).

Mean Scores on Three Assessments of Creativity.
Post-graduate Student Teachers.

	All P.G. Students 282	First Group 141	Second Group 141	Arts Students 173	Science Students 109	Women 183	Men 99
Unusual Uses	26.8	26.1	27.6	27.6	25.6	26.4	27.7
Imaginative Drawing	5.3	5.5	5.1	5.5	5.0	5.3	5.4
Product Im- provement	9.0	9.0	9.1	9.9	7.7	8.9	9.4

It is not entirely fair to make direct comparisons between results obtained
from testing a highly homogeneous group of graduate students with
Hudson's sample. Different assessment conditions, environmental circumstances, qualifications, career determination and so forth could very well
influence differences in the nature of response. What was most surprising
was, firstly, the wide range of marks obtained from an otherwise fairly
homogeneous group of students, and, secondly, no single curriculum subject claimed a monopoly of fluency, originality or ingenuity. Responses
were quite frequently subject-based, particularly in the unusual uses of
articles sub-test and reflected both undergraduate training and a variety of
cultural and sporting interests.

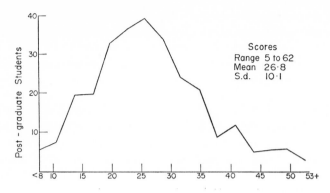

FIG. 34. Distribution of scores on unusual use of objects scale.

Teachers should not feel unduly worried about the technical problems involved in the measurement of creativity, for their role is to recognize talent and to provide a climate in which it is likely to develop. The extent to which it is capable of being fostered is arguable and few would attempt to organize anything but a small part of the curriculum with this uppermost in mind. There are ample opportunities for imaginative, original and personal contributions in a normal school day provided the teacher has foresight to think beyond formal exercises and repetitive stereotypes. How many geography periods are reduced to a dull routine by asking for sketch maps to be drawn towards the end of every lesson, or history periods by filling in blanks with names and dates on cyclostyled sheets? Foster creativity through a variety of challenging exercises with opportunities for personal contributions after a stimulating and thought-provoking introduction. The success of the series of textbooks introduced by Honeybone (1956) and his colleagues in Geography has been equally due to the lively and stimulating text with meaningful and realistic examples as to the wealth of practical individual work and exercises it suggests.

In a subject like Drama, opportunities for self-expression are endless. Taught by an expert it is of inestimable value in the educational and personal development of a child or student, irrespective of intellectual attainment and artistic ability. Practical drama of the kind promoted by S.C. Evernden and G. W. Canham at Loughborough College of Education called for an active contribution from every participant, a high standard of self-discipline and a total commitment to the work in progress. Their objectives were achieved with so-called difficult and disadvantaged children who found the freedom of expression and movement in a recognizable framework so rewarding and enjoyable that any attempt to interfere with the flow of activity by a potentially disruptive minority was simply not tolerated.

A common but improper misconception is that creativity is a compensatory activity, a poor substitute for sustained work of the more formal and traditional kind, and that freedom of expression constitutes a licence for disorder and unruly behaviour. This is of course nonsense, the exact opposite is more likely to be true. Conventional learning and creativity are complementary to each other, one sustains the other. Inventiveness is not conjured from ignorance, imagination from insensibility or ingenuity from indolence.

From America there is growing evidence that certain aspects of productive creativity are capable of development by training. Creative problem-solving courses for university students, industrial organizers and serving officers have proved successful in raising standards of competence. At the University of Buffalo, courses developed by Parnes (1959) are based on Osborn's *Applied Imagination* (1953). Students are made aware of a variety of blocks to creative thinking including the inability to isolate a problem, a restricted listing of attributes, inadequate generation of questions, perceptual failure, the effects of conformity and perfectionism and fear of making mistakes. Emphasis is also laid on the principle of deferred judgement which advocates that a new idea should not be evaluated immediately but suspended until a variety of suggestions have been accumulated. Interested readers are recommended to the publications of Parnes, particularly *Education and Creativity* which is more readily available in Britain in Vernon's *Readings* (1970).

Closely related to the principle of deferred judgement is a study by Kagan (1971) into the role of reflection and visual analysis in cognitive development. Reflection affords a child time to organize stimuli and evaluate alternative possibilities, whereas impulsive behaviour often produces an immediate and incorrect response in problem-solving situations. Failure and anxiety lead to the following kind of cycle: problem → impulsive action → failure → anxiety → second impulsive action → failure and so on to a state of withdrawal. That personality factors are involved in the cycle are obvious, but are they largely constitutional?

Evidence from several sources suggests that hyperactive preschool children, exceedingly restless and easily distractable, are more likely to develop into impulsive school children than those quiescent from birth. The time taken to respond to a problem normally increases with age, but whether this is due to longer reflection times or to factors such as wanting to avoid making incorrect answers is not clear. In some arts subjects the generation of creative answers may actually be impaired by too much reflection and cause a total mental blockage, yet sequences of impulsive and quite outrageous ideas occasionally lead somewhere worth while and prove productive. Controlled research into the fostering of creativity in particular school subjects including a practical study of effective styles of teaching is urgently needed. Such an investigation necessitates broad terms of reference and would have to cover personality factors and intellectual dispositions.

Two parallel researches by Haddon and Lytton (1968) and Lytton and Cotton (1969) were designed to evaluate the effects of two contrasting teaching approaches on divergent thinking abilities in British primary and secondary schools respectively. The hypothesis that informal, progressive teaching would more effectively promote divergent thinking than formal, subject-centred teaching was confirmed for primary-school but not for secondary-school children. The results of the primary-school research study clearly showed that convergent and divergent thinking are more independent of each other at higher ability levels, but they tend to overlap more closely at lower levels. This research was not into good or bad schools, permissive or authoritarian, but into the degree of emphasis laid upon self-initiated learning and patterns of interpersonal relationships.

The investigation by Haddon and Lytton (1968) into the promotion of divergent thinking abilities through progressive and less formal primary-school teaching techniques has been followed up after a period of 4 years. They hypothesized that, irrespective of the type of secondary school attended, the effects of informal primary-school teaching would still be measurable on a test of divergent thinking ability. Their hypothesis was convincingly upheld (1971), and substantiated the argument made earlier that the primary school is an important and formative influence in the development of divergent abilities. They found no significant difference in level of divergent thinking ability between arts and science specialists at the age of 15.

Failure to confirm the hypothesis in secondary schools was mainly attributed to the lack of a clear-cut contrast between formal and informal teaching approaches, which tended to vary within schools from department to department. Correlation coefficients between assessments of divergent thinking and verbal reasoning quotients were very low ($+$.17) for 143 children, pointing to the existence of independent factors.

In some quarters hostility has been expressed against the possible introduction of standardized objective testing techniques into external and public examinations on the grounds that they will stem the production of divergent thought and lead to greater conformity. There is a grain of truth in this; but many experienced examiners after having read so many stereotyped essays would need a lot of convincing and would challenge the view that traditional type essays necessarily offer much greater scope for originality of contribution. This reflects a naïve way of looking at the purpose and function of an examination; it is not simply a matter of essay versus objective type question, but of the kind of ability, attainment or thought process which has to be assessed. There is no logical reason why all academic subjects should be measured by a formal and limited examination technique; on the contrary, aim for as much breadth and variety of assessment as possible. Measure factual knowledge on standardized tests of attainment, set stimulating and thought-provoking questions which allow some freedom of expression, assess practical skills in the laboratory and field, encourage individual studies and provide opportunities for oral contributions.

The University of Cambridge Local Examinations Syndicate give Advanced Level candidates in Geography and History the option of submitting a study on a topic or theme approved by the Syndicate's examiners. In the past, topics which have proved successful are those which ask a definite question or attempt to solve a specific problem, preferably in a local area where a pupil has access to primary sources and opportunities for field observation and recording.

Other than guidance in the preliminary stages on choice of theme, methods of work and suggestions on possible sources, no other help must be given by teachers. The writing of the essay and its presentation is wholly unaided; it is the candidate's personal work. After the essays have been read by an examiner external to the school, each candidate is interviewed and is required to bring notes and field records to the interview.

Meetings between the Syndicate's examiners and school teachers are held to discuss the scheme in general and to clarify details of procedure. The educational value of an examination scheme of this kind is inestimable to pupil and teacher alike. An active and lively department will quickly accumulate a comprehensive survey and document of local knowledge for use with children of all ages throughout the school. Candidates not only learn in the narrower academic sense and gain experience of new skills and techniques, but in getting out of school into the local community they are brought into direct contact with real-life problems and socially meet people face to face who have first-hand and expert knowledge.

It is expected that the proposed merger of G.C.E. "O" level and C.S.E. will initiate more realistic examining techniques and give opportunities for the genuinely creative and divergent child to show his talent and originality. Changes in methods of assessment are needed to parallel changes in curriculum content. The question of the increased costs of newer techniques is not insurmountable, provided teachers themselves are willing to accept greater responsibility and play a more active role in the organization, setting and co-ordinated marking stages of an external examination system with some regional affiliations.

Additional Reading

ANASTASI, A. (1961) *Psychological Testing*, 2nd edn. New York: Macmillan.

BERRY, J. W. and DASEN, P. R. (Eds.) (1974) *Culture and Cognition: Readings in Cross-Cultural Psychology*. London: Methuen.

BURT, C. (1966) The genetic determination of differences in intelligence: a study of monozygotic twins reared apart. *Brit. J. Psychol.* **57**, 137–53.

BURT, C. (1974) *The Gifted Child*. London: Univ. of London Press.

BUTCHER, H. J. and LOMAX, D. E. (Eds.) (1972) *Readings in Human Intelligence*. London: Methuen.

CATTELL, R. B. and BUTCHER, H. J. (1968) *The Prediction of Achievement and Creativity*. Indianapolis: Bobbs-Merrill.

FOSTER, J. (1973) Creativity. *Educ. Res.* **15**, No. 3.

FREEMAN, J., BUTCHER, H. J. and CHRISTIE, T. (1968) *Creativity*. London: Society for Research into Higher Education, Monograph, No. 5.

HEIM, A. W. (1970) *The Appraisal of Intelligence*. New edn. London: N.F.E.R.

HUNT, J. McV. (1961) *Intelligence and Experience*. New York: The Ronald Press.

JENSEN, A. R. (1969) How much can we boost I.Q. and scholastic achievement? *Harvard Educ. Rev.* **39**, 1–123.

JENSEN, A. R. (1973) *Educational Differences.* London: Methuen.

LYTTON, H. (1971) *Creativity and Education.* London: Routledge & Kegan Paul.

MACFARLANE SMITH, I. (1964) *Spatial Ability.* London: Univ. of London Press.

MITTLER, P. (Ed.) (1970) *Psychological Assessment of Mental and Physical Handicaps.* London: Methuen.

SPEARMAN, C. E. and WYNN JONES, LL. (1950) *Human Ability.* London: Macmillan.

TAYLOR, C. W. (Ed.) (1964) *Creativity: Progress and Potential.* New York: McGraw-Hill.

TORRANCE, E. P. (1964) *Education and Creativity.* In TAYLOR, C. W. (Ed.).

VERNON, P. E. (1956) *The Measurement of Abilities,* 2nd edn. London: Univ. of London Press.

VERNON, P. E. (1960) *Intelligence and Attainment Tests.* London: Univ. of London Press.

VERNON, P. E. (1964) Creativity and intelligence. *Educ. Res.* **6**, 163–9.

VERNON, P. E. (1971) Effects of administration and scoring on divergent thinking tests. *Brit. J. Educ. Psychol.* **41**, Pt. 3, 245–57.

WARBURTON, F. W. *et al.* (1970) Some problems in the construction of individual intelligence tests. In MITTLER, P. (Ed.).

WARD, J. and FITZPATRICK, T. W. (1970) The New British Intelligence Scale: Construction of logic items. *Res. in Educ.* **4**, 1–24.

WECHSLER, D. (1958) *The Measurement and Appraisal of Human Intelligence.* Baltimore: Williams & Wilkins.

CHAPTER 9

Personality

Concept of Personality

A familiar platitude in most psychological textbooks is to the effect that every individual is unique with personal differences in attitudes, behaviour, feelings, interests and habits. However, there are times when it is necessary to describe one person to another using either a broad typology like extravert or a number of traits like sociable, boisterous or restless. The fact that it is possible to communicate a generalized biographical sketch implies that certain characteristics of a person's behaviour are consistent and to an extent predictable.

The concept of personality is complicated by a colloquial usage of the term expressed in a phrase such as "he has tremendous personality", which is not used in the broader sense adopted by most psychologists. However, there is no universal agreement on its scope and breadth; the majority would include temperament, some might include aptitude, but most would exclude intelligence. Educational psychologists tend to treat intelligence separately yet remain fully aware of the interaction between ability, learning and personality. A word or concept like temperament also presents difficulties; witness the gulf between the familiar expression "he is a bit temperamental today" and the more formal psychological definition "generalized emotional disposition". Most psychologists recognize the difference between a temporary state, which may alter according to social influences, for example, if status is involved; and a more permanent propensity to react consistently to given situations. Others would include expressions like innate and constitutional characteristics in referring to temperament, even though there is no reliable method known of assessing the contribution of genetic inheritance to personality.

Personality Assessment

Superficial judgements of personality are made in everyday social exchanges and they very often prove utterly misleading when based on brief acquaintances and hearsay. A psychologist requires more specific and controlled information than is normally obtained from a single interview to assist him in diagnosis, remedial programming and guidance. Consequently, scales of personality have been constructed in every imaginable form for every conceivable purpose but unfortunately with every shade of validity and reliability from acceptability to incredulity. Fortunately most children under the English educational system have not been plagued by assessments of personality. Tests have normally only been administered in clinical practice and for research purposes.

Insight into the difficulty of constructing personality tests is self-evident immediately one attempts to set down and classify a list of traits which come to mind in describing people. There might well be over 5000 descriptions in such a mini-Thesaurus, which in practice would be unmanageable and difficult to group because traits are almost identical in meaning. On the other hand, it could be argued that it is more rewarding to group people into types of personality rather than attempt a seemingly impossible classification of traits. There is some justification for both approaches and it will vary according to needs and objectives.

A fairly common classification of personality tests is into projective and non-projective types; albeit somewhat arbitrary and overlapping it is probably better than classifying them according to whether they are given to groups or individuals, or whether they consist of single or multiple-choice questions or demand closed or open-ended responses. The term projective is based on the assumption that a person projects his personality in making a response to stimuli which are presented to him visually; as, for instance, in constructing a story around a specific set of pictures or in describing imaginative responses to a series of ink-blots. The set stimulus is deliberately of vague and ambiguous content in order to elicit a variety of responses which are recorded for subsequent analysis. It would be impossible to refer to other than a minute fraction of all the personality tests at present available for professional use and wherever possible in this text reference will be made to the junior or children's version of a published scale. The principal source of reference for the serious student of personality are those massive and comprehensive volumes edited by Buros (1970 and 1972), which in this country are normally only to be found in the larger public reference and university libraries.

Methods of Personality Assessment

1. PERSONAL INTERVIEW
   (a) Free-ranging, unstructured.
   (b) Standardized questions.
2. OBSERVATIONAL METHODS
   (a) Direct.
   (b) Concealed—tape recording, video recording, one-way window.
3. REAL-LIFE SITUATIONS
   (a) Simulation techniques—aptitude.
   (b) Actual situations—selection board problems (Armed Forces).
4. RATING SCALES
   (a) Observer rating—teacher's record card.
   (b) Self-rating.
   (c) Rating by peers—sociometry, leadership qualities.
5. PHYSIOLOGICAL
   (a) Body type.
   (b) Blood pressure, heart rate, galvanic skin response.
6. NON-PROJECTIVE TESTS
   Cattell Sixteen Personality Factor Questionnaire.
   Eysenck Personality Inventory.
   Brook Reaction Test.
7. PROJECTIVE TESTS
   Rorschach Inkblot Test.
   Thematic Apperception Test.
   Bender-Gestalt.
8. OTHER TESTS
   Attitude, prejudice, interest, values.
   Social adaptation.
   Motivation, achievement need.

Theories of Personality Development

Most psychological tests and assessments are a direct offspring from well-defined theories of personality. In this country, Eysenck (1953) and his colleagues have researched intensively into two basic dimensions; neuroticism/stability and introversion/extraversion.

Figure 35 indicates how four main personality types are derived from two dimensions and their relationship to the classical Greek temperaments. Eysenck arrived at his model from the use of factor analysis, a statistical method which enables a researcher to identify the major factors which emerge from a large number of intercorrelated tests. It is a sophisticated

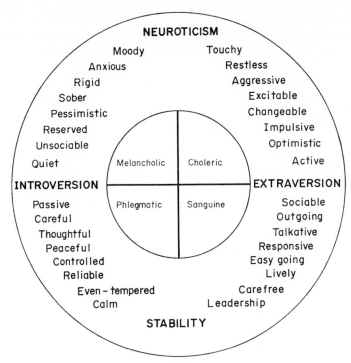

FIG. 35. Four temperaments of Hippocrates and Galen related to
Eysenck's factor analytic dimensions (after Eysenck and Eysenck, 1963).

method of extracting factors common to a battery of tests and assessments.
The aim is to make a mass of data more manageable and intelligible.
Eysenck's division of personality into four basic types has not met universal
approval. Some psychologists argue that it is too broad a classification and
that it would be more profitable to study separate personality traits.
There is room for both approaches, they are not mutually exclusive; on
the contrary, they should be taken as being complementary to each other.

Eysenck does not simply allocate individuals to one of four groups and
label them as such, but spreads the population along scales in a normal "distribution" with few at the extremes and the majority around the average.
His use of only two dimensions may appear unnecessarily restrictive, yet
in clinical practice and research their conciseness is a strong and appealing

virtue. These two scales have proved useful and informative in the study of the relationship between anxiety and performance.

Cattell's Sixteen Source Traits or Primary Factors

RESERVED
  Detached, stiff, cool, aloof, prefers
  things to people.

A OUTGOING
  Warm-hearted, good-natured,
  co-operative, attentive to people.

LESS INTELLIGENT
  Dull, concrete thinking, low
  mental capacity.

B MORE INTELLIGENT
  Bright, abstract thinking, high
  mental capacity.

AFFECTED BY FEELINGS
  Immature, less stable, evasive, low
  ego strength, neurotically fatigued.

C EMOTIONALLY STABLE
  Mature, faces reality, calm, high
  ego strength.

HUMBLE
  Submissive, conforming, modest,
  unsure, retiring.

E ASSERTIVE
  Dominant, self-assured, confident,
  aggressive.

SOBER
  Serious, taciturn, pessimistic,
  subdued.

F HAPPY-GO-LUCKY
  Cheerful, enthusiastic, enjoys
  excitement, energetic.

EXPEDIENT
  Irresponsible, unreliable, gives in
  easily, low regard for moral
  principles.

G CONSCIENTIOUS
  Responsible, high regard for
  moral standards, perseverant.

SHY
  Withdrawn, timid, more easily
  embarrassed.

H VENTURESOME
  Sociable, adventurous,
  uninhibited.

TOUGH-MINDED
  Insensitive, tough, self-reliant,
  realistic.

I TENDER-HEARTED
  Sensitive, dependent, fastidious,
  impractical.

TRUSTING
  Not jealous, adaptable, works well
  in a group.

L SUSPICIOUS
  Mistrusting, sceptical, self-
  opinionated.

PRACTICAL
  Conventional, does the right thing,
  careful.

M IMAGINATIVE
  Bohemian, unconventional,
  aesthetic, more creative.

FORTHRIGHT
  Natural, vague, artless.

N SHREWD
  Calculating, experienced, polished,
  social climbing.

SELF-ASSURED
  Self-confident, untroubled, low
  anxiety.

O APPREHENSIVE
  Worried, depressive, guilt-prone,
  blames himself, anxious.

CONSERVATIVE
  Traditional, cautious, not very
  resourceful.

Q1 EXPERIMENTING
  Radical, critical, analytical, likes
  change.

GROUP DEPENDENT	Q2 SELF-SUFFICIENT
Enjoys social approval, prefers to work with other people, committee type.	Independent, makes own decisions, self-reliant.
UNDISCIPLINED SELF–CONFLICT	Q3 CONTROLLED
Casual, not dependable, inconsiderate, untidy.	Self-disciplined, reliable, socially approved behaviour.
RELAXED	Q4 TENSE
Calm, tranquil, patient, not easily irritated.	Excitable, overwrought, restless, impatient, fretful.

Cattell (1965), on the other hand, favours a model based on surface and source traits. Surface traits are the more obvious and self-evident personality traits which are intercorrelated and form easily recognizable clusters. Source traits are more basic, deeper and less readily identified. They are factors derived by factorial analysis. The adult version of Cattell's test was constructed around sixteen such factors or source traits.

Subjectivity in the interpretation of factors obtained by statistical methods cannot be dismissed lightly, therefore it is reasonable to inquire as to whether Cattell's structure is but one of a number of "acceptable" models and might it be possible to identify other source traits from different yet equally valid factorial techniques? On this point psychologists are unlikely to agree. The contribution of the Cattell test to clinical and educational assessment is undeniable and it has been widely accepted as a useful diagnostic and research instrument.

Grygier's Dynamic Personality Inventory (1970) is a more recent example of a scale developed from psychoanalytic theory. In a general text on learning it would be unrealistic to touch upon anything but the fringe of the subject, mainly because no single theory of psychoanalysis has proven acceptable to all those seriously interested in this area of study. To a certain extent psychoanalytic theories of development are losing ground to the psychometric models of the statistical psychologist who has masses of test data, sophisticated mathematical techniques and computer technology at his command.

The notion of broad stages of development in human growth is already familiar to readers. Freud recognized six distinctive phases in psychosexual development:

(i) Oral—corresponding to gratification obtained from "mouth" actions like sucking or biting in the child; for instance thumb sucking.

(ii) Anal—referring to toilet activity and its subsequent training in the child.

(iii) Phallic—handling of the sexual organs.

(iv) Oedipus/Electra Complex—attachment of a child to a parent of the opposite sex: son to mother/daughter to father and antagonism to parent of the same sex.

(v) Latent—the period between infantile sexuality and the beginning of adolescence.

(vi) Genital—normal heterosexual development.

The basis of Freud's theory is that an individual's personality reflects the manner in which he progressed through the various stages of psycho-sexual development. Difficulties arise when a child's normal progression becomes arrested at a particular stage and aspects of this stage are subsequently manifested in adult life. The oral stage is revealed either in the person who shows a constant need for reassurance and is rather immature and dependent, or in characteristics such as frustration and aggression. In the first case the correspondence is with the sucking or passive oral character, and in the latter, to the biting or sadistic type.

Anal characteristics are manifested in three intercorrelated personality traits: obsession with orderliness, obstinacy and stinginess. Fixation at the phallic stage shows itself in narcissism, gratification through self-admiration and possibly in exhibitionism.

It is not easy to judge objectively the significance of the psychoanalytic approach to personality study because so little of the underlying theory is accessible for measurement. The better known psychometrists like Cattell have not yet identified a factor or source trait wholly corresponding to anal-erotic characteristics.

Physique and Temperament

Teachers of physical education should know something about the relationship between body build and personality, more usually referred to as the study of physique and temperament. Historical references to a correlation between them are abundant, some going back to the fourfold classification of Hippocrates and Galen in classical times:

The Four Temperaments

Sanguine — shallow and carefree.
Phlegmatic — sluggish in movement and thought.
Choleric — aggressive and impulsive.
Melancholic — reserved and anxious.

In literature, the following quotations serve as an introduction:

> ... but for sweet Jack Falstaff, kind Jack Falstaff, true Jack Falstaff, valiant Jack Falstaff: banish not him—banish plump Jack and banish all the world.
>
> *(Henry IV, Pt. 1)*

> The smith, a mighty man is he,
> With large and sinewy hands;
> And the muscles of his brawny arms
> Are strong as iron bands.
>
> *(The Village Blacksmith)*

> Yond' Cassius has a lean and hungry look;
> He thinks too much; such men are dangerous.
>
> *(Julius Caesar)*

or in the writings of Kretschmer (1965) who distinguished three types:

Pyknic   Athletic   Asthenic

and Sheldon (1942):

Physique	—	Endomorphic	Mesomorphic	Ectomorphic
Temperament	—	Viscerotonic	Somatotonic	Cerebrotonic

Sheldon photographed over 4000 male students in three different positions and from the standardized prints obtained body measurements which were classified into three groups. Each of the three body components was given a rating on a scale from 1 to 7.

(i) *Endomorphy*—prominence of the endoderm suggesting roundness and a capacity to put on fat. The somatic structure, bone, muscle and connective tissue, tends to be weak and specific gravity is low. They have a highly developed and massive digestive viscera.

(ii) *Mesomorphy*—prominence of the mesoderm suggesting massive limbs and well-developed muscles. They have a very strong somatic structure, high specific gravity, upright physique, large arteries and blood vessels and a relatively thick skin with large pores.

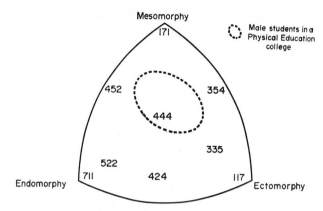

FIG. 36. Distribution of somatotypes.

(iii) *Ectomorphy*—prominence of the ectoderm suggesting linearity and fragility of structure. Weak development of the viscera and stringy muscles. Because of greater surface exposure to sensory perceptions they have a poorly protected nervous system.

In Fig. 36 note how the rating is always given in the same order: endomorphy, mesomorphy and ectomorphy. In common with normal distributions there are comparatively few individuals located at the extremes.

Having assigned somatotypes or body build groups to students Sheldon next interviewed and rated them for temperament on three, seven-point scales:

(i) *Viscerotonia*—generally relaxed, sociable and enjoy comforts. They love to be well thought of and respond well to affection. Enjoy food almost to the point of gluttony to satisfy their digestive tract.

(ii) *Somatotonia*—a tendency towards extraversion and when motivated exert tremendous drive and physical activity. Tolerant of spartan conditions and generally tough in mind and body.

(iii) *Cerebrotonia*—much more introverted and inhibited, they avoid drawing attention to themselves. Repress emotional expression and enjoy solitude. They show restraint in habits and activities like eating, drinking and sport.

Correlations were calculated between physique and temperament and remarkably high coefficients were obtained:

Endomorphy and Viscerotonia	+ .79
Mesomorphy and Somatotonia	+ .72
Ectomorphy and Cerebrotonia	+ .83

Replications of this kind of investigation by Parnell (1958) at Oxford and Evans Robson and Cross at Loughborough indicate that correlations of between +.3 and +.4 are more realistic. They took actual body measurements and scores from standardized personality rating scales whereas Sheldon used photographic techniques and his own temperament scale. Even if anthropometric measurements have been taken with accuracy, a problem remains: which parts of the body does one choose, how many and with what weightings in averaging them out?

Physical types do not necessarily remain stable throughout life, women would be the first to agree. Also were Sheldon's students too homogeneous a group for a worth-while study? Statistically it could be argued that there is no real justification for the division of body type into three groups, two would be adequate but with lower correlations. Also if high correlations are obtained it is reasonable to argue that if physique accurately predicts temperament, the converse to a large extent must also hold true, but in fact it does not.

There is adequate evidence for a small and positive relationship between physique and temperament which cannot be ignored by teachers of physical education in the assessment of athletic potential. Possibly in vocational guidance decisions as to suitability for certain occupations should take into consideration personality and somatotype, particularly if working conditions involve repetitive tasks or periods of stress or sheer physical strength. In mental health, an assessment of physique merits some attention even though it plays a minor role in the diagnosis of a patient. Kretschmer's relationship between the pyknic (endomorph) and manic depression, and between the asthenic (ectomorph) and schizophrenia has been confirmed in a number of studies (Parnell).

Assessment in Schools

Is there a case for more widespread use of personality tests in schools today with greater teacher involvement? No, certainly not; the backwash effects would prove disastrous and create unbearable anxiety among children and parents alike, particularly because gross errors of judgement can be so easily made in the interpretation of multi-trait profiles.

Warburton (1969) sums up the case against the introduction of personality tests into schools in a highly sensible statement: "Since personality tests are partly fakable they should not be set in Britain in competitive situations, such as academic and vocational selection. They can probably be used, however, in any form of guidance in which the subject is actively seeking out advice." He goes on to outline areas of research in which personality testing is justified, stressing guidance rather than selection and general understanding of human behaviour rather than specific application to individuals.

Fakability is a real problem in test construction, because it is normal for an individual to want to show himself in the best possible light as a socially desirable person: "One likes to feel clever, more honest, more likeable and kinder than the next" (A. Heim, 1970). In Grygier's Dynamic Personality Inventory there is a scale called "liking for children". Prospective candidates for places in colleges and departments of education tend to score more highly on this scale than student teachers actually taking professional education courses, especially if they are tested at the end of a week of gruelling teaching practice!

Teachers are rarely called upon to make assessments of personality other than grading attitudes and characteristics such as conduct, co-operativeness, persistence, reliability and sociability. A practical difficulty in allocating grades to children is in attempting to avoid the "halo" effect; namely having given a child "A" for one or two desirable traits it is only too easy to give the same child high gradings for all other socially acceptable traits, and vice versa. Similarly in writing reports, references and, more especially, testimonials there is a tendency to over-generalize and to be insufficiently discriminating between personal attributes. Open testimonials are quite worthless and should be immediately abolished by the teaching profession. It would be astonishing and quite revealing to understand the motives of a candidate who willingly submits a bad testimonial with his formal application.

Interviews, too, are notoriously unreliable unless carefully controlled questioning techniques are employed. Initial impressions and opening responses, probably of little significance to the main aim and function of the interview, too easily colour the evaluation of subsequent responses and impair overall judgement. From this one should not imply that all interviews are undesirable; on the contrary, it gives a candidate an excellent opportunity to see a college or school and to ask questions before he commits himself to it.

Anxiety and Achievement

As the central theme of the text is the psychology of classroom learning it is necessary to examine the nature of the relationship between anxiety and educational achievement. For a recent and more detailed study of this topic and a fairly representative list of references to research in a number of countries readers are referred to Gaudry and Spielberger (1971).

Like personality itself, anxiety is not a clearly defined concept therefore research workers tend to adopt an operational definition of the term based on observable behaviour. At present there is no generally accepted way of distinguishing between anxiety and fear; yet it is a fairly common practice to associate fear with an emotional reaction to a specific situation or object, and anxiety with a more generalized condition characterized by an almost permanent state of anticipation. Freud describes the latter as "free-floating", implying a feeling of apprehension which may be attached quite irrationally to any situation or object. Many feelings of general anxiety are perfectly normal and heighten performance; such as in anticipating and preparing for important examinations. Specific and intense fears impair efficiency, a condition known too well to many student teachers as they await the initial visit of a supervising tutor on teaching practice and his comments at the end of the lesson.

The nature of the behaviour response, shown by an increase or decrease in efficiency and performance under conditions of anxiety and stress, has attracted a number of research projects in recent years. Physiological measurements of glandular secretions like adrenalin, blood pressure, heart rate and perspiration level provide some indication of emotional state, but this kind of information is not readily available to psychologists who prefer to analyse personal responses to standardized rating scales. Subjects are normally asked questions about their general and specific emotional feelings. Unfortunately, responses are introspective and subjective in that they rely upon the attitude, integrity and self-evaluating skill of the testee.

Anxiety-arousing situations are found in many aspects of school life including highly competitive classroom exercises, difficult problem-solving tasks, important tests and examinations and in social and sporting activities. The expression "I cannot think any more" is a sympton of stress implying that the functioning of the mental system has become impaired and possibly grossly overloaded. Contestants on "quiz" pro-grammes, which necessitate a personal appearance before a large and seemingly more knowledgeable audience under conditions of intense competition and demanding speed of response, often make elementary mistakes and fail to recollect information normally easily retrievable from the memory system. Similarly in sitting an examination a student might become worried and over-anxious because he knows from memory of his notes that there are seven possible causes of an event, but can only immedi-

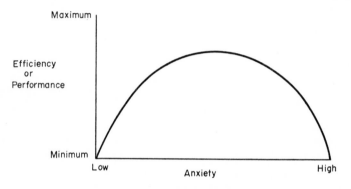

FIG. 37. Yerkes–Dodson (1908) curvilinear relationship between anxiety and efficiency.

ately recall five of them and therefore wrongly assumes that he is doomed to failure.

There is obviously a level at which anxiety acts as a motivator—"keyed up and ready to go". However, it is equally pertinent to inquire about the conditions under which it is said to inhibit performance. For a number of years the Yerkes–Dodson (1908) law of a curvilinear relationship between anxiety and efficiency has been accepted as reasonable. Figure 37 should be self-explanatory. There have been recent reports showing that the relation-ship is affected by the difficulty of the task and also by the age and ability of the pupil or student. In primary schools the negative relationship between anxiety and performance becomes more marked as children grow older and they are made more aware of their individual competence in, say, reading and arithmetic compared with the class norm.

At secondary-school level, grammar-school children generally show less anxiety than non-selective modern school children; on the other hand, it is reasonable to expect "successful", i.e. top-stream secondary-modern children, to be less anxious than bottom stream grammar-school children who have become conditioned to seeing themselves as failures. Lynn (1971) has studied the problem and suggests that children who are good at school work have less to feel anxious about and that intelligent children anticipate and cope with anxiety-arousing situations or else take avoiding action.

It is frequently said that for university and college students there is a positive correlation between academic success and high anxiety because intelligent young adults are capable of building up sound defence mechanisms and display greater "ego-strength" and control over their emotions than children. Yet many experienced counsellors working in student guidance point to individual examples of the detrimental effect of over-anxiety on scholastic progress culminating in academic failure and dropping out.

Alleviating Stress

Accepting the hypothesis that highly anxious children are more likely to be impaired by exposure to stressful conditions, how does one minimize anxiety-provoking situations in school? Ideally an educational programme should be tailored to meet the needs of each individual child, but short of using carefully graded project techniques and complex technology like computer-based instruction and sophisticated programmed-learning machines this is a practical impossibility. A successful teacher has learned from experience how to exercise personal judgement in general class management. He intuitively knows in certain subjects and at given times those children who need to be motivated and stimulated and those who need reassurance, encouragement and a reduction in tension.

Lengthy over-demanding question-and-answer sessions, frequent slip tests and formal examinations are known to raise the emotional temperature of highly anxious children. Questions should be structured and phrased so as to give a child a reasonable chance of making a correct response, if necessary in a step-by-step progression. Children are quick to spot the teacher who asks questions in a deadly dull routine fashion, or who shows his authority by trying to catch out the unwary, as opposed to the teacher who genuinely questions for diagnostic purposes in an attempt to help slower learners eradicate mistakes and sources of error. A lively, stimulating opening to a lesson, followed by a few worth-while questions, often sets the right climate for the remainder of the period. Endless interrogation frequently heightens tension, causes frustration and finally leads to aversion and passivity.

In planning a test ensure that there are some easy questions at the beginning and reserve the more difficult items for the end. This helps the anxious child from early wrestling with a problem, including wrestling with himself and mental exhaustion before he has an opportunity to show his real worth. If objective tests are to be introduced in external examinations like G.C.E. and C.S.E. a short practice session with an opportunity for asking questions immediately before the main test might prove helpful for children who for various reasons are slow to warm up. The Alice Heim tests of high-grade intelligence are models of excellence in this respect.

Attempts to alleviate examination stress by reducing memory load include permitting candidates to bring dictionaries, reference books and atlases into the examination hall, specifying exactly which topics are to be examined and by circulating a list of questions in advance of the examination from which a selection is subsequently made. As an alternative, continuous coursework assessment can be substituted for a formal examination or it may be combined with a shorter examination in a predetermined proportion, with or without compensation between the two parts.

Teachers of mixed ability classes claim that one of the advantages of the unstreamed system is that it minimizes the sense of failure in the slow learner. At the height of selection procedure and streaming there was very little clinical evidence to confirm or refute the allegation of increased anxiety in children at the age of 10 or 11.

Changes in the organization of the curriculum and in the grouping of primary-school children in recent years have done much to reduce competition between children and to promote greater co-operation across age groups. Possibly the introduction of educational technology has tended to reduce classroom tension. It would be interesting to know for certain whether, in particular, the use of teaching machines has made a special contribution in this direction or not. A child working through a programme competes against himself at his own pace, and is not constantly reminded of his progress in comparison with others. It would be valuable if research could show whether certain children are more likely to profit from a formal school routine as opposed to a child-centred system in which self-discovery plays a dominant role.

Personality and Achievement

For a statistical analysis of the relationship between personality, ability and achievement scores of 4000 eleven-year-old primary-school children readers are referred to Eysenck and Cookson (1969). The personality dimensions, extraversion/introversion and neuroticism/stability, were assessed by the Junior Eysenck Personality Inventory (1965), the teachers subjectively rated emotional stability, perseverance, sociability and impulsiveness. Two Moray House tests of verbal reasoning, the Schonell Graded Word Reading Test, secondary-school selection tests of Mathematics and English and grammar-school pass or failure were also incorporated to give a broad assessment of academic ability and achievement.

Analysis of results showed the superiority in scholastic achievement and verbal reasoning of extraverted over introverted children. Whereas unstable extraverted girls did unexpectedly well, unstable extraverted boys performed rather poorly when interaction effects were studied. Personality determined performance more closely in the case of girls than boys. The authors tentatively suggest that introverts are late developers compared with extraverts but they would like further follow-up studies on this hypothesis before arriving at a firm conclusion.

Anthony (1973) argues, from a study of peaks of development, that on the contrary, it is the introvert in late school years who is the early developer. The ability score of the introvert is more typical of those pupils who are older rather than of peers of the same age. Entwistle (1972) has surveyed the literature on personality and attainment very thoroughly and finds evidence to confirm the suggestion that young school extraverts, say between 7 and 13 years of age, tend to do better than young introverts; but among older pupils, the reverse holds true. He makes the point that "shifts in relationships between personality and attainment with age might then be explained as much in terms of changes in personality within contrasting academic environments as in changes in attainment". The change could be affected by teaching style, class size, classroom organization and formality of approach, including the personality of the teacher. Possibly senior pupils who are highly motivated introverts succeed because they have good study methods, work carefully, think ahead and are conscientious.

Although evidence for a positive relationship between personality and achievement is undeniable it must be kept in perspective. In the case of some children emotionality is a dominant factor affecting behaviour; however, for the child population as a whole it is so small as to be of little practical consequence, particularly in predictive use (Butcher, 1968). The emotionally disturbed child presents a totally different problem to the specialist teacher compared with the highly anxious child in a normal classroom. It is important to recognize the highly anxious child as quickly as possible and help him build up his self-confidence, self-esteem and self-image, particularly before the onset of adolescent development. Such a child needs a lot of positive encouragement to join in as wide a variety of school activities as possible because he tends to lack an adventurous spirit and avoid the unfamiliar. Never make a child feel different or inadequate because this only confirms in his mind the very lowly self-concept which is in need of modification. The aim is to promote an adequate self-concept, not to reinforce a poor one.

In adolescence a youth with poor self-esteem sometimes finds it difficult to gain acceptance among his peers, becomes an isolate, then withdraws from the social group and channels his frustrations into undesirable outlets. It is the responsibility of every school to make provision for a wide range of social, cultural and sporting activities. By encouragement and guidance, rather than compulsion, it should ensure that all pupils take part in at least one or two activities each term, if necessary on a basis of rotation. In very large schools this demands a great deal of organization and careful supervision but its value in terms of the development of the self-concept in individual pupils is inestimable. Recall the broad definition of learning: a school should offer its pupils far more than academic learning, it must foster social adjustment, too.

Additional Reading

ALLPORT, G. W. (1961) *Pattern and Growth in Personality*. New York: Holt, Rinehart & Winston.

ARGYLE, M. (1967) *The Psychology of Interpersonal Behaviour*. London: Penguin.

CATTELL, R. B. (1957) *Personality and Motivation: Structure and Measurement.* New York: World Books.

ENTWISTLE, N. J. and WELSH, J. (1969) Correlates of school attainment at different ability levels. *Brit. J. Educ. Psychol.* **39**, 57–63.

EPPS, P. and PARNELL, R. W. (1952) Physique and temperament of women delinquents compared with women undergraduates. *Brit. J. Med. Psychol.* **25**, 249–55.

EVANS, K. M. (1965) *Attitudes and Interests in Education.* London: Routledge & Kegan Paul.

EYSENCK, H. J. (1947) *The Dimensions of Personality.* London: Routledge & Kegan Paul.

EYSENCK, H. J. (1952) *The Scientific Study of Personality.* London: Routledge & Kegan Paul.

EYSENCK, H. J. (1957) *Sense and Nonsense in Psychology.* London: Penguin.

NAYLOR, F. D. (1972) *Personality and Educational Achievement.* Sydney: Wiley.

SAVILLE, P. (1972) *The British Standardization of the 16 PF., Supplement of Norms, Forms A and B.* Windsor: N.F.E.R.

SAVILLE, P. and FINLAYSON, L. (1973) *The British Supplement to the High School Personality Questionnaire.* Windsor: N.F.E.R.

SEMEONOFF, B. (Ed.) (1966) *Personality Assessment.* London: Penguin.

SIDNEY, E. and BROWN, M. (1961) *The Skills of Interviewing.* London: Tavistock.

STOTT, D. H. and SYKES, E. G. (1956) *The Bristol Social Adjustment Guides.* London: Univ. of London Press.

SUMNER, R. and WARBURTON, F. W. (1972) *Achievement in Secondary School: Attitudes, Personality and School Success.* London: N.F.E.R.

THOMAS, A., CHESS, S. and BIRCH, H. G. (1968) *Temperament and Behaviour Disorders in Children.* London: Univ. of London Press.

TROWN, A. (1970) Some evidence on the "interaction" between teaching strategy and personality. *Brit. J. Educ. Psychol.* **40**, Pt. 2, 209–11.

VERNON, P. E. (1964) *Personality Assessment.* London: Methuen.

WARBURTON, F. W. (1961) The measurement of personality. *Educ. Res.* **4**, 2–17.

YARLOTT, G. (1972) *Education and Children's Emotions.* London: Weidenfeld & Nicolson.

CHAPTER 10

Educational Technology

Introduction

In post-war years the growth and expansion in the number and variety of mechanical aids at the disposal of the teacher has been accompanied by enthusiasm, doubts and misgivings according to experience, changing philosophy or downright prejudice. A familiar cycle in the reception of technological innovation is one of initial euphoria, hotly contested claims and counter-claims, followed by relative quiessence and a gradual acceptance. To the progressives this is no doubt frustrating in the extreme but in the long term it has proved beneficial in educational practice, particularly in the Western World, where technology is changing so rapidly that redundancy and obsolescence in the function and design of equipment is inevitable. Given greater financial assistance for the purchase of modern teaching aids some members of the profession would still show little overt enthusiasm and would prefer alternative ways of spending any extra money.

An argument frequently put forward in opposition to the increased use of technology in the classroom is that human relationships should never be devalued, they cannot be replaced by anything which is bought. True, if one thinks solely of an automated classroom managed by technicians; but it is wildly exaggerated in the context of providing assistance for the teacher in order to free him from mass exposition and give him additional time to spend with individuals needing his personal attention and guidance. A good teaching aid is one which positively supplements the teacher in his normal work, no more and no less. Not all aids are necessarily good or bad, they can be used effectively or stupidly.

Programmed Learning

Programmed learning is the preferred term for it covers programmed books, programmed or teaching machines and computer-assisted instruction. It represents another aspect of child-centred education in which the focus of a classroom moves away from the teacher and his output to the child's input and active engagement in learning.

The earliest "teaching" machine was not designed for this function by Pressey in 1926, it was a self-scoring machine for tests. Immediately upon obtaining a correct answer to a question the testee would continue to move on to the next problem until an error was made and corrected. The total number of errors indicated his score. It was soon realized that a machine of this kind was also an effective method of teaching but it did not gain acceptance in this role. Nowadays the function of a machine is exactly the opposite, to teach rather than test. If anything it is the efficiency of the program which is on test because one of the characteristics of a good program is that the chance of making errors is reduced to a minimum.

Readers should refer back to Professor Skinner's work on operant conditioning for the psychological theory underlying linear programs in machine or book form. The word "linear" is used in the sense of students proceeding along a straight line without branching; that is, they all cover the same steps in a program in exactly the same sequence, only the pace differs.

The basic principles of Skinner's technique of instruction are summarized below:

1. Break down the material to be learned into very small steps or frames.
2. From given information the student is required to construct a response.
3. The chance of a successful response must be maximized; that is, students are normally expected to respond correctly, the steps should not deliberately be made progressively more difficult.
4. Reinforce each step by knowledge of results, immediately informing the student of a correct response.

There is no need for expensive machines to accommodate linear programs, a simple box-like structure will suffice. In fact there is no real need for a machine at all because a programmed book may very well prove equally as effective. Machines certainly have a novelty value, particularly with younger children; they make it less easy for a child to cheat; but of course, they are more costly and more space consuming.

Experience with teaching machines in U.S. Air Force training schedules made Crowder (1959) challenge the whole concept of the need for continuous reinforcement. He was convinced that in teaching, errors prove helpful in diagnosing the exact source of a mistake. He designed programs with branching sub-routes thus making it possible for students to follow different sequences to the final goal. The route is determined by the particular nature of the answer chosen by the student from a small number of alternative responses. In this context a correct answer is recognized rather than constructed. Obviously these programs are fairly sophisticated and need to be presented in a more complex machine which incorporates film transport and back projection devices. Sometimes the name "skip-branching" is given to a program with many different sub-routes. The quick learner goes ahead rapidly, if necessary, taking short cuts between principles. The slower student takes longer because he is forced to work through more detailed and simplified explanations as he progresses along most of the sub-routes.

Crowder claims that students are less quickly bored with a branching program because it avoids needless repetition, that more advanced concepts are capable of being taught by this method and that linear techniques can be incorporated whenever it is found necessary to explain especially difficult principles. Again, it is possible to write books using this technique but they are tedious and cumbersome compared with machines and, of course, it is even more difficult to prevent readers from cheating. However, they are much cheaper than machines and also quieter in operation.

The various technical methods of constructing programs are not explained in this textbook, suffice to say that a good program is based on sound teaching principles and makes excessive demands on meticulous standards of lesson preparation. A sequence should be planned with the utmost care and precision, the maintenance of logical order is imperative. Steps should be manageable but not so short that they proliferate and lead to long and boring programs. Evaluation and revision is essential before rushing into publication; the basic objective is to facilitate learning, to teach efficiently and effectively, not to test and tease.

Just how effective is programmed learning compared with conventional teaching methods? This is a very difficult question to answer, regretfully the evidence is rather inconclusive. A small number of surveys and reviews of the relevant research literature have been published, notably by Hartley (1965) in the U.K. and Schramm (1962a) in the U.S.A. (Tables 2 and 3).

TABLE 2

HARTLEY	Studies	Programmed Instruction Group		
		Superior	Same	Worse
Time taken	90	47	37	6
Test	110	41	54	15
Retest	33	6	24	3

In terms of speed, program learning has certain advantages over conventional learning and it seems to do little harm.

TABLE 3

SCHRAMM	Compared with conventional teaching		
Studies	Superior	Same	Worse
36	17	18	1

Earlier research centred round the merits and defects of linear and branching techniques produced no proof of the superiority of one over the other. Nowadays investigations are made into the optimum length of various programs, the nature of appropriate subject material for inclusion in programs, the design of programs for specific age, ability and experience ranges and the integration of programmed instruction into normal classroom methods either in individual or group work and whether it should be paced or not. Also, in the earlier reports there are suggestions that programmed techniques are suitable only for teaching basic factual material akin to rote learning. Recently programs have been designed to teach difficult concepts, the elements of logic and art appreciation.

From research reviews one obtains the impression that many of the reported experiments are of the short-term type and that few investigations have been made into the effects of prolonged periods of programmed learning once the initial motivation and novelty has worn off. Similarly it would be useful to know for what age groups the techniques are proving most rewarding; one tends to hear more reports of programmed learning with polarized groups, in initial or higher education and with dull or brilliant pupils. Certainly in higher educational establishments, including the armed services and industry, teaching machines have been most helpful, particularly in crash courses because it dispenses with the arrangement of detailed and elaborate time-tables for sub-groups. A programmed course in statistics for post-graduates is valuable to students wanting to know the fundamentals of the subject in order to understand the research literature more readily or to gain insight into the design of experiments and methods of analysis.

Sometimes the by-product of research into something like computer-assisted education proves equally as fascinating as the central objective. Atkinson (1968) found that in learning to read by this method girls do not progress more rapidly than boys; they normally do so in conventional classrooms.

Tait (1973) and his colleagues used computer-assisted arithmetic instruction in an investigation into the effect of different feedback procedures on young children learning the process of multiplication. They claim that contrary to Skinner's assertion, many researches report no significant increase in learning due to feedback. Guthrie (1971) found no evidence to show that feedback strengthens the tendency to give correct answers; however, it does improve post-test performance on questions which are initially answered incorrectly. From this it is concluded that feedback is important in helping a learner correct his mistakes, not as a reinforcement. When few errors are made, feedback assumes lesser importance; yet, it was noted previously in this book that programs are specifically designed to keep errors at a minimum level.

The results of the experiment showed that feedback techniques had greatest impact on the least advanced children, thus affirming the hypothesis that feedback helps a pupil to correct his errors. Feedback groups made significantly better progress than children taught in groups without knowledge of results. However, there was only a slight improvement in performance for groups taught by active as opposed to passive feedback techniques. Active feedback methods demanded an overt response to each step in the computing procedure, whereas the passive feedback group only received a printed feedback message which sometimes short-circuited detailed steps in computation. The real significance of this kind of research using a computer-assisted educational technique lay in the diagnosis of pupils' errors and in the subsequent planning of specific remedial teaching.

References to the relationship between programmed learning and the role and status of the teacher are more commonly found in the writings of the demurrers who abhor the thought of an automated classroom controlled and organized by technicians. Some of the exaggerated claims of the opponents read like science fiction. Teachers are not made redundant by the introduction of educational technology into the classroom, they are freed for different tasks such as giving extra guidance to pupils in difficulty who need personal help. There is quite a mythology in the teaching profession, particularly in secondary quarters, about the nature of the relationship between a teacher and his class, which is regarded as sacred, inviolate and inevitably good. Anything likely to impair this so-called relationship is naturally viewed with suspicion.

A poor teacher out of communication with his pupils will do far more damage to the image of a subject than a machine and an indifferent program. But why discuss this in terms of a dichotomy rather than one working in conjunction with the other? A carefully controlled investigation by Wallis and Saville (1964) into teaching electronics to Royal Navy mechanics clearly demonstrated the superiority of integrated human and machine teaching over conventional instruction and over a well-tried machine program alone. The integrated method was well received by students and instructor alike because there was available time to discuss difficulties with individual ratings in a class as large as the other two combined.

In some primary schools it is not uncommon to see small groups of children busily engaged at their machines and more often than not it is another child rather than the teacher who helps the slower learner to surmount a difficulty. Faster and slower groups might be observed progressing through programs specifically designed for their respective ability levels and pace of working. The teacher's time is used more efficiently concentrating on individuals and smaller groups, sorting out problems and difficulties which might otherwise have been overlooked in a large formal class situation. A child who has missed a key lesson due to unavoidable absence soon catches up with the group, given some preliminary instruction.

Many of the earlier critics of programmed learning argued that it was a form of indoctrination made worse by its inflexibility, that it emphasized rote learning rather than insight and understanding and that in making learning too easy, children did not gain experience of wrestling with difficulties. The latter argument has little to commend it. Many children already spend too large a proportion of their working day trying to surmount difficulties and have little progress to show in the end. A limited feeling of success and progress increases confidence, stimulates further interest and generates a faster pace of working.

It would be foolish to deny that programmed learning raises educational and financial problems and that in practice it is free of limitations. Complex machines are costly, if sound-proofed cubicles are essential to keep mechanical noise at a tolerable level costs soar upwards. A good program is difficult to write: it is a painstaking process demanding an overview of highly specific objectives, a grasp of apparently insignificant detail and a feeling for a simple yet logical pattern of interrelationships. A worthwhile exercise in a subject method course for teachers in training is to ask students to write out a short program in an area of study with which they are familiar and evaluate it in group discussion.

In American literature references to computer-assisted instruction are sometimes made, but even in a country with a wealth of resources the development and utilization of the technique appears to have moved little beyond the experimental stage. Typically a pupil observes information and instructions projected on a TV-type screen. Beneath this is a keyboard similar to that of a typewriter which is used for making responses to a set question. Feedback is almost immediate. Incorrect answers back-track the program and the necessary information to make the likelihood of a correct response is projected.

Computer-assisted instruction is too expensive to be used in British schools even on a shared facility basis. The advantage of this method lies in its greater flexibility and adaptability, serving the needs of individual pupils according to their level of knowledge and competence. There is no point arguing that savings on staff salaries could be used to offset payment for sophisticated educational aids; one does not supplant the other, they are complementary.

Audio-Visual Aids

The purpose of this section is not to describe the technical specifications of all the classroom aids currently available to the teacher or to discuss which aids should be utilized under given circumstances, but rather to justify them on psychological principles and to look at their effectiveness as reported in educational research.

Many experienced teachers agree that the most important principle underlying the employment of a teaching aid in the classroom is precisely that which is implied by the word "aid" itself, namely assistance, help or support. For a student rummaging through a stock room and coming across an attractive hardware model or an inviting piece of mechanical equipment the temptation to take it out and use it as quickly as possible must seem absolutely irresistible. One intuitively sympathizes with the view, "here is something too good to miss during my relatively short period of teaching practice, therefore how can I work it into my lesson planning and preferably make the most of it when my visiting tutor next comes to hear me teach". A good intention which seldom works in practice; it is the children who need educating, not the tutor entertained.

The majority of principles underlying the use of simple aids like the chalkboard, flannelgraph, magnetic board, picture, model and projected slide are based on common sense; yet so many demonstrations go astray that one must attribute this in part to technical failure, but more often to poor planning, inadequate preparation, inefficient organization and incompetence in handling machines and materials. How many problems of classroom control reflect a casual and shoddy approach to preparation?

Informing student teachers that they should ensure that a visual aid is visible or an audio aid is audible to the *whole* class seems too ridiculous for words yet countless times tutors have heard statements to the effect, "if you could have seen the bottom of the screen you would have noticed . . .". Statements of this kind are frustrating and irritating; no wonder children soon lose interest, become restless and adopt distraction tactics like making shadowgraphs. Similarly a chalkboard so cluttered as to make it look worse than a scruffy schoolboy's rough pad is utterly useless. An effective board is preplanned and organized, it is not a jotter for random thoughts, diagrams and sketches. Models and specimens too should be clearly visible, otherwise hand them round for individual inspection with specific instructions on what points should be observed. With three-dimensional models extra care and time is mandatory.

Consideration for other classes is important when playing back a tape recording or projecting a sound film. Quite often the volume chosen is so unreasonably high it detracts from clarity of hearing and induces listening fatigue. By careful planning it is not difficult to make an almost imperceptible change from conventional to audio-visual teaching techniques. Have the machine in position, ready-loaded or threaded, at a prepared focus and volume setting. Drill the children into a quiet and efficient routine of lowering the blackout screen and lights. It is not always essential to have a room completely darkened; merely exclude sufficient light for adequate visibility, particularly when working with an overhead projector and children are expected to make notes. Other practical points like having a spare bulb available, easy access to a light switch, avoiding trailing wires, not moving a hot projector and, of course, knowing how to handle equipment in accordance with the recommendations in the instruction manual all minimize the chance of technical failure.

If attention to physical conditions enhances smooth technical running, what psychological conditions are likely to ensure that a child effectively learns from audio-visual aids? This is difficult to answer objectively because there is a serious lack of specific research evidence on the effectiveness of teaching aids, including optimum times and methods of utilization with groups of different ages and abilities in various subjects of the curriculum. Teachers are forced to rely on past experience, general observation of class reaction and to some extent on intuition. It would certainly be wrong to take for granted that a seemingly attractive aid is better for children than no teaching aid at all.

A statement often heard is to the effect that "a picture explains more than a thousand words"; partly true, provided attention is directed by cues, prompts, suggestions and highlighting. Children are not necessarily looking at or interpreting detail in the same perceptual sense as the teacher, what the teacher considers significant is possibly meaningless and irrelevant to the class. A good illustration or picture should leave more than a vague visual impression in the mind of the child, it must have some salient feature which is easily recognizable and capable of retention. This does not mean that it should only convey facts, on the contrary, a picture with good visual impact gives insight into beauty of form and texture, colour and life in all its riches, poverty and moods. In teaching the geography of Japan a colour slide of a rural and traditional padi cultivator primitively working his fields contrasted against an express super-train in the background never fails to astonish and stimulate comment. It is as if the children have lived for a moment in that environment.

A practical question often asked by students is how long should a picture remain projected on the screen? This is almost impossible to answer as so much depends on the particular merit of the illustration and whether or not it has been chosen as a basis for analytical questioning and discussion. Under normal circumstances a single frame or slide should be shown for no less than 30 seconds; allow about 2 minutes on average and vary the rate according to feedback from the children in terms of stimulation and boredom.

Teachers nowadays prefer a series of slides to the continuous film strip because they allow more flexibility in planning a presentation, say, from panoramas to close-up or from human to technical interest. The main temptation in projecting a published film strip is to show every frame, rushing from one scene to another with pictures literally flashing on and off the screen. Another error characteristic of the inexperienced teacher is too heavy reliance on the handbook which accompanies the script, it so effectively bores children that they switch off and no longer listen. Write your own brief commentary from the booklet, make it lucid and focus on essentials only.

The chalkboard can be used effectively in conjunction with the projector. One useful device is to project a slide of say a landscape on to the board and draw round it with chalk to give an outline with good perspective. Film strips and slides in the form of abstracted stills taken from a moving picture are invaluable aids in revision and in the explanation of difficult sequences. However, for on-going sequences, moving films and loops are unequalled.

One of the attractions of the continuous loop projector is that it can easily be made accessible and children should be encouraged to use it in their own time. The film cassettes or cartridges can be indexed and stored like books on a library shelf and they need not all have been commercially published. School-produced 8-mm films are easily loaded into cartridges for continuous-loop projection. Slow and normal motion sequences of movements in subjects like physical education, handicrafts and drama are efficiently demonstrated by ciné-photographic loop techniques.

In the Faculty of Education at King's College, University of London, a mobile television recording unit, initiated by a grant from the Gulbenkian Foundation, has been designed and developed by J. V. Muir and I. Harris. For the past 6 years it has been recording classroom lessons for subsequent playback to student teachers on closed-circuit television. The overwhelming advantage of this technique is its unobtrusiveness, only a minimum of equipment is located in the classroom. Cameras and microphones are remote-controlled from a van, which is placed in position prior to the commencement of a lesson. A teaching period is free to run its own course under normal conditions without any rehearsal or staging of incidents.

The mobile unit has successfully captured natural and spontaneous classroom situations which have most effectively stimulated lively and worth-while discussion of teaching styles, a variety of approaches to similar objectives, recent curriculum developments and patterns of teacher-pupil interaction. Students televised in the classroom gain far greater insight into their own teaching competence from an extended recording of a lesson than from the normal processes of self-evaluation in which only the depths or highlights tend to be recalled.

There are many similarities between film and television instruction. Until video recorders are reduced in cost and universally adopted as a basic essential of school equipment, the film will continue to cause fewer difficulties in making time-table arrangements. Fortunately the broadcasting companies give ample notice of their programmes and it is feasible to integrate them into conventional work in school. Unless the whole syllabus is carefully preplanned to incorporate broadcasted lessons the teacher is forced to make haphazard arrangements of the kind which were generally found so undesirable in attempting to build a lesson around a visual aid merely because it was available.

For a discussion of the advantages and disadvantages of television instruction, Gryde (1966) is an excellent source of reference. Film and television are economical means of mass teaching; although the initial capital outlay for production is apparently high, the shared cost per child for expert teaching is in reality fairly low. Do not underestimate the importance of "expert" in the context of teaching for in it lies one of the greatest strengths of the media; namely, bringing highly skilled demonstrators, working in detailed close-up, straight into the heart of the classroom. The scope and flexibility of filmed material is an asset which cannot be matched in a normal classroom. Material which is not generally accessible is an obvious benefit; so also is the variety of technique which can be incorporated into a film such as animated sequences, slow-motion, time-lapse, graphs, flow diagrams, exploded drawings, overlay maps, printed words and arrow-pointings to direct attention.

Against these advantages at least three limitations should be noted but they are in no way unsurmountable. A mass audience by implication includes children of different ages and of different attainment and ability. No film or television programme can possibly cater for all individuals throughout the full screening time; some will find parts completely incomprehensible, others will comment on its elementary nature. In producing an important film on a vital topic in health education surely it is not impossible to make more than one version or at least record different commentaries? Taking into consideration how much film footage is discarded in the cutting room, some of it must be particularly appropriate for children of higher or lower ability.

Secondly, there is little or no feedback from the class during the actual transmission, neither is there much active engagement by the pupils other than observation and possibly note making. Feedback can be delayed, it will be activated in the discussion session which should follow every film or broadcast. Similarly, normal class questioning, practical exercises and creative activities are not ruled out because a film has been shown, they are only put back in time.

A third point is the amount of redundant and repeated material in the average film compared with conventional teaching. To a certain extent this is unavoidable, particularly if it is the producer's intention to highlight significant points, concepts and principles otherwise hidden in a wealth of perceptual detail.

Gryde's observation that a film or television broadcast is not necessarily an end in itself is highly relevant; both create learning opportunities, they have a potential which teachers must learn to use effectively. This is also true of course for the tape recorder and language laboratory. Taped recordings of "live" events and performances were the norm in the early days when rather bulky recorders were first introduced into schools. The development of good-quality portable machines, particularly of the cassette type demanding a minimum of technical expertise, has done much to broaden the scope of recording activities by teachers and children alike.

Many departments build up libraries of tapes of recordings from radio broadcasts and store them for later use in appropriate and convenient lessons, thus overcoming the problem which arises through inflexibility in time of transmission and the time-tabling of classes. Another excellent technique is the synchronization of tapes with projected slides; examples are marketed by the B.B.C.

Teachers of languages have found the tape recorder an almost indispensable aid at a time when emphasis is moving from written to oral work. A good recording affords an opportunity for all children to hear a foreign tongue spoken with correct pronunciation and intonation. The more sophisticated kind of language laboratory is designed so that the pupil not only listens to a phrase, but can imitate it and hear comments on his response from a teacher sitting at a console. Costs of such an installation compare favourably with setting up, say, a full technical workshop or science laboratory; even so, is the expenditure justified in terms of increased efficiency in learning?

From published research comparing laboratory and conventional teaching of languages the evidence is rather inconclusive, neither method has definitely proved superior to the other. On the other hand, there are reports of children being stimulated and thoroughly enjoying the laboratory work, consequently adopting a better attitude towards learning a foreign language. Possibly written proficiency has taken too dominant a place in the evaluation of successful learning at the expense of oral fluency.

What looked like a promising method of teaching children to read, the "talking page", has recently been withdrawn from manufacture in spite of favourable comments on its efficiency. Children found the colourful reading books highly attractive in themselves, they enjoyed operating the machine and gained satisfaction when they made real progress.

Games and Simulation

Some of the best teaching aids are not necessarily of mechanical construction; on the contrary, they are wholly based on printed material either compiled by the teacher himself or purchased commercially. In particular, the introduction of games and simulation methods into subjects like geography as advocated by Taylor and Walford (1973) has proved most successful.

Examples of Games and Simulation

Community	local, national and international government.
Conservation	planning, amenities, pollution.
Economy	national, products, economics.
Farming	crop growth and production.
Historical	Congress of Vienna.
Industrial	commercial decisions, marketing.
Newspaper	simulation of newspaper production.
Transport	historical routes and contemporary networks.

Taylor and Walford justify the inclusion of role-play, gaming and simulation techniques as a classroom activity and method of teaching along the following grounds:

1. They motivate children both initially and throughout the period of role-play. The interest promoted tends to be sustained by involvement.
2. Active participation by teacher and pupil in a dynamic learning situation, encountering novel situations and problems.
3. Children monitor the results of their actions, much of the feedback is instant.
4. Engagement in problem-solving activity and insight into decision-making processes at a level varying with the ability of individual participants.
5. Children formulate and adopt new strategies when new patterns of interrelationships develop or chance factors arise.
6. The teacher assumes a less formal and authoritarian role—he guides, inspires and stimulates. In doing so, he shares insights with pupils in a corporate venture.
7. Children learn social skills in working together in groups and in role-play gain awareness of how others feel and react.
8. The approach is often interdisciplinary and in cutting across narrow subject divisions brings outside reality into the heart of the classroom.

The authors are aware of the reservations some teachers hold about introducing these techniques into normal classroom work, but the writer who has observed and played a variety of gaming periods in Geography teaching has found few problems to be insoluble in practice. That they are time-consuming is undeniable but they are no worse in this respect than a worth-while project or sample study; in any case, they can be played in an abbreviated form. Commercially published kits are beyond the purchasing powers of some departments with a meagre financial allowance. This need not deter an enthusiast who will gain far more insight from constructing his own tailor-made and more readily adaptable kit than from a prepackaged item.

Other reservations are sometimes expressed about the new role of the teacher in a changed and less formal classroom situation, including motivating the inhibited child at one extreme and calming down the high-spirited or intentionally disruptive child at the other. Traditional rows of single desks are neither conducive to the right atmosphere nor do they facilitate role-playing and gaming, large tables are much more appropriate for informal group work. Unfortunately there is very little evidence available at this stage of development from validation studies comparing simulation methods with conventional classroom teaching. The design of such a study is likely to prove highly complex because of the number of interrelated factors involved and also it needs to consider both short- and long-term effects.

Algorithms

In higher education, Beard (1970) advocates the development of algorithms for trouble-shooting and problem-solving exercises in subjects like mathematics, chemistry, medicine and law, having noticed their effectiveness in industry. An algorithm is basically a flow-chart of instructions which a reader follows and by a process of successive elimination arrives at a decision. It needs very careful planning if it is to prove efficient in practice and avoid time-wasting. A simple algorithm which could be used in tracing the source of a fault in a "high-fidelity" sound reproducing system with separate loudspeakers, amplifier and record player is shown in Fig. 38.

There is no reason why this technique should not be more widely explored for use in normal educational practice as an aid to problem-solving, particularly when specific properties are to be identified from a mass of data containing a number of alternatives.

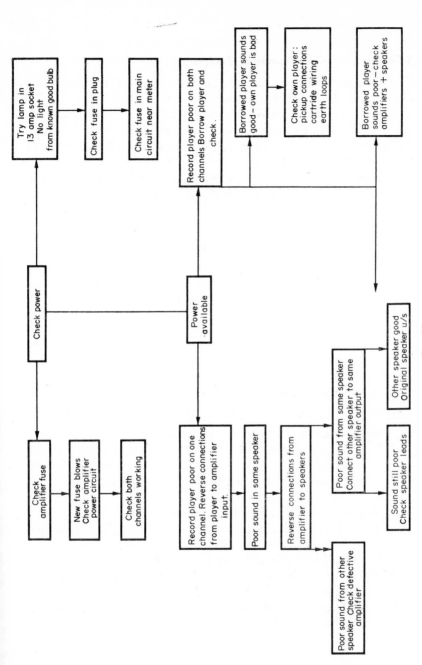

FIG. 38.

Effectiveness of Audio-visual Techniques

For a balanced summary and assessment of research into the comparative effectiveness of audio-visual techniques in teaching, readers are referred to chapter 20 in Thouless (1969). It would certainly be unwise to take for granted that visual aids are always and necessarily better than traditional methods of the socratic type in which personal interaction is dominant (Vernon, 1953 and 1954).

Schramm (1962b) examined research evidence reporting comparisons between television and conventional lessons and tabled the following results:

	TV better	No different	TV less efficient
Primary schools	63	109	20
High schools	11	57	21
Science in schools	20	29	7
Science in colleges	1	26	1

Barrington (1965) confirmed the findings of Schramm, and from a comprehensive survey of international researches in the field of instructional television arrived at the following conclusions:

1. There appears to be no significant difference in achievement between pupils taught by television and by conventional methods.
2. The few experiments aimed at measuring the intangibles of the learning situation have also failed to discover significant differences between television and conventionally taught pupils.
3. Follow-up work after a television lesson is vital.
4. Television lessons hold the pupil's attention.
5. The evidence indicates that the optimum length of a television lesson is about 25 minutes.
6. Sound should be closely related to what can be perceived.
7. The effect of television teaching on the achievement of pupils of different levels of ability has not been resolved.
8. Pupils favour two-way communication between the classroom and studio. But the absence of two-way communication does not effect

the level of achievement of the pupils. There is evidence to indicate that it may impede the learning taking place.

9. It has not been satisfactorily resolved whether television teaching helps or hinders retention of learning. When pupils are engaged in making active responses during a television lesson, retention is much improved.

10. The attitude of pupils to television instruction is affected by the subject being taught and by the television teacher.

11. The less able pupils and younger pupils are enthusiastic about television lessons. The pupil's attitude becomes unfavourable as he climbs the educational ladder from primary to secondary and higher education. However, the attitude of the pupil towards television lessons does not appear to be related to his level of achievement in the subject being taught.

12. Pupils appear to favour the direct teaching type of lesson rather than the enrichment type of lesson.

One of the difficulties in attempting a subjective review of the effectiveness of audio-visual aids in classroom teaching lies in the evaluation of teachers' attitudes. A well-equipped stockroom or resource centre is no guarantee or evidence for the widespread and regular employment of the equipment it contains. Why do some teachers resist the introduction of educational technology so stubbornly?

Teachers with deep-rooted fears of mechanical aids and those who tend to be accident prone in front of children dread the thought of wrapping a reel of 16-mm film round themselves like a cobra, or projecting a slide upside-down or erasing a recording instead of playing it back. Others genuinely believe that time taken (i) to learn how to use an aid, (ii) to organize and plan its utilization and (iii) for its actual running in the classroom is not time well spent compared with formal and traditional methods of teaching. Admitted, the initial claims for some new item of equipment or game are often exaggerated and their alleged superiority is not always substantiated in practice, but this attitude should not be transferred like stimulus generalization to all aids.

This is only part of the story, at times one feels that many teachers so enjoy formal teaching that they intuitively dislike and suspect anything which might undermine their authoritarian role in the classroom and alter the nature of existing interpersonal relationships. Naturally there are grounds for misgivings particularly if a super-mechanical classroom is visualized. This, thank goodness, is completely out of the question for economic reasons; conventional work with the assistance of teaching aids is likely to remain the standard pattern for a long time to come. Effectively used, an aid should not reduce interaction in the classroom but foster and promote it. Lively discussion of issues raised, exploration of hypotheses and analytical questioning are by no means ruled out; neither are humour, intrinsic motivation and a general reduction in tension.

Too much stimulation is equally undesirable and would ultimately prove self-defeating. Children need quiet moments for reflection and time to organize and absorb material into their personal schemata. From the country which leads the world in the practical use of education technology is a plea by Travers (1973) for a technology which can be used in an "open" classroom situation, for a technology which is not preoccupied with developing a packaged curriculum to be used for providing a uniform pupil product and for a technology that would free man from many of the controls that the rest of technology imposes on him.

Additional Reading

APTER, M. J. (1968) *The New Technology of Education*. London: Macmillan.

ATKINSON, R. C. and WILSON, H. A. (Eds.) (1969) *Computer-assisted Instruction—A Book of Readings*. London: Academic Press.

AUSTWICK, K. (Ed.) (1964) *Teaching Machines and Programming*. Oxford: Pergamon.

FEIGENBAUM, E. A. and FELDMAN, J. (Ed.) (1963) *Computers and Thought*. New York: McGraw-Hill.

FIRTH, B. (1968) *Mass Media in the Classroom*. London: Macmillan.

GLASER, R. (Ed.) (1965) *Teaching Machines and Programmed Learning*. 11: *Data and Directions*. Washington, D.C.: NEA.

HARTLEY, J., HOLT, J. and HOGARTH, F. W. (1971) Academic motivation and programmed learning. *Brit. J. Educ. Psychol.* **41**, Pt. 2, 171–83.

KAY, H. (1964) General introduction to teaching machine procedures. In AUSTWICK, K. (Ed.).

KAY, H., DODD, B. T. and SIME, M. E. (1968) *Teaching Machines and Programmed Instruction*. London: Penguin.

KAYE, B. (1970) *Participation in Learning*. London: Allen & Unwin.

LANGLEY, C. (Ed.) (1972) *Games and Simulations*. London: B.B.C.

LEEDHAM, J. and UNWIN, D. (1965) *Programmed Learning in Schools*. London: Longmans.

LEITH, G. O. M. (1966) *A Handbook of Programmed Learning*, 2nd edn. Birmingham: Univ. of Birmingham Inst. of Educ.

LEITH, G. O. M. and BRITTON, R. J. (1973) The influence of learning techniques of programmed instruction on teaching performance in school. *Educ. Res.* **15**, No. 3.

MABEY, R. (1972) *Children in Primary School: The Learning Experience*. London: Penguin.

RICHMOND, W. K. (1967) *The Teaching Revolution*. London: Methuen.

ROWNTREE, D. (1966) *Basically Branching: A Handbook for Programmers*. London: MacDonald.

TANSEY, P. J. (Ed.) (1971) *Educational Aspects of Simulation*. New York: McGraw-Hill.

WHEATLEY, D. M. and UNWIN, A. W. (1973) *The Algorithm Writer's Guide*. London: Longmans.

CHAPTER 11

Moral Behaviour

Concept of Morality

The concept of morality is no less complex or polymorphous than, say, intelligence and is equally as difficult to define even at an operational level. Moreover, it is almost impossible to separate the psychological from the philosophical, historical and sociological aspects of the subject and it would in fact be very unwise for a student teacher to attempt to do so. It is recommended that Wilson *et al.* (1967) is read before Wright (1971); both are essential reading for they raise a variety of significant contemporary moral issues for which there are few ready answers and solutions.

An entry under "moral" in a dictionary or thesaurus normally includes concepts and synonyms such as goodness, trust, socially acceptable behaviour, altruism, virtuous conduct, justice, conformity to generally accepted customs, conventions and formulated rules, guilt, sense of duty, feeling an obligation, conscience and so on. These terms give some indication of the dimensions of the subject, with one serious and fundamental omission; namely, the right intentions, reasons and motives for human behaviour: "In morals the action is judged by the intention" (Swinburne, 1837–1909).

How does one justify including a chapter on moral education in a textbook on the psychology of classroom learning? First, in referring back to the broad definition of learning adopted at the beginning of this book; secondly, in the belief that education involves far more than accumulating knowledge and developing skills; thirdly, in that a school is an institution with a varied corporate life, a complex structure of social sub-groups with values, conventions, traditions, rules and norms; and fourthly, in that a school with a good moral tone and discipline is likely to facilitate rather than inhibit learning and personality development.

Historically, the older generation has usually considered the up and coming generation to be a race of barbarians characterized by a consistent decline in standards of behaviour, but rarely do they admit even partial responsibility for this alleged state of affairs. Whether moral standards as a whole are falling or not is debatable; that they are changing in certain areas, is not. How does society draw up a national balance sheet of moral behaviour with say a genuine concern for the aged and the deprived on the credit side and the so-called growth of permissiveness and delinquent acts on the other? Surely this is an impossible task, culminating in a wholly unrealistic and worthless collection of subjective value judgements. The study of limited and restricted aspects of moral behaviour, whether counting heads to investigate incidence, or testing hypotheses about causation, has proved exceedingly difficult in practice. They have raised numerous methodological problems, particularly regarding the collection of accurate and reliable data. Exaggeration, self-denigration, under-assessment and anxiety to please or to conform to a peer group image are human traits too well known to every serious investigator of social behaviour. No wonder the results of many small-scale researches are apparently in direct conflict and exceedingly difficult to evaluate.

Piaget's Theory

It is to Piaget's (1932) seminal work that one normally turns for an introduction to some of the psychological aspects of moral development. Readers should recall his non-statistical but nevertheless rewarding technique of observing, conversing and playing with children, and should also bear in mind that his investigations were into moral insight: namely, the growth of a child's thinking about moral problems. For simplicity it is probably easier to follow Wright's (1971) example and study children in two broadly based age groups; contrasting the immature development of moral concepts approximately between the years 5 to 8 with the more mature concepts which develop from about 10 years of age onwards. Emphasis must be placed on the deliberate use of the words "broad" and "approximate" in referring to age groups. Also, examples of immature thinking are sometimes encountered at the adult level, one kind of reasoning does not necessarily supersede or extinguish the other.

The earlier stage is called "moral realism"; to the child it is an externally imposed morality rooted in authority. Whilst playing games of marbles with young children, Piaget questioned their understanding of the rules of the game and observed that although they claimed a rule to be inviolable and derived from some semi-mystical source, they frequently disobeyed them in actual play. This observation not only indicates that a young child's conception of a rule is absolute but typifies the divergence, not infrequently found in assessing moral development, between a person's stated belief and actual behaviour pattern.

Children were told short stories in an attempt to evaluate the criteria by which they made moral judgements; "Mary thought she would help Mummy who was out shopping by laying the table ready for tea, but in doing so broke an expensive tea pot. Joan who had been told not to climb up to the shelves to get some sweets whilst Mummy was out, did so, and broke an old tea cup. Which child was the naughtier and deserved punishment for her action?" Responses to this type of question suggest that the value of the object broken is equally or possibly of greater significance in the moral judgement of a young child than intention or motive. Similarly, punishment is retributive and they argue it is right for children to suffer for transgressing and breaking rules. It is almost of necessity that a wrongdoing is balanced by punishment; even if a class or group is made to suffer for an individual's misdemeanour, only a little sense of injustice is felt by those who are not responsible.

Young children at the immature stage also believe in the concept of immanent justice; for example, the young boy sent to bed early for misbehaving at tea thinks that the early evening thunderstorm raging outside his window is a punishment decreed by some form of authority. Piaget considers this stage of moral realism or "heteronomy" to be a natural outcome reflecting limitations in the child's intellectual development which have been imposed by thinking at the pre-operational level; to which one must add, of course, the child's limited social contacts and group experiences.

As the child grows up and broadens his intellectual and social life his concept of morality inevitably changes. Rules are no longer sacred, if a change in them is deemed necessary for the benefit of the group as a whole, then it is not thought wrong to modify them. Intention and motive must be taken into consideration in judging an infringement of a rule and disobedience is not necessarily wrong in every circumstance. The need for rules to facilitate the efficient and harmonious running of an institution like a school is accepted, particularly if the pupils feel that they have had an opportunity to discuss with teachers their nature, number, content and enforcement. Open discussion of rules in house groups and elected school councils can make an invaluable contribution to moral education, provided the meetings are conducted in a democratic fashion and that decisions are honoured and not intentionally subjected to delay.

Attitudes to punishment undergo changes; older children realize it has a deterrent function and a reciprocal effect in that it should be made to fit the crime. A decision on the nature of punishment should be based on the individual and personal characteristics of the offender as much as on the offence itself. It is not necessary to punish every misdeed or violation of a rule. Punishment of the innocent, like keeping a whole class in detention because an individual offender cannot be found out or because a few members are misbehaving, is considered unjust and is not acceptable. Neither does it serve any useful purpose for a teacher to cover up or defend his action by stating that group punishment balances past misdeeds for which individuals were not publicly found out.

Piaget has called this stage a "morality of co-operation" in which children foster and develop mutual respect for each other. They become increasingly aware of the need to be tolerant of different points of view whether or not they coincide with their own deep-rooted personal beliefs or those of authority. The maturation of moral insight is a correlate of intellectual and social development, part of the complex and changing structure of cognitive growth.

Kohlberg's Theory

Kohlberg and colleagues (1971) researching in the U.S.A. in the same cognitive field and tradition as Piaget have in many ways extended and refined his work on moral development. Children and students listened to stories, and the questioning which followed, placed them in a moral predicament such as having to make a choice between undesirable alternatives:

"In Europe, a woman was near death from a very bad disease, a special kind of cancer. There was one drug that the doctors thought might save her. It was a form of radium for which a druggist was charging ten times what the drug cost him to make. The sick woman's husband, Heinz, went to everyone he knew to borrow the money, but he could only get together about half of what it cost. He told the druggist that his wife was dying, and asked him to sell it cheaper or let him pay later. But the druggist said, 'No, I discovered the drug and I'm going to make money from it'. So Heinz got desperate and broke into the man's store to steal the drug for his wife."

Should the husband have done that? Why?

From some very deep probing and really penetrating questions on the reasons for making moral decisions Kohlberg identified six developmental stages:

Stage 1. Conformity and obedience to those in authority who have power to reward or punish. Rules are obeyed to avoid punishment.

Stage 2. Conformity to rules results in rewards and favours for himself and there is only a little regard for the fate of others. Beginnings of a naïve notion of fair play and reciprocal bargaining between children.

Stage 3. Conformity in order to gain the approval of others, "the good boy" orientation. One behaves correctly to please and help others even though it possibly involves making a sacrifice, such as giving up some unacceptable form of behaviour which previously gave personal satisfaction.

Stage 4. Conformity to avoid the disapproval of authority and to maintain social order. Rules have to be obeyed and it is right to do one's duty and not let authority down.

Stage 5. Morality of contract involving both a respect for the rights of an individual and the democratic laws of society. Rules can be changed if it is the will of the majority. One must avoid violating the rights of others.

Stage 6. Morality of individual principles of conscience, if necessary, in defiance of authority. Belief in abstract concepts like equality of rights, justice and mutual respect.

Kohlberg claims that his stages of moral development have cross-cultural validity and that they have been identified in Israel, Mexico and Taiwan. Not all children attain the final stages because they demand a fairly high level of cognitive functioning and an intellectual development capable of handling advanced abstract concepts which need to have been carefully thought out by the individual himself.

Moral Development and Learning Theory

Does moral development or learning differ in any respect from general learning; if not, can it be explained or interpreted in the light of learning theories outlined earlier in this book? To date no really convincing argument has been made for a separate learning theory to explain moral growth; yet on the other hand it would be highly speculative, on the basis of present knowledge and research, to suggest say cybernetic principles as an explanation.

Many learning theorists outside the psychoanalytic school have turned to instrumental learning, more particularly to anxiety conditioning, to explain moral learning. A useful revision exercise would be to reread the section on learning theories and see how adequate they are in attempting to explain one aspect of a child's moral development such as honesty.

Psychologists are particularly interested in the study of individual differences in moral development; why does only one member of a family brought up under practically identical environmental conditions become delinquent but not his brothers and sisters? Are isolated cases of deviance attributed to differences in personality development? But surely this will prove an inadequate explanation without making reference to a child's social relationships. The sociologist quite rightly adds group influences, roles and pressures to purely psychological theories of moral development.

A third approach to the theoretical study of moral growth is via psychoanalysis, which postulates that parental patterns of upbringing in the formative years of a child's life are subsequently revealed in the development of feelings of guilt. However, empirical research into a typical area of study, say the relationship between guilt and self-punishment, does not always substantiate the hypothesis put forward by the Freudian school. This does not imply that all their work has been unproductive, on the contrary, they opened up new fields and identified important problems.

Discipline and Order

Reference back to general learning principles and theories of reward and punishment is again necessary for an understanding of key concepts like authority, discipline and order as applied to the work of the teacher. Before the commencement of teaching practice no other topic is raised more frequently in general discussion than class control and discipline. At the back of nearly every student teacher's mind there is a nagging doubt about personal competence to maintain order in the classroom and how to cope should disintegration seem imminent. The problems they raise are real, very real and possibly too real for comfort, particularly because there are very few ready-made solutions a tutor can offer his students in all sincerity. An ocean divides the gentile discussion of a hypothetical disciplinary problem in a college tutorial and the heat and tension generated by an actual incident in the classroom.

Offering temporary palliatives merely to delay or suppress anxiety in the student teacher like "don't worry it might not happen to you" or "as a student you have the authority of the school and the normal classroom teacher behind you, leave the serious problems to them" or "being nearer the children in age you should not find it difficult to identify and sympathize with their difficulties and frustrations" are too negative for practical value. A much more positive approach is required, and even then, no guarantee of success is assured because many of the so-called tips for teachers are based on common sense and past experience and have little psychological evidence to substantiate them. A ploy that works for one teacher does not necessarily work successfully for another.

Two imperatives to be constantly borne in mind by every student teacher are anticipation and action. Sitting at the back of a class, visiting tutors, peacefully dozing after a hectic journey to observe a lesson at an appointed time, even notice signs and incidents which are likely to lead to trouble if ignored by the student teacher. Quite often an offender is made aware of the fact you have spotted something wrong from a glance or pained facial gesture, and is enough to warn him without interrupting the whole class. Anticipate trouble when children begin to show a blank look of interest and become restless and cause distractions like asking ridiculous questions or making repeated requests to open and shut windows for the sake of physical movement.

It is probably wiser in the long term to begin on a firm and polite basis than attempt to gain the co-operation of a class by suggesting that you are on "their" side, tolerant and opposed to the shortcomings of authority. The latter course is rarely successful because if discipline does go astray one has to cope with a growing problem alone or be forced to call upon the same authority you have previously and publicly undermined. Children are not slow in detecting the "with it" young teacher who thinks he is free to jump on and off the adolescent cultural bandwaggon at will. Take a genuine interest in their culture and aspirations, get to know them as individuals with varied personalities, discuss their problems and difficulties and listen to their views, attitudes and opinions but never lose your identity as a teacher with special responsibilities to children, parents and society generally.

This applies probably more pertinently to less formal out-of-school activities than in the classroom. For example, on a field study it is not difficult to become drawn into a suggested or implied criticism of a senior colleague whose theoretical knowledge of an aspect of, say, land-formation is somewhat dated compared with the current state of the art freshly acquired from college. In fairness to student teachers, it is in school departments where they treat the teacher in training as an intruder with status slightly above that of a prefect and do not welcome him as an inexperienced member of staff that this is likely to happen. It is not unknown for trained teachers to turn to senior pupils for sympathy and support when it is not forthcoming from colleagues in a small department.

The concepts of authority and authoritarian are bedevilled with difficulties and are not capable of easy and precise definition. Having authority is not the same as being authoritarian; one implies potential access to or being a representative of a powerful institution, the other suggests a personal attitude or the climate in which duties and responsibilities are carried out. All teachers have authority, nowadays few are authoritarian in their relationships with children. Being an intellectual authority with power to influence the cognitive development of others is yet another sense in which the term may be validly used. For a philosophical discussion of these terms, Peters (1966) is recommended as essential reading.

Similarly, a distinction should be drawn between order and discipline. Order has been described as a state of affairs externally imposed upon the child, discipline as an internal state of mind emerging from within the child. A well-disciplined class does not always give an appearance of being orderly; in some lessons children are noisy, mobile and variable in work output but they know their limits and are fully aware that certain levels are intolerable and lead to disruption. Asked to obey and pay attention to a difficult point they do so willingly because they have learned how to control themselves; they are self-disciplined. They accept sensibly moments when absolute concentration is demanded and know when the atmosphere is more relaxed; an experienced teacher respects their judgement and responds by not continually pressurizing and dominating such a class.

An orderly class may superficially appear well disciplined to the outsider, but if they are orderly for negative reasons like avoidance of punishment or because they are delaying a true expression of inner feelings, they cannot be described as self-disciplined. A passive and submissive class certainly makes the life of a teacher less fatiguing, but are children deriving much benefit if they are too frightened or inhibited to learn and have little opportunity for self-expression? Anxiety and fear are powerful weapons in the teacher's armoury, misused they are as dangerous as other more sophisticated forms of destruction.

Very well, one might ask, an acceptable distinction has been drawn between order and discipline and a valid case has been made for the latter, how can a child become a self-disciplined person without being submitted to some form of order? This is difficult to answer, it is a problem facing many teachers of reception classes in infants schools and makes them plead for an expansion of nursery education facilities. Few will deny that in school some form of order is essential for the safety of children, the maintenance of social harmony and the routine organization of activities and their efficient functioning. A statement of objective and rationale is easy enough to make, how can it be implemented by the teacher? It is suggested that it is, first, the teacher's personal manner and attitude and, secondly, his actions which will determine whether a class becomes truly self-disciplined or merely submissive. Self-discipline is fostered by a sincere and sympathetic understanding of children, the use of encouragement and praise, establishing a stable routine with a minimum of rules, promoting community rather than self-interest, planning worth-while and purposeful activities, stimulating adventure and curiosity and in the provision of creative experiences.

Rules

Notifying children and parents of the rules and regulations of a school is not sufficient, their purpose and need should be explained. Participation in their formulation is worth encouraging. Arguments to the effect that schools could manage without rules are sterile. Society is governed directly and indirectly by rules, lack of knowledge of them is no defence in law.

Learning to obey rules is mandatory otherwise a child will find the period of transition from school to the wider non-school environment hazardous and penalizing. It is not implied that rules should always be accepted blindly; by all means challenge, question and suggest improvements, but use normal democratic channels, rather than attempt to force minority pressure group changes or employ devious underhand tactics.

Formal school rules, irksome in print, are often magnified to an importance not really warranted because they exert a relatively minor influence on behaviour compared with conventions, traditions, customs and norms. Moral rules themselves are not necessarily formalized like the rules of golf with clearly defined penalties for every transgression. Society would crumble if it abandoned moral concepts like altruism, trust and justice. For the teacher, the important question is how to "teach" obedience of rules so that children want to accept them. Inwardly they must feel it is right to obey, not out of self-interest, but for the maintenance of harmonious social relationships.

The notion of "teaching" moral rules in the sense of imparting knowledge is in itself misleading and is probably unprofitable in practice. What is more desirable is to provide situations, models and examples in the corporate life of a school from which children learn socially acceptable lines of conduct by direct experience and active participation. Many moral decisions are taken by children themselves in play without a teacher or parent being present. They learn that failure to make group decisions could cause the abandonment of an activity and all would suffer the loss of pleasure which stems from a team effort.

Punishment

On the assumption that some state of order is essential for the promotion of worth-while activities in school, how does the teacher deal with the disruptive element determined both to destroy the rights of other children to engage in work and play and to undermine the authority of the teacher? This introduces forms of punishment which vary from a facial sign of displeasure to suspension or expulsion and includes:

    (i) verbal admonition;
    (ii) detention after normal school hours;
    (iii) sending out of class (a) to stand in the corridor,

     (b) to work with another class,
     (c) to work in a special counselling centre;
(iv) extra work or repeated work;
 (v) additional duties;
(vi) informing parents verbally or by "conduct" cards; .
(vii) deprivation of privileges;
(viii) placing on report with a "satis"/"non-satisfactory" card to be signed after each lesson.

   The absence of physical punishment from the above list might surprise readers, but here the author takes a firm stand with the majority of professional psychologists who are opposed to it in any form and actively support movements for its total abolition in schools. This has been achieved without difficulty in other institutions in this country and in schools in most of the so-called culturally advanced nations. Many head teachers defend their position arguing that it is commonly used by parents, regulations control its use, its abolition could lead to the use of undesirable alternatives and in any case it is used more sparingly as each year passes.

   Psychologists question the effectiveness of physical punishment in modifying behaviour patterns, they maintain that it provides yet another model of aggressive behaviour, it has undesirable and often permanent psychological side-effects, that the deliberate infliction of pain causes loss of dignity to both parties, it induces fear and anxiety in sensitive children who are not actually being punished but feel they are under the threat of it and that in mixed schools there are problems arising from the differential treatment of boys and girls.

   From more than 20 years experience as a supervisory tutor visiting many kinds of school in different parts of the country the author is convinced that schools who have dispensed with corporal punishment are characterized by a far better ethos, have higher standards of self-discipline and are frequently more progressive and liberal in their teaching methods. There is a great deal of evidence to suggest that in certain schools the same boys are punished over and over again with little effect other than hardening their attitudes or reinforcing and intensifying maladjustment. The ineffectiveness of corporal punishment in reducing the amount of smoking by boys in secondary schools is well known. The fact that children sometimes express a preference for corporal as opposed to other forms of punishment is no logical justification for its continued use in schools, it simply makes one suspect the motives behind the alleged preference.

There are times when children have to be punished for transgressing codes of conduct; what guidance therefore does one offer the teacher in deciding what form it should take and under what circumstances? It is impossible to work out a scale of punishments for committed offences, parallel to guides for sentencing in law. It is equally impossible to define what is a suitable punishment for a particular misdemeanour, so much depends on the individual child, his past attitude and the likely effect it will have upon him, including his subsequent relationships with the teacher. Also, on whether the child had acted on impulse or had been under emotional stress and whether his action was premeditated and intentional. Certainly the teacher must point out the nature of the offence and explain precisely how it infringes accepted codes of behaviour. The child should be made to understand that punishment is inevitable if a further offence is committed following a firm and final warning. Repeated threats without subsequent action are useless, they merely alter the delicate balance between teacher and taught; the teacher's authority and morale is lowered, that of the offender is boosted. It is exceedingly difficult to reverse the position should a class get out of hand and judge a teacher to be ineffectual, soft and easy-going; they will show little sympathy or respect for a lack of positive approach. Appealing to them from a weak defensive position is useless; equally as bad is the practice of ignoring a desperate situation in the expectancy that something will turn up or if you can hold on you will eventually be saved by the bell.

Investigate offences thoroughly, take immediate action and aim for positive rather than negative forms of punishment. Never give group punishments for individual misdemeanours and do not keep punishing the same child over and over again without consulting a colleague, a head of department, house or school. To improve his standards a teacher must be sincere in his self-criticism and ask to what extent did lack of organization, anticipation and action force one to employ a negative force when some early positive movement might possibly have avoided it.

Discipline: the School and the Community

Many disciplinary troubles inside the classroom are projected from outside the school by agencies including aspects of peer group culture like current trends in fashion, the influence of mass media, neighbourhood gangs, lack of parental responsibility, earlier maturation of adolescents, health problems and the backwash effect of social and political unrest. Problems are likely to be caused by the compulsory raising of the school leaving age (ROSLA). Open hostility to the extra year will be demonstrated quite belligerently by pupils who consider it a waste of wage-earning time. There is also certain to be a growth in the number of married pupils in school in the future, some of whom will be young mothers.

Immigrant children will continue to cause difficulties, not especially in urban areas with an already high proportion of immigrant population but more particularly in schools accepting children over 13 years of age who cannot speak a word of English. Special provision will have to be made for these pupils who will possibly come from the European continent and have not had the Commonwealth tradition of some contact with British culture.

Research is needed into the effect on school discipline of changes in the planning of buildings, curriculum development, secondary school reorganization and staffing policy. Under the heading "planning" a number of factors need investigating like the optimum size of a school, mixed or single-sex, its role in the local community, open or traditionally planned classrooms and special smaller room accommodation for counselling, vocational guidance and sixth-form study. Too much physical movement in large schools and possibly in small open-planned buildings may contribute to restlessness among children of certain temperament. Some children feel more secure working in a more permanent environment under a fairly fixed routine with fewer changes of subject teacher, others thrive on mobility with constantly changing social contacts.

As purchasers of cars, cameras, "hi-fi" equipment and other pieces of sophisticated engineering know to their cost the latest design does not always live up to the manufacturers' specification of performance and reliability. This fact is well known yet there is no shortage of buyers who will spend out a fortune simply to possess the current model with distinctive design and greater gadgetry but no corresponding improvement in output, quality or ease of operation. How many schools adopt a similar unstable outlook towards educational technology, innovation in teaching methods, syllabus content and curriculum development? Consider very carefully the consequences of change. Like a high rate of staff turn-over, too many changes in technique are equally unsettling for children and unless one considers them absolutely essential they are better avoided or reserved until more evidence is made available.

If children detect a feeling of dissent in a teacher's manner, or worse, if they are subjected to an illogical assortment of teaching techniques, class morale is certain to fall and so are standards of attainment and behaviour. Not all parents are sympathetic to newer methods of teaching and feel frustrated when they are unable to help their children at home. Of course, many of them are capable of so doing, but dismiss the perplexed child with "we didn't do it that way at school, I don't understand it, either". If home attitudes reinforce those of the uncertain teacher, weeds of doubt will choke the seeds of learning.

Movement from school to school and frequent changes in class groupings are not conducive to feelings of security which emerge from membership of relatively permanent groups and well-established circles of friendship. In urban areas and in rural areas where larger multi-purpose institutions are replacing the local village schools, traditional patterns of movement known to at least three generations are being radically changed by reorganization schemes. Neighbourhood pride, often accompanied by a strong "tribal" discipline is usually destroyed, and as yet nothing of merit has been discovered to replace it.

Frequent changes in the staff of a school obviously militate against stability and security; they reflect the social unrest of our times, the search for better prospects, pay, accommodation and working environment. Who can blame them; like Gresham's law bad schools drive out good teachers.

An authority with problem schools and difficult children must square up to the situation, in private rather than public, and give the teachers as many supplementary services and aids as possible. Some schools desperately need trained counsellors blessed with personal qualities which will gain them the confidence and respect of children and parents alike in school and at home. For maladjusted children special educational provision urgently needs expanding. Some authorities are setting up a variety of experimental units. It will be interesting to see how residential units attached to normal schools, possibly with temporary, investigatory or remedial functions, work out in practice.

The school's psychological service is hopelessly overworked throughout the country; in areas with ratios of one trained psychologist to 10,000 children it is wholly unrealistic to expect them to function efficiently. They are forced by circumstance to take short cuts either in reporting back to schools or by refraining from making lengthy investigations or by limiting the essential follow-up of case studies. Similarly with other services including child guidance and probation, the child suffers and ultimately society pays the price over and over again at a later date.

It would be wrong and misleading to end on a note of pessimism suggesting that school discipline is inevitably breaking down and the teacher is an helpless bystander. The alert teacher has many opportunities to take positive action before an incident arises and to project his personality in a firm yet sympathetic manner. Display a genuine interest in children for they have talents and attributes which often go unnoticed, listen to their problems and difficulties, do things with them and not always for them and provide them with a choice of purposeful and worth-while activities outside the traditional subjects of the curriculum. It is impossible to achieve self-discipline without the active co-operation of children who naturally and willingly submit to a code of behaviour which has evolved over a period of time in a school characterized by good ethos. A school of this kind places truth and integrity above expediency, consciously promotes altruistic attitudes and fosters a mutual and reciprocal respect between teacher and pupil.

Children learn sympathy and consideration for others, the denial of self-interest and personal gain for the good of the community and a sense of willing obligation at the expense of self-sacrifice by living in and actively contributing to formal and informal, large or small groups with acceptable standards of morality. An unsatisfactory home atmosphere might not be conducive to the development of altruism for various reasons including deprivation, personality disturbance, lack of stability and the pursuit of wrong and deviant aims. No school is ever like this but how much positive good it exerts over home, peer and media influences is not easy to assess; at times one suspects it to be small in neighbourhoods with a traditional "them and us" attitude towards any institution identified as part of the "authority".

A school which works in the local community and for the local community rather than simply drawing pupils from it will inevitably stand to benefit in the long run. Telling children about the moral goodness of others in history, geography and religious education palls by comparison with the direct engagement of children in charitable work, welfare services and other voluntary organizations. Sermonizing teachers are a bore to most children and heaven help them if they are found to be hypocritical and deceitful in their own conduct. Mutual respect develops out of sympathy, trust, justice, consideration, stability, firmness, good manners and politeness; in short, by the moral standards and codes shown to children by the example of their elders.

It is no use setting up standards which children find impossible to attain for thereby lies the road to anxiety, guilt and neuroticism. Finally, must teachers always equate the slow learner and a class which too obviously displays academic shortcomings with poor standards of behaviour and moral development? Do some teachers approach such a child or group with a predetermined attitude or with an expectancy of trouble which might be completely unwarranted? A pupil with a permanent and deep-rooted sense of failure and low self-esteem carries a heavy enough burden, no teacher worthy of membership of the profession need overload it by impulsive action and unguarded comments tantamount to ridicule which cause deeper humiliation and ultimate alienation.

Additional Reading

BENNETT, S. N. and YOUNGMAN, M. B. (1973) Personality and behaviour in school. *Brit. J. Educ. Psychol.* **43**, Pt. 3, 228–33.

BULL, N. J. (1969) *Moral Education*. London: Routledge & Kegan Paul.

BULL, N. J. (1969) *Moral Judgement from Childhood to Adolescence*. London: Routledge & Kegan Paul.

EYSENCK, H. J. (1960) The development of moral values in children. VII: The contribution of learning theory. *Brit. J. Educ. Psychol.* **30**, Pt. 1, 11–21.

GNAGEY, W. J. (1968) *The Psychology of Discipline in the Classroom*. New York: Macmillan.

GRAHAM, D. (1972) *Moral Learning and Development*. London: Batsford.

HIGHFIELD, M. E. and PINSENT, A. (1952) *A Survey of Rewards and Punishments in Schools*. London: Newnes.

HUGHES, P. M. (1971) *Guidance and Counselling in Schools*. Oxford: Pergamon.

KAHN, J. H. and NURSTEN, J. (1968) *Unwillingly to School*, 2nd edn. Oxford: Pergamon.

KAY, W. (1968) *Moral Development*. London: Allen & Unwin.

KOHLBERG, L. (1964) Development of moral character and ideology. *Rev. Child Dev. Res.* **1**, Russell Sage Fd.

KOHLBERG, L. (1971) *From Is to Ought*. In MISCHEL, T. (Ed.).

MISCHEL, T. (Ed.) (1971) *Cognitive Development and Epistemology*. New York: Academic Press.

MORRIS, J. F. (1958) The development of adolescent value judgements. *Brit. J. Educ. Psychol.* **28**, Pt. 1, 1–14.

NEWELL, P. (Ed.) (1972) *A Last Resort? Corporal Punishment in Schools.* London: Penguin.

PETERS, R. S. (1960). Freud's theory of moral development in relation to that of Piaget. *Brit. J. Educ. Psychol.* **30**, Pt. 3, 250–8.

PETERS, R. S. (1971) *Moral Developments: A Plea for Pluralism.* In MISCHEL, T. (Ed.).

STENHOUSE, L. (Ed.) (1967) *Discipline in Schools.* Oxford: Pergamon.

STRATTA, E. (1970) *The Education of Borstal Boys.* London: Routledge & Kegan Paul.

TAYLOR, W. J. (1972) *School Counselling.* Basic Books. London: Macmillan.

TURNER, B. (Ed.) (1973) *Discipline in Schools.* London: Ward Lock.

TYERMAN, M. J. (1968) *Truancy.* London: Univ. of London Press.

WARD, J. (1971) Modification of deviant classroom behaviour. *Brit. J. Educ. Psychol.* **41**, Pt. 3, 304–13.

WILLIAMS, P. (Ed.) (1974) *Behaviour Problems in School: A Source Book of Readings.* London: Univ. of London Press.

WILSON, J. (1973) *The Assessment of Morality.* London: N.F.E.R.

Notes on Some Statistical and Technical Terms used in Psychometrics

CONSIDER two sets of marks or scores obtained by the same six children on two different tests, X and Y.

Test One (X)	Test Two (Y)
118	106
109	101
121	100
118	99
100	98
94	96

Plot the scores for the two tests on a graph and the distribution shows three facts (Fig. 39).

(a) Test One (X) has a higher average or mean score; 110 compared with 100.

(b) Test One has a larger variability in spread of scores about the mean; i.e. a larger standard deviation or σ.

(c) There is a positive relationship between the two sets of scores, i.e. they are positively correlated or r is $+$.

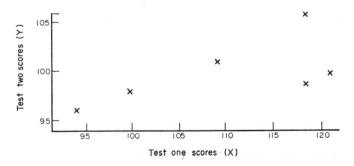

FIG. 39.

259

Standard Deviation

A measurement of the variability of marks about a mean, the greater the variability the larger the standard deviation. It is *not* the same as the range of marks from highest to lowest scores. In mathematical terms it is the square root of the mean of all the squared deviations of scores from the arithmetical mean of the distribution, hence it is the root–mean–square deviation:

$$\sigma = \sqrt{\left(\frac{\Sigma x^2}{N}\right)} \quad \text{(note: } \Sigma \text{ is the sum of)}$$

Test One (X)			Test Two (Y)		
X	x	x^2	Y	y	y^2
118	+ 8	64	106	+6	36
109	− 1	1	101	+1	1
121	+11	121	100	0	0
118	+ 8	64	99	−1	1
100	−10	100	98	−2	4
94	−16	256	96	−4	16

Mean = 110 $\Sigma x^2 = 606$ Mean = 100 $\Sigma y^2 = 58$
N = 6   N = 6

$\therefore \sigma x = \sqrt{101} = 10.00 \quad \therefore \sigma y = \sqrt{9.66} = 3.11$

If two or more sets of marks are to be added together to make a combined score for each individual child it is essential to note that the means and standard deviations of each set are approximately equal, otherwise one set of scores will exert greater weight in the final total than the other. If a discrepancy is noted between the means and standard deviations then it is necessary to scale one set of scores against the other set. A scaling technique does not change the rank order of marks or scores obtained by individual children; so the top child will still be top before and after scaling and the same with the bottom child and all other children—their relative position does not change as a result of scaling.

It would be grossly wrong to combine scores without first scaling them for the two distributions shown in Fig. 40.

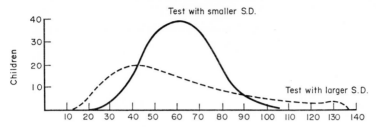

FIG. 40. Scores for two tests.

Correlation Coefficient

A coefficient of correlation *r* indicates numerically the nature of the relationship between one variable, say marks for an attainment test, and another variable, say scores on a verbal reasoning scale. The measurement of agreement or disagreement between two such variables is expressed as a coefficient on a scale:

$$+ 1 = \text{perfect positive correlation,}$$
$$0 = \text{no correlation,}$$
$$- 1 = \text{perfect negative correlation. (See Fig. 41.)}$$

Correlation is a relative and not an absolute indication of relationship and care should be taken in its interpretation. A coefficient should be evaluated with the following in mind:

(a) The characteristics or nature of the variables correlated; for instance, one would expect a higher correlation (say +.85 or higher) between test and retest scores on an intelligence test than between academic attainment and anxiety.

(b) The size of the sample and degree of homogeneity. Total populations with wide variability will normally generate higher coefficients than small homogeneous groups.

(c) The statistical significance of the coefficient, or the probability of a coefficient occurring by chance, say once in twenty or a hundred times. This is obtained from prepared tables.

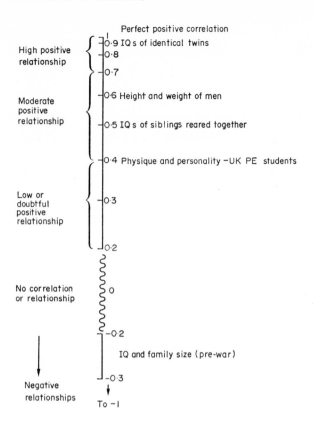

FIG. 41.

(d) The reliability of the traits or tests themselves.
(e) The method of calculation of the coefficient; Pearson's product moment or Spearman's rank or Kendall's tau.
(f) The use one makes of the coefficient; for background information or a trend compared with using it to predict an attribute.

Finally, a positive correlation should not necessarily be taken as implying causation, it simply indicates a degree of relationship.

Pearson's Product-moment

$$r = \frac{\Sigma xy}{N\sigma x\sigma y}$$

X	x	x^2	Y	y	y^2	xy
118	$+8$	64	106	$+6$	36	$+48$
109	-1	1	101	$+1$	1	-1
121	$+11$	121	100	0	0	0
118	$+8$	64	99	-1	1	-8
100	-10	100	98	-2	4	$+20$
94	-16	256	96	-4	16	$+64$

$$\sigma x = 10.0 \qquad\qquad \sigma y = 3.11 \qquad\qquad \Sigma xy = 123$$

$$r = \frac{123}{6 \times 10 \times 3.11},$$

$$r = +.659$$

From significance tables the value of .659 is not significant at the 5 per cent (1 in 20) or 1 per cent (1 in 100) levels. For this small group of children, proof of a relationship between marks on Test One and Test Two has not been firmly established, it could be due to chance factors.

Spearman's Rank Correlation

$$\text{rho} = 1 - \frac{6\Sigma d^2}{N(N^2 - 1)}$$

X	X Rank	Y	Y Rank	Rank difference	$\left(\dfrac{\text{Rank}}{\text{difference}}\right)^2$
118	2=	106	1	1.5	2.25
109	4	101	2	2	4
121	1	100	3	2	4
118	2=	99	4	1.5	2.25
100	5	98	5	0	0
94	6	96	6	0	0

$$\Sigma d^2 = 12.5$$

$$\text{rho} = 1 - \frac{6 \times 12.5}{6(36 - 1)}$$
$$= 1 - \frac{75}{210}$$
$$= 1 - .357$$
$$= + .643$$

The rho value of $+.643$ approximates the product-moment coefficient $+.659$; however, it cannot be tested for significance. The rank correlation technique should only be used in quick exploratory investigations, and preferably when there are few tied scores to be ranked. It is generally much more profitable to use the product-moment method which can be tested for statistical significance and it also more readily facilitates the computation of the mean and standard deviation of the variables.

Reliability of a Test

A psychologist wants to feel assured that the test he is using is both a reliable and valid instrument. Reliability may be defined in two senses:

(i) The extent to which a test yields consistent results on testing and retesting after an interval of time.

(ii) The extent to which a test is internally consistent. No test is perfectly reliable and variations are possibly due to:

(a) Familiarity of the testee with a particular test; through practice, an individual gains in test sophistication.

(b) Coaching in different methods of approach to the various sub-scales, coaching in pacing or self-timing and coaching to give insight into the basis of test construction.

(c) Environmental conditions under which a test is taken; in familiar surroundings and in a favourable "climate" for thinking.

(d) Physical and mental health of the testee including effects of emotional stress and fatigue.

(e) Motivation of the testee; particularly under competitive conditions like selection.

(f) Fluctuations in attitude, attention, memory and so forth during the test itself, including discouragement when the testee makes an apparently poor opening or quickly encounters difficulty.

(g) Inability to understand instructions and possibly poor rapport with the examiner.

(h) Guesswork, including using a simple permutation in a speed-test.

Validity

Validity is the extent to which a test actually measures what it purports to measure. A test which is claimed to measure mechanical aptitude and in fact measures manual dexterity and memory of a few scientific principles would certainly not be called a valid instrument. It is often very difficult in practice to define an acceptable criteria and even more difficult to obtain a relatively "pure" measurement of stated criteria.

The term is used in various ways by psychologists; for instance, they talk about a test's predictive validity and its construct validity. Predictive validity implies detailed analysis of a test in, say, a selection procedure and measurement of the subsequent success or failure of a test by means of a follow-up study using correlation techniques. Construct validity is in itself a term used differently by a number of authorities; it is employed fairly frequently to describe the extent to which a test measures an hypothetical construct or the underlying theoretical concept of a dimension like neuroticism in the study of personality.

Objectivity in Marking

An objective test is scored so accurately that every marker would mark each question in the same way and would arrive at an identical final score. The marking is completely independent of a marker's personal judgement; in fact, it could be marked and is frequently marked in practice by machine methods. A more subjective test, like a creativity item, necessitates a measure of judgement by the scorer.

Standardization for Age

Attainment and reasoning tests are normally standardized to take into account differences in the age of children. Norms are carefully calculated for specified age groups and they should not be extrapolated beyond the limits of the conversion tables provided in the test handbook.

P.L.—K

Titles and Publishers of Tests Mentioned in the Text

OBVIOUSLY the list represents only a minute fraction of the total number of tests of ability, achievement, aptitude, intelligence, interests and personality which have been published throughout the world in the present century.

Readers are warned that psychological tests are instruments which must be used with professional care and that test agencies take every possible precaution to ensure that tests do not fall into the hands of unsuitable persons. All prospective purchasers must produce evidence of their level of qualification, and in the case of certain tests, evidence of specific training in the use of clinical techniques. Before embarking on an ambitious research project involving assessment and testing, check with a test agency like the National Foundation for Educational Research (N.F.E.R.) that tests will be made available to you.

It must not be taken for granted that the N.F.E.R. is the test publisher in every case; on the contrary, in many instances it acts solely as a test agency and distributor on behalf of publishers at home and abroad. Qualified testers will also find the catalogue of psychological tests marketed by SWETS and ZEITLINGER, Keizersgracht 487, Amsterdam, The Netherlands, quite informative and an alternative source of supply—but again with the same restriction on distribution of tests to authorized and qualified users.

(Age group in brackets)

A.H. 4, 5, 6. Group Tests. HEIM, A. *et al.* Windsor: N.F.E.R. A.H. 4 (10+ to Adult); A.H. 5 (13+ Highly Intelligent); A.H. 6 (18+ Student Selection).
Bender-Gestalt. BENDER, L. *et al.* Six Forms (4+ and over). Windsor: N.F.E.R.
Blacky Pictures. BLUM, G. S. Windsor: N.F.E.R.
Bristol Social Adjustment Guides. STOTT, D. H. and SYKES, E. G. London: Univ. of London Press and Windsor: N.F.E.R.

Brook Reaction Test. HEIM, A. W., WATTS, K. P. and SIMMONDS, V. Windsor: N.F.E.R.

Children's Personality Questionnaire. PORTER, R. B. and CATTELL, R. B. (8–12). Windsor: N.F.E.R.

Dynamic Personality Inventory. GRYGIER, T. G. (18+). Windsor: N.F.E.R.; also *Likes and Interests Test for Apprentices et al.* (15+).

Early School Personality Questionnaire. COAN, R. W. and CATTELL, R. B. (6–8). Windsor: N.F.E.R.

Eysenck Personality Inventory. EYSENCK, H. J. and EYSENCK, S. B. G. Forms A, B (9–16. and Adults). London: Univ. of London Press and N.F.E.R.

Family Relations Test. BENE, E. and ANTHONY, J. (3–7) (7–15) (Adults). Windsor: N.F.E.R.

High School Personality Questionnaire. CATTELL, R. B. and BELOFF, H. (12–16). Windsor: N.F.E.R.

Junior Eysenck Personality Inventory. EYSENCK, S. B. G. (7–15). London: Univ. of London Press and N.F.E.R.

Kohs Block Design Test. KOHS, S. C. Windsor: N.F.E.R.

Manchester Scales of Social Adaptation (adaptation of *Vineland Social Maturity Scale*). LUNZER, E. A. (6–15). Windsor: N.F.E.R.

Minesota Multiphasic Personality Inventory. HATHAWAY, S. R. and McKINLEY, J. C. (16+). Available in three formats: Individual, old group (booklet) form and new group (R) form. Windsor: N.F.E.R.

Moray House. Dept. of Educ., Edinburgh Univ. London: Univ. of London Press.

N.F.E.R. Publishing Company, 2 Jennings Buildings, Thames Ave., Windsor, Berkshire.

Porteus Maze Test. PORTEUS, S. D. British Edn. London: Harrap.

Progressive Matrices. RAVEN, J. C. Various forms, e.g. Coloured and Advanced for all age groups. London: H. K. Lewis & Co. and N.F.E.R.

Rorschack. Various titles, e.g. *Inkblots in colour.* Windsor: N.F.E.R.

Schonell Diagnostic Tests of English and Arithmetic. SCHONELL, F. T. Windsor: N.F.E.R.

Sixteen Personality Factor Questionnaire. CATTELL, R. B. and EBER, H. W. (16+). Windsor: N.F.E.R.

Stanford–Binet Intelligence Scale, 3rd Revision. British Edn. London: Harrap and N.F.E.R.

Study of Values. ALLPORT, G. E., VERNON, P. E. and LINDZEY, G. (10–16) and (Adults). British Edn. Revised 1964 by RICHARDSON, S. Windsor: N.F.E.R.

Thematic Apperception Test. MURRAY, M. A. (4+ and over). Windsor: N.F.E.R.

Torrance Tests of Creative Thinking. TORRANCE, E. P. Individual (5–9); Group (10+). Windsor: N.F.E.R.

Vineland Social Maturity Scale. DOLL, E. A. (Infancy to Adults). Windsor: N.F.E.R.

Wechsler Intelligence Scale. WECHSLER, D. New York: Psychological Corporation and N.F.E.R.

References to Authors Cited in the Text

ABERNETHY, E. M. (1940) The effect of changed environmental conditions upon the results of college examinations. *J. Psychol.* **10**, 293–301.

ALLEN, L. E. (1965) Toward autotelic learning of mathematical logic by the WFF'N PROOF games: Mathematical Learning. *Mon. Soc. Res. Child Dev.* **30**, No. 1.

ANNETT, J. (1969) *Feedback and Human Behaviour.* London: Penguin.

ANTHONY, W. S. (1973) The development of extraversion, of ability, and of the relation between them. *Brit. J. Educ. Psychol.* **43**, Pt. 3, 223–7.

ATKINSON, R. C. (1968) Computerized instruction and the learning process. *Amer. Psychol.* **23**, 225–39.

AUSUBEL, D. P. and ROBINSON, F. G. (1969) *School Learning.* New York: Holt, Rinehart & Winston.

AVITAL, S. M. and SHETTLEWORTH, S. J. (1968) *Objectives for Mathematics Learning: Some Ideas for the Teacher.* Toronto: Ontario Inst. for Studies in Educ.

BAHRICK, H. P. and BAHRICK, P. O. (1964) A re-examination of the inter-relations among measures of retention. *Q.J. exp. Psychol.* **16**, 318–24.

BARTLETT, F. C. (1932) *Remembering.* London: Cambridge Univ. Press.

BARTLETT, F. C. (1943) Fatigue following highly skilled work. *P. Roy. Soc. B.* **131**, 247–57.

BARRINGTON, H. (1965) A survey of instructional television researches. *Educ. Res.* **8**, 8–25.

BASSON, A. H. and O'CONNOR, D. J. (1959) *Introduction to Symbolic Logic*, 3rd Edn. London: Univ. Tutorial Press.

BEARD, R. (1969) *An Outline of Piaget's Developmental Psychology.* London: Routledge and Kegan Paul.

BEARD, R. (1970) *Teaching and Learning in Higher Education.* London: Penguin.

BERNSTEIN, B. (1961) Social structure, language and learning. *Educ. Res.* **3**, 163–76.

BERNSTEIN, B. (1970) A sociolinguistic approach to socialization. In GUMPERZ, J. J. and HYMES, D. (Eds.).

BERNSTEIN, B. and HENDERSON, D. (1969) Social class differences in the relevance of language to socialization. *Sociology,* **3**.

BERLYNE, D. E. (1966) Curiosity and exploration. *Science,* **153**, 25–33.

BITTERMAN, M. E. (1965) Phyletic differences in learning. *Amer. Psychol.* **20**, 396–410.

BLOCK, J. H. (Ed.) (1971) *Mastery Learning: Theory and Practice.* New York: Holt, Rinehart & Winston.

BLOOM, B. S. (Ed.) (1956) *Taxonomy of Educational Objectives.* New York: Longmans.

BLOOM, B. S. (1971) Mastery learning. In BLOCK, J. H. (Ed.).

BRAINE, M. D. S. (1963) The ontogeny of English phrase structure. *Language,* **39**, 1–13.

BROADBENT, D. E. (1958) *Perception and Communication*. Oxford: Pergamon.

BRUNER, J. S., GOODNOW, J. and AUSTIN, G. A. (1956) *A Study of Thinking*. New York: Wiley.

BUROS, O. K. (Ed.) (1970) *Personality Tests and Reviews*. New Jersey: Gryphon Press.

BUROS, O. K. (Ed.) (1972) *The Seventh Mental Measurements Yearbook*. New Jersey: Gryphon Press.

BURT, C. (1940) *The Factors of the Mind*. London: Univ. of London Press.

BURT, C. (1970) *The Genetics of Intelligence*. In DOCKRELL, W. B. (Ed.).

BUTCHER, H. J. (1968) *Human Intelligence*. London: Methuen.

BUTLER, R. A. (1971) *The Art of the Possible*. London: Hamish Hamilton.

CAMPBELL, R. and WALES, R. J. (1970) The study of language acquisition. In LYONS, J. (Ed.).

CARMICHAEL, L. *et al.* (1932) An experimental study of the effect of language on perceived form. *J. Exp. Psychol.* **15**, 78–86.

CARMICHAEL, L. (Ed.) (1954) *Manual of Child Psychology*. New York: Wiley.

CASHDAN, A. and WHITEHEAD, J. (Eds.) (1971) *Personality Growth and Learning*. London: Longman (Open Univ. Press).

CATTELL, R. B. (1965) *The Scientific Analysis of Personality*. London: Penguin.

CAZDEN, C. (1965) On individual differences in language competence and performance. *J. Special Educ.* **1**, 135–49.

CHOMSKY, N. (1957) *Syntactic Structures*. The Hague: Mouton.

CHOMSKY, N. (1959) Review of verbal behaviour by B. F. Skinner. *Language*, **35**, 26–58.

CHOMSKY, N. (1965) *Aspects of the Theory of Syntax*. Cambridge, Mass.: M.I.T. Press.

CHOMSKY, N. (1968) *Language and Mind*. New York: Harcourt, Brace.

CLARK, H. H. (1970) Word associations and linguistic theory. In LYONS, J. (Ed.).

COCHRAN, A. J. and STOBBS, J. (1968) *The Search for the Perfect Swing*. London: Heinemann.

CORDER, S. PIT. (1973) *Introducing Applied Linguistics*. London: Penguin.

CRAIK, K. J. W. (1948) Theory of the human operator in control systems. II: Man as an element in a control system. *Brit. J. Psych.* **38**, 142–8.

CROWDER, N. A. (1959) Automatic tutoring by means of intrinsic programming. In GALANTER, E. H. (Ed.).

DE CECCO, J. P. (Ed.) (1967) *The Psychology of Language, Thought and Instruction*. New York: Holt, Rinehart & Winston.

DE SAUSSERE, F. (1915) *Course in General Linguistics*. 1959 Translation. New York: Philosophical Library.

DEUTSCH, J. A. and CLARKSON, J. K. (1959) Reasoning in the hooded rat. *Q.J. exp. Psychol.* **11**, 150–4.

DEWEY, J. (1910) *How We Think*. Boston: Heath.

DOCKRELL, W. B. (Ed.) (1970) *On Intelligence*. London: Methuen.

DUNCKER, K. (1945) On problem-solving. *Psychol. Mono.* **58**, 5.

EBBINGHAUS, H. (1885) *Memory: A Contribution to Experimental Psychology*. 1913 Translation. Columbia Univ.

EL KOUSSY, A. A. H. (1935) The visual perception of space. *Brit. J. Psychol. Monog.* Suppl. 20.

ENTWISTLE, N. J. (1972) Personality and academic attainment. *Brit. J. Educ. Psychol.* **42**, Pt. 2, 137–51.

EPSTEIN, W. (1961) The influence of syntactical structure on learning. *Amer. J. Psychol.* **74**, 80–85.

ESTES, W. K. (1944) An experimental study of punishment. *Psychol. Monog.* **57**, No. 263.

EYSENCK, H. J. (1953) *The Structure of Human Personality.* London: Methuen.

EYSENCK, H. J. and EYSENCK, S. B. G. (1963) *The Eysenck Personality Inventory.* London: Univ. of London Press.

EYSENCK, H. J. and COOKSON, D. (1969) Personality in primary school children. *Brit. J. Educ. Psychol.* **39**, 109–22. Also in CASHDAN, A. and WHITEHEAD, J. (Eds.).

EYSENCK, S. B. G. (1965) *The Junior Eysenck Personality Inventory.* London: London Univ. Press.

FESTINGER, L. (1942) Wish, expectation and group standards as affecting level of aspiration. *J. Ab. Social Psychol.* **37**, 184–200.

FJERDINGSTAD, E. J. *et al.* (1965) Effect of RNA extracted from the brain of trained animals on learning in rats. *Scand. J. Psychol.* **6**, 1–6.

FODOR, J. A. and BEVER, T. G. (1965) The psychological reality of linguistic segments. *J. Verb. Learn. Verb. Behav.* **4**.

FORSTER, K. I. (1966) Left to right processes in the construction of sentences. *J. Verb. Learn. Verb. Behav.* **5**.

FOSS, B. M. (Ed.) (1966) *New Horizons in Psychology.* London: Penguin.

FREUD, S. (1922) *Introductory Lectures on Psycho-Analysis.* London: Allen & Unwin.

GAGNÉ, R. M. (1965) *The Conditions of Learning.* New York: Holt Rinehart & Winston.

GALLANTER, E. H. (Ed.) (1959) *Automatic Teaching: The State of the Art.* New York: Wiley.

GALTON, F. (1869) *Hereditary Genius.* London: Macmillan.

GARDNER, R. W. *et al.* (1959) Cognitive controls: a study of individual consistencies in cognitive behaviour. *Psychol. Issues* **1**, No. 4.

GARRETT, M., BEVER, T. G. and FODOR, J. A. (1966) The active use of grammar in speech perception. *Percept. Psychophys.* **1**.

GAUDRY, E. and SPIELBERGER, C. D. (1971) *Anxiety and Educational Achievement.* Sydney: John Wiley.

GETZELS, J. W. and JACKSON, P. W. (1962) *Creativity and Intelligence.* New York: Wiley.

GRYDE, S. K. (1966) The feasibility of "programmed" television instruction. *AV Communication Rev.* **14**. Abridged in STONES, E. (Ed.).

GRYGIER, T. G. (1970) Recent studies with the Dynamic Personality Inventory. *Int. Cong. Rorschach and other Proj. Techn.* **7**.

GUILFORD, J. P. (1950) Creativity. *Amer. Psychologist* **5**, 444–54. Also in CASHDAN, A. and WHITEHEAD, J. (Eds.).

GUILFORD, J. P. (1956) The structure of intellect. *Psychol. Bull.* **53**, 267–93.

GUILFORD, J. P. (1958) A system of the psychomotor abilities. *Amer. J. Psychol.* **71**, 164–74.

GUILFORD, J. P. (1967) *The Nature of Human Intelligence.* New York: McGraw-Hill.

GUMPERZ, J. J. and HYMES, D. (Eds.) (1970) *Directions in Sociolinguistics.* New York: Holt, Rinehart & Winston.

GUTHRIE, J. T. (1971) Feedback and sentence learning. *J. Verb. Learn. Verb. Behav.* **10**, 23–28.

HADDON, F. A. and LYTTON, H. (1968) Teaching approach and the development of divergent thinking abilities in primary schools. *Brit. J. Educ. Psychol.* **38**, 171–80. Also in CASHDAN, A. and WHITEHEAD, J. (Eds.).

HADDON, F. A. and LYTTON, H. (1971) Primary education and divergent thinking abilities—four years on. *Brit. J. Educ. Psychol.* **41**, Pt. 2, 136–47.

HALLWORTH, H. J. (1961) Anxiety in secondary modern and grammar school children. *Brit. J. Educ. Psychol.* **31**, 281–92.

HARDYCK, C. D. *et al.* (1966) Feedback of speech muscle activity during silent reading: rapid extinction. *Science* **154**.

HARLOW, H. F. (1949) The formation of learning sets. *Psychol. Rev.* **56**, 51–65. Also in RIOPELLE, A. J. (Ed.) (1967).

HARLOW, H. F. (1953) Mice, monkeys, men and motives. *Psychol. Rev.* **60**, 23–62.

HARRIS, Z. S. (1957) Co-occurrence and transformation in linguistic structure. *Language* **33**, 283–340.

HASAN, P. and BUTCHER, H. J. (1966) Creativity and intelligence: a partial replication with Scottish children of GETZELS and JACKSON's study. *Brit. J. Psychol.* **57**, 129–35.

HARTLEY, J. (1965) Linear and skip-branching programmes: a comparison study. *Brit. J. Educ. Psychol.* **35**, 320–8.

HEBB, D. O. (1949) *The Organisation of Behaviour: A Neuropsychological Theory.* New York: Wiley.

HEIM, A. (1970) *Intelligence and Personality.* London: Penguin.

HENDRICKSON, G. and SCHROEDER, W. H. (1941) Transfer of training in learning to hit a submerged target. *J. Educ. Psychol.* **32**, 205–13.

HEZLETT DEWART, M. (1972) Social class and children's understanding of deep structure in sentences. *Brit. J. Educ. Psychol.* **42**, Pt. 2, 198–203.

HICK, W. E. (1952) On the rate of gain of information. *Q. J. Exp. Psychol.* **4**, 11–26.

HILGARD, E. R. *et al.* (1953) Rote memorization, understanding and transfer: an extension of Katona's card-trick experiments. *J. Exp. Psychol.* **46**, 288–92.

HOCKETT, C. F. (1958) *A Course in Modern Linguistics.* New York: Macmillan.

HONEYBONE, R. C. *et al.* (1956) *Geography for Schools, Books* 1–5. London: Heinemann.

HUDSON, L. (1966) *Contrary Imaginations.* London: Methuen.

HULL, C. L. (1952) *A Behaviour System.* New Haven: Yale Univ. Press.

HUNTER, I. M. L. (1957) *Memory: Facts and Fallacies.* London: Penguin.

HUSEN, T. (1967) *International Study of Achievement in Mathematics.* Stockholm: Almqvist & Wiksell. London and New York: Wiley.

HYDÉN, H. (1965) Activation of nuclear RNA in neurons and glia in learning. In KIMBLE, D. P. (Ed.).

INHELDER, B. and PIAGET, J. (1958) *The Growth of Logical Thinking from Childhood to Adolescence*. Basic Books.

INHELDER, B. and PIAGET, J. (1964) *The Early Growth of Logic in the Child*. London: Routledge & Kegan Paul.

JENKINS, J. G. and DALLENBACH, K. M. (1924) Obliviscence during sleep and waking. *Amer. J. Psychol.* **35**, 605–12.

JENSEN, A. R. (1973) *Educability and Group Differences*. London: Methuen.

JOHNSON-LAIRD, P. N. (1970) The perception and memory of sentences. In LYONS, J. (Ed.).

JUDD, C. H. (1908) The relation of special training to general intelligence. *Educ. Rev.* **36**, 28–42.

KAGAN, J. (1971) Developmental studies in reflection and analysis. In CASHDAN, A. and WHITEHEAD, J. (Eds.).

KALMYKOVA, Z. I. (1962) Psychological prerequisites for increasing the effectiveness of learning in problem solving in arithmetic. In SIMON, B. and J. (Eds.).

KATONA, G. (1940) *Organizing and Memorizing*. New York: Columbia Univ. Press.

KIMBLE, D. P. (Ed.) (1965) *Learning, Remembering and Forgetting*, Vol. 1. Palo Alto: Science and Behaviour Books.

KNAPP, B. (1963) *Skill in Sport*. London: Routledge & Kegan Paul.

KOCH, S. (Ed.) (1959) *Psychology: A Study of a Science, General Systematic Formulations, Learning and Special Processes*. London: McGraw-Hill.

KOFFKA, K. (1935) *Principles of Gestalt Psychology*. New York: Harcourt Brace.

KOHLBERG, L. and TURIEL, E. (1971) *Recent Research in Moral Development*. New York: Holt.

KOHLER, W. (1925) *The Mentality of Apes*. London: Routledge & Kegan Paul.

KOHLER, W. (1929) *Gestalt Psychology*. New York: Liveright.

KRATHWOHL, D. R. *et al.* (1964) *Taxonomy of Educational Objectives:* Handbook II: *Affective Domain*. New York: David McKay.

KRETSCHMER, E. (1925) *Physique and Character*. London: Routledge & Kegan Paul.

KREUGER, W. C. F. (1929) The effect of over learning on retention. *J. Exp. Psychol.* **12**, 71–78.

KUENNE, M. R. (1946) Experimental investigation of the relation of language to transposition behaviour in young children. *J. Exp. Psychol.* **36**, 471–90.

LADEFOGED, P. and BROADBENT, D. E. (1960) Perception of sequence in auditory events. *Q. J. Exp. Psychol.* **12**, 162–70.

LAMBERT, W. E. and JAKOBOVITS, L. A. (1960) Verbal satiation and changes in the intensity of meaning. *J. Exp. Psychol.* **60**, 376–83.

LAWTON, D. (1968) *Social Class, Language and Education*. London: Routledge & Kegan Paul.

LENNEBERG, E. H. (1967) *Biological Foundations of Language*. New York: Wiley.

LESSINGER, L. M. (1963) Test building and test banks through the use of the taxonomy of educational objectives. *Calif. J. Educ. Res.* **14**, 195–201.

LEVINSON, B. and REESE, H. W. (1963) Patterns of discrimination learning set. . . . *Final Report, Co-op Research Proj.* 1059. U.S. Dept. of Health, Educ. and Welfare.

LEWIS, M. M. (1963) *Language, Thought and Personality in Infancy and Childhood.* London: Harrap.

LITTELL, W. M. (1960) The Wechsler Intelligence scale for children—a review of a decade of research. *Psychol. Bull.* **57**, 132–62.

LIUBLINSKAYA, A. A. (1957) The development of children's speech and thought. In SIMON, B. (Ed.), and in STONES, E. (Ed.) (1970).

LORENZ, K. Z. (1952) *King Solomon's Ring.* London: Methuen.

LOVELL, K. (1961) *The Growth of Basic Mathematical and Scientific Concepts in Children.* London: Univ. of London Press.

LUNZER, E. A. (1965) Problems of formal reasoning in test situations. In MUSSEN, P. H. (Ed.).

LUNZER, E. A. (1968) *The Regulation of Behaviour.* London: Staples.

LUNZER, E. A. and MORRIS, J. F. (1968) *Development in Learning.* London: Staples.

LURIA, A. R. (1961) *The Role of Speech in the Regulation of Normal and Abnormal Behaviour.* Oxford: Pergamon.

LURIA, A. R. and YUDOVITCH, F. J. (1960) *Speech and the Development of Mental Processes in the Child.* London: Staples.

LYNN, R. (1971) *An Introduction to the Study of Personality.* London: Macmillan.

LYONS, J. (Ed.) (1970) *New Horizons in Linguistics.* London: Penguin.

LYTTON, H. and COTTON, A. C. (1969) Divergent thinking abilities in secondary schools. *Brit. J. Educ. Psychol.* **39**, 188–90. Also in CASHDAN, A. and WHITEHEAD, J. (Eds.).

McCARTHY, D. (1954) *Language Development in Children.* In CARMICHAEL, L. (Ed.).

McCLELLAND, D. C. *et al.* (1953) *The Achievement Motive.* New York: Appleton–Century-Crofts.

McCONNELL, J. V. (1962) Memory transfer through cannibalism in planarions. *J. Neuropsychiat.* **3** (Suppl. 1), 542.

MASLOW, A. H. (1968) *Toward a Psychology of Being.* New York: Von Nostrand.

MASLOW, A. H. (1970) *Motivation and Personality.* New York: Harper & Row.

MAXWELL, A. E. (1959) A factor analysis of the Wechsler intelligence scale for children. *Brit. J. Educ. Psychol.* **29**, 119–32.

MAYS, W. (1965) Logic for Juniors. *Teaching Arithmetic* **3**, 3–10.

MELTON, A. W. (1941) Review of Katona's: "Organizing and Memorizing". *Amer. J. Psychol.* **54**, 455–7.

MEYER, V. and CHESSER, E. S. (1970) *Behaviour Therapy in Clinical Psychiatry.* London: Penguin.

MILES, T. R. (1957) On defining intelligence. *Brit. J. Educ. Psychol.* **27**, 153–65. Also in WISEMAN, S. (Ed.).

MILLER, G. A. (1962) Some psychological studies of grammar. *Amer. Psychol.* **17**.

MILLER, G. A. (1967) *The Psychology of Communication.* London: Penguin.

MILLER, G. A., GALANTER, E. and PRIBRAM, K. H. (1960) *Plans and the Structure of Behaviour.* New York: Henry Holt.

MILLER, G. A. and McKEAN, K. O. (1968) A chronometric study of some relations between sentences. In OLDFIELD, R. C. and MARSHALL, J. C. (Eds.).

MORAN, L. J. *et al.* (1964) Idiodynamic sets in word association. *Psych. Monog.* **78**, No. 579.

MORRIS, J. F. and LUNZER, E. A. (Eds.) (1969) *Contexts of Education.* London: Staples.

MUSSEN, P. H. (Ed.) (1965) European research in cognitive development. *Mon. Soc. Res. Child Dev.* **30**, No. 2.

NEWELL, A. *et al.* (1958) Elements of a theory of human problem solving. *Psychol. Rev.* **65**, 151–66.

O'CONNOR, K. (1968) *Learning.* Basic Books. London: Macmillan.

OLDFIELD, R. C. and MARSHALL, J. C. (Eds.) (1968) *Language: Selected Readings.* London: Penguin.

OSBORN, A. F. (1953) *Applied Imagination.* New York: Scribner.

OSGOOD, C. E. (1952) The nature and measurement of meaning. *Psych. Bull.* **49**, 197–237.

PARNELL, R. W. (1958) *Behaviour and Physique.* London: Arnold.

PARNES, S. J. (1959) *Instructor's Manual for Semester Courses in Creative Problem-solving.* Creative Educ. Fdn., Buffalo, New York. Summarized in VERNON, P.E. (Ed.) (1970).

PAVLOV, I. P. (1941) *Lectures on Conditioned Reflexes* (2 vols.). London: Lawrence & Wishart.

PAVLOV, I. P. (1955) *Selected Works.* Moscow: Foreign Languages Publishing House.

PEEL, E. A. (1960) *The Pupil's Thinking.* London: Oldbourne.

PEEL, E. A. (1971) *The Nature of Adolescent Judgment.* London: Staples.

PETERS, R. S. (1966) *Ethics and Education.* London: Allen & Unwin.

PIAGET, J. (1932) *The Moral Judgement of the Child.* London: Routledge & Kegan Paul.

PIAGET, J. (1950) *The Psychology of Intelligence.* London: Routledge & Kegan Paul.

PLOWDEN REPORT (1967) *Children and Their Primary Schools.* London: H.M.S.O.

PRESSEY, S. L. (1926) A simple apparatus which gives tests and scores and teaches. *School and Society* **23**, 373–6.

PRIDE, J. B. (1970) *Sociolinguistics.* In LYONS, J. (Ed.).

RIOPELLE, A. J. (Ed.) (1967) *Animal Problem Solving.* London: Penguin.

RUSHTON, J. (1966) The relationship between personality characteristics and scholastic success in eleven-year-old children. *Brit. J. Educ. Psychol.* **36**, 178–84.

RYLE, G. (1949) *The Concept of Mind.* London: Hutchinson.

SAVIN, H. B. and PERCHONOCK, E. (1965) Grammatical structure and the immediate recall of English sentences. *J. Verb. Learn. Verb. Behav.* **4**.

SCHRAMM, W. (1962a) *The Research on Programmed Instruction: An Annotated Bibliography.* Inst. of Comm. Research, Stanford Univ.

SCHRAMM, W. (1962b) Learning from instructional television. *Rev. Educ. Res.* **32**, 156–67.

SCHWAB, R. S. (1953) Motivation in measurements of fatigue. In *Symposium on Fatigue*. London: H. K. Lewis.

SCOTTISH COUNCIL FOR RESEARCH IN EDUCATION (1949) *The Trend of Scottish Intelligence*. Pub. 30, Univ. of London Press.

SCOTTISH COUNCIL FOR RESEARCH IN EDUCATION (1953) *Social Implications of the 1947 Scottish Mental Survey*. Pub. 35, Univ. of London Press.

SEARS, P. S. (1940) Levels of aspiration in academically successful and unsuccessful children. *J. Ab. Social Psychol.* **35**, 498–536.

SHANNON, C. E. and WEAVER, W. (1949) *The Mathematical Theory of Communication*. Urbana: Univ. of Illinois Press.

SHELDON, W. H. and STEVENS, S. S. (1942) *The Varieties of Temperament*. New York: Harper.

SIMON, B. (Ed.) (1957) *Psychology in the Soviet Union*. London: Routledge & Kegan Paul.

SIMON, B. and SIMON, J. (Eds.) (1962) *Educational Psychology in the U.S.S.R.* London: Routledge & Kegan Paul.

SIMPSON, E. J. (1966) *The Classification of Educational Objectives: Psychomotor Domain*. U.S. Office of Educ., Urbana: Univ. of Illinois.

SKINNER, B. F. (1953) *Science and Human Behaviour*. New York: Macmillan.

SKINNER, B. F. (1957) *Verbal Behaviour*. Appleton–Century–Crofts.

SLAMECKA, N. J. and CERASO, J. (1960) Retroactive and proactive inhibition of verbal learning. *Psychol. Bull.* **57**, 449–75.

SLOBIN, D. I. (1966) Grammatical transformations and sentence comprehension in childhood and adulthood. *J. Verb. Learn. J. Verb. Behav.* **5**.

SPEARMAN, C. E. (1904) "General intelligence": objectively determined and measured. *Amer. J. Psychol.* **15**. Also in WISEMAN, S. (Ed.) (1967).

SPEARMAN, C. E. (1927) *The Abilities of Man*. London: Macmillan.

STONES, E. (Ed.) (1970) *Readings in Educational Psychology*. London: Methuen.

SWENSON, E. J. (1942) Generalization and organization as factors in transfer and retroactive inhibition. *Proc. Indiana Acad. Sci.* **51**.

TAIT, K. *et al.* (1973) Feedback procedures in computer assisted arithmetic instruction. *Brit. J. Educ. Psychol.* **43**, Pt. 2, 161–71.

TALLAND, G. A. (1968) *Disorders of Memory and Learning*. London: Penguin.

TAYLOR, J. L. and WALFORD, R. A. (1972) *Simulation in the Classroom*. London: Penguin.

TERMAN, L. M. (1925) *Genetic Studies of Genius* I. Stanford Univ. Press.

THOMSON, G. H. (1951) *The Factorial Analysis of Human Ability*. London: Univ. of London Press.

THOMSON, R. (1959) *The Psychology of Thinking*. London: Penguin.

THORNDIKE, E. L. (1949) *Selected Writings from a Connectionist's Psychology*. New York: Appleton–Century–Crofts.

THORNDIKE, E. L. and WOODWORTH, R. S. (1901) The influence of improvement in one mental function upon the efficiency of other functions, I. II. III. *Psychol. Rev.* **8**.

THOULESS, R. H. (1958) *General and Social Psychology*, 4th edn. London: Univ. Tutorial Press.

THOULESS, R. H. (1969) *Map of Educational Research*. London: N.F.E.R.

THURSTONE, L. L. (1924) *The Nature of Intelligence*. London: Routledge & Kegan Paul.

TINBERGEN, N. (1951) *The Study of Instinct*. London: Oxford Univ. Press.

TOLMAN, E. C. (1959) Principles of purposive behaviour. In KOCH, S. (Ed.).

TOLMAN, E. C. and HONZIK, C. H. (1930) Introduction and removal of reward and maze performance in rats. *Univ. of California Pub. in Psychol.* **4**.

TRAVERS, R. M. W. (1973) *Educational Psychology*. New York: Macmillan.

TREISMAN, A. M. (1966) Our limited attention. *Advancement of Science*, Feb., pp. 600–11.

UNDERWOOD, B. J. (1966) *Experimental Psychology*. New York: Appleton–Century–Crofts.

UNDERWOOD, B. J. and POSTMAN, L. (1960) Extra-experimental sources of interference in forgetting. *Psychol. Rev.* **67**, 73–95.

VERNON, M. D. (1953) The value of pictorial illustration. *Brit. J. Educ. Psychol.* **23**, Pt. 3, 180–7.

VERNON, M. D. (1954) The instruction of children by pictorial illustration. *Brit. J. Educ. Psychol.* **24**, Pt. 3, 171–9.

VERNON, M. D. (1962) *Psychology of Perception*. London: Penguin.

VERNON, P. E. (1950) *The Structure of Human Abilities*. London: Methuen.

VERNON, P. E. (1969) *Intelligence and Cultural Environment*. London: Methuen.

VERNON, P. E. (Ed.) (1970) *Creativity-Readings*. London: Penguin.

VYGOTSKY, L. S. (1962) *Thought and Language*. New York and London: Wiley.

WALFORD, R. A. (1969) *Games in Geography*. Longman.

WALLACH, M. A. and KOGAN, N. (1965) *Modes of Thinking in Young Children*. New York: Holt, Rinehart & Winston.

WALLIS, D. and SAVILLE, R. (1964) An experimental use of programmed instruction to increase the productivity of technical training. SP (N) Report 2/64. London: Min. of Defence.

WARBURTON, F. W. (1966) Construction of the new British Intelligence Scale. *Bull. Brit. Psychol. Soc.* **19**, 68–70.

WARBURTON, F. W. (1969) The assessment of personality traits. In MORRIS, J. F. and LUNZER, E. A. (Eds.).

WALTER, W. GREY (1961) *The Living Brain*. London: Penguin.

WARD, J. (1972) The saga of Butch and Slim. *Brit. J. Educ. Psychol.* **42**, Pt. 3, 267–89.

WASON, P. C. (1966) Reasoning. In Foss, B. M. (Ed.).

WECHSLER, D. (1944) *The Measurement of Adult Intelligence*. Baltimore: Williams & Wilkins.

WELFORD, A. T. (1968) *Fundamentals of Skill*. London: Methuen.

WERTHEIMER, M. (1945) *Productive Thinking*. New York: Harper.

WHITEHEAD, A. N. (1950) *The Aims of Education*, 2nd edn. London: Benn.

WHITEHEAD, A. N. and RUSSELL, B. (1925) *Principia Mathematica*. London: Cambridge Univ. Press.

WILSON, J. B., WILLIAMS, N. and SUGARMAN, B. N. (1967) *Introduction to Moral Education*. London: Penguin.

WISEMAN, S. (Ed.) (1967) *Intelligence and Ability*. London: Penguin.

WOODROW, H. (1927) The effect of type of training upon transference. *J. Educ. Psychol.* **18**, 159–72.

WRIGHT, D. (1971) *The Psychology of Moral Behaviour*. London: Penguin.

YERKES, R. M. and DODSON, J. D. (1908) The relation of strength of stimulus to rapidity of habit-formation. *J. Comp. Neur. Psychol.* **18**, 459–82.

YNGVE, V. H. (1962) The depth hypothesis. *Scientific American* **206**, No. 6, 68–76.

Author Index

279

Subject Index